bes the Catholic Ren-
...t is my guess that he
will pay particular attention to the emergence, during the
great wars and at the darkest moment before the dawn, of
the great 'doctors' who were the prophets of the new age.
He will point to men like Etienne Gilson and Jacques
Maritain and Edward Watkin and, certainly, to Christopher Dawson. Perhaps he will see that with these erudite
and devoted men the Church moved out of that state of
siege in which it had been living for four centuries and
assumed her rightful role of leadership in the West.

"Christopher Dawson is not a controversialist. He is a
confident, intellectual Catholic, who by a life of dedicated
research has become the greatest living sociologist and philosopher of history, although not as yet the best known.
. . . It is a great source of gratification to all Catholic
scholars that his authority is of that unquestionable and
self-validating sort which simply cannot be ignored by the
serious student of these fields.

" 'Religion,' says Dawson, 'is the key to history.' It is his
insistence upon the primacy and autonomy of religious
knowledge in the formation of any human culture which
is Dawson's unique contribution. . . . In *Religion and the
Rise of Western Culture,* Dawson applies his general thesis
to the specific case of Western culture.

"He tells the story of the Dark Ages and the High Middle Ages in an incomparably interesting and informed style.
It is a twice-told tale for him, and one over which he has
worked and meditated until he is at home in every depart-
ment of its complex history. The wonder of this book is
the skill of its selection and arrangement of materials so
as to bring out the significance of whole epochs and to allow the original sources to tell their own story. The student
of medieval history will find great integrating insights; the
beginner will find the account fascinating and understand-
able. . . . The story of the thin thread of Christian learning in the West preserved with supernatural courage
against wave after wave of barbarian invaders has never
been so well told." *Integrity*

Religion and the Rise of Western Culture

by

Christopher Dawson

---

*Gifford Lectures Delivered in
the University of Edinburgh
1948–1949*

Image Books

A DIVISION OF
DOUBLEDAY & COMPANY, INC., GARDEN CITY, NEW YORK

Image Books edition 1958

Image Books edition published February, 1958
1st printing .... December, 1957
2nd printing .... July, 1960
3rd printing .... November, 1961

COVER BY RONALD CLYNE

TYPOGRAPHY BY EDWARD GOREY

ACKNOWLEDGMENTS

The author wishes to express his gratitude to Mr. E. I. Watkin for reading the proofs and making the Index. He gratefully acknowledges the kindness of those named hereunder in granting him permission to use copyright material in this book:

The Clarendon Press, Oxford, for an extract from Rashdall's *Medieval Universities*, edited by Powicke and Emden.

W. Heffer & Sons, Ltd., Cambridge, for extracts from E. Monsen's translation of Snorre Sturlason's *Heimskringla* (Cambridge, 1932).

CONTENTS

CONTENTS

Chapter I

Introduction: The Significance
of the Western Development

IN MY previous series of lectures I abstained as far as possible from dealing with the history of Christian culture, not because this lies outside the scope of the Gifford Lectures, but because it is the culture to which we all in some sense belong, and therefore it is impossible for us to study it in the same way as the cultures of the remote past which we can see only through the opaque medium of archaeology or the cultures of the non-European world which we have to understand from the outside and from a distance. This involves a difference in the quality of our knowledge which may almost be compared to the difference between the astronomer's knowledge of another planet and the geographer's knowledge of the earth on which we live. There is not only a far greater mass of material available for the study of Western culture than for that of any other; but our knowledge is also more intimate and internal. Western culture has been the atmosphere we breathe and the life we live: it is our own way of life and the way of life of our ancestors; and therefore we know it not merely by documents and monuments, but from our personal experience.

Hence any study of religion which ignores and leaves on one side the accumulated experience of the Christian past and looks exclusively to the remote and partially incomprehensible evidence derived from the study of alien religious traditions or even to our own abstract notions of the nature of religion and the conditions of religious knowledge is bound to be not merely incomplete but insubstantial and unreal. And this is most of all the case when we are considering, as in these lectures, the problem of Religion and Culture—the intricate and far-reaching network of relations that unite the social way of life with the spiritual beliefs and values, which are accepted by society as the ultimate laws of life and the ultimate standards of individual and social behaviour; for these relations can only be studied in the concrete, in their total historical reality. The great world religions are, as it were, great rivers of sacred tradition which flow down through the ages and through changing historical landscapes which they irrigate and fertilize. But as a rule we cannot trace them to their source, which is lost in unexplored tracks of the remote past. It is rare indeed to find a culture in which the whole course of this religious development can be traced from beginning to end in the full light of history. But the history of Christendom is an outstanding exception to this tendency. We know the historical environment in which Christianity first arose: we possess the letters of the founders of the Churches to the first Christian communities in Europe, and we can trace in detail the successive stages by which the new religion penetrated the West.

Thenceforward, at least during the last sixteen centuries, the mass of material available for study is so huge that it exceeds the capacity of the individual mind to grasp it.

Consequently the study of Western religion and Western culture is difficult from the opposite reason to that which renders the study of prehistoric and ancient oriental religions difficult: because we know too much rather than too little—because the vast field of study has had to be divided among a number of different sciences, each of which is further subdivided into specialized branches of study which in turn become autonomous fields of study.

But while this process of specialization has increased our knowledge of almost every aspect of history, it has had an unfortunate influence on the study with which we are concerned, since it has tended to separate and divide the elements that we have to unite and bring together. On the one side, the scientific historian has concentrated his researches on the criticism of sources and documents; on the other, the student of Christianity has devoted himself to the history of dogma and ecclesiastical institutions, with the result that we have a number of highly developed separate studies—political history, constitutional history, and economic history, on the one side, and ecclesiastical history, the history of dogma, and liturgiology on the other. But the vital subject of the creative interaction of religion and culture in the life of Western society has been left out and almost forgotten, since from its nature it has no place in the organized scheme of specialized disciplines. It has been left to the amateur and to the man of letters. It is only thanks to some exceptional foundation like that of the Gifford Lectures that it is possible to find an opportunity to bring it into relation with academic studies.

But meanwhile, outside the academic world, new social forces have been at work which have used history, or a particular version of history, for social ends, as a means to change men's lives and actions. And the rise of these new political ideologies and ideological theories of history has shown that the development of scientific specialism has in no way lessened man's need for an historical faith, an interpretation of contemporary culture in terms of social processes and spiritual ends, whether these ends are defined in religious or secular formulae. This conflict of ideologies, the Marxian doctrine of historical materialism and the attempt of the new totalitarian states to create historical myths as a psychological basis of social unity, have all made us realize that history does not consist in the laborious accumulation of facts, but has a direct bearing on the fate of modern society. To vote in an election or a plebiscite to-day has ceased in many European countries to be a purely political action. It has become an affirmation of faith in a particular social philosophy and a theory of history; a decision between two or three mutually exclusive forms of civilization. I do not say this is a good thing; on the contrary, it means that history and social philosophy are being distorted and debased by political propaganda and party feeling. Nevertheless much the same thing happened in the past in the sphere of religion, and yet these ages of religious controversy were also ages of high religious achievement.

This transportation of the ultimate problems of history and culture from the study to the market-place and the hustings is not the result of any *trahison des clercs*, but is the inevitable result of the awakening of public opinion to their significance and relevance. And it is of vital importance that the gap between the popular political interests in these questions and the scientific and philosophic study of them should not be too wide. The increasing specialization of modern higher studies creates a real danger in this respect, so that a situation may conceivably arise in which the specialist exists solely to provide expert advice to the politician and the journalist, and no one is left to criticize the official ideology which is imposed on the community not so much by deliberate propaganda as by the bureaucratic control of education, information and publicity.

It would be a strange fatality if the great revolution by which Western man has subdued nature to his purposes should end in the loss of his own spiritual freedom, but this might well happen if an increasing technical control of the state over the life and thought of its members should coincide with a qualitative decline in the standards of our culture. An ideology in the modern sense of the word is very different from a faith, although it is intended to fulfil the same sociological functions. It is the work of man, an instrument by which the conscious political will attempts to mould the social tradition to its purpose. But faith looks beyond the world of man and his works; it introduces man to a higher and more universal range of reality than the finite and temporal world to which the state and the economic order belong. And thereby it introduces into human life an element of spiritual freedom which may have a creative and transforming influence on man's social culture and historical destiny as well as on his inner personal experience. If therefore we study a culture as a whole, we shall find there is an intimate relation between its religious faith and its social achievement. Even a religion which is explicitly other-worldly and appears to deny all the values and standards of human society may, nevertheless, exert a dynamic influence on culture and provide the driving forces in movements of social change. "Religion is the key of history," said Lord Acton, and to-day, when we realize the tremendous influence of the unconscious on human behaviour and the power of religion to bind and loose these hidden forces, Acton's saying has acquired a wider meaning than he realized.

It is true that this factor does not seem to play a large part in the history of modern civilization. The great changes that have transformed the conditions of human life in every continent and have gone a long way towards the creation of a single world society seem at first sight to be the result of purely secular and economic causes. Yet none of these causes seems adequate to explain the magnitude of the European achievement.

How did it come about that a small group of peoples in Western Europe should in a relatively short space of time acquire the power to transform the world and to emancipate themselves from man's age-long dependence on the forces of nature? In the past this miraculous achievement was explained as the manifestation of a universal Law of Progress which governed the universe and led mankind by inevitable stages from apehood to perfection. To-day such theories are no longer acceptable, since we have come to see how much they depend on an irrational optimism which was part of the phenomenon they attempted to explain. Instead we now tend to ask ourselves what were the factors in European culture which explain the peculiar achievement of Western man? or to use the brutal and expressive American phrase, "What makes him tick?" But when we reach this point we shall find the religious factor does have a very important bearing upon the question.

For as I wrote eighteen years ago: "Why is it that Europe alone among the civilizations of the world has been continually shaken and transformed by an energy of spiritual unrest that refuses to be content with the unchanging law of social tradition which rules the oriental cultures? It is because its religious ideal has not been the worship of timeless and changeless perfection but a spirit that strives to incorporate itself in humanity and to change the world. In the West the spiritual power has not been immobilized in a sacred social order like the Confucian state in China and the Indian caste system. It has acquired social freedom and autonomy and consequently its activity has not been confined to the religious sphere but has had far-reaching effects on every aspect of social and intellectual life.

"These secondary results are not necessarily of religious or moral value from the Christian point of view—but the fact remains that they are secondary to and dependent on the existence of a spiritual force without which they either would not have been or would have been utterly different.

"This is true of the humanist culture in spite of the secularism and naturalism which seem so characteristic of it. The more one studies the origins of humanism, the more one is brought to recognize the existence of an element which is not only spiritual but definitely Christian.

"It may be objected that this is only one and not the most important aspect of the Humanist movement. But even the purely naturalistic achievements of the Renaissance were dependent on its Christian antecedents. Humanism was, it is true, a return to nature, a rediscovery of man and the natural world. But the author of the discovery, the active principle in the change was not the natural man; it was Christian man—the human type that had been produced by ten centuries of spiritual discipline and intensive cultivation of the inner life. The great men of the Renaissance were spiritual men even when they were most deeply immersed in the temporal order. It was from the accumulated resources of their Christian past that they acquired the energy to conquer the material world and to create the new spiritual culture."[1]

Now what I said here about the origins of the Humanist culture seems to me to be equally true of the age of the Enlightenment and the nineteenth century, when Western culture conquered and transformed the world. It is easy enough to present the history of this European expansion as a process of imperialistic aggression and economic exploitation. But aggression and exploitation are nothing new in world history, and if they suffice to explain the European

[1] From *Christianity and the New Age*, pp. 94–96 (1931).

achievement, it might have been realized hundreds or thousands of years earlier by any of the world empires that have successively held the stage of history.

The peculiar achievement of Western culture in modern times is due to a new element which was not present in the older type of imperialism.

For, side by side with the natural aggressiveness and the lust for power and wealth which are so evident in European history, there were also new spiritual forces driving Western man towards a new destiny. The activity of the Western mind, which manifested itself alike in scientific and technical invention as well as in geographical discovery, was not the natural inheritance of a particular biological type; it was the result of a long process of education which gradually changed the orientation of human thought and enlarged the possibilities of social action. In this process the vital factor was not the aggressive power of conquerors and capitalists, but the widening of the capacity of human intelligence and the development of new types of creative genius and ability.

The other great world cultures realized their own synthesis between religion and life and then maintained their sacred order unchanged for centuries and millennia. But Western civilization has been the great ferment of change in the world, because the changing of the world became an integral part of its cultural ideal. Centuries before the achievements of modern science and technology Western man had conceived the idea of a *magna instauratio* of the sciences which would open new ways for human understanding and change the fortunes of the human race.

Nor was this the unique vision of a solitary genius. We can see to-day that Francis Bacon was much nearer to the Middle Ages in his thought than Macaulay and his generation believed; indeed in some respects his thought is nearer to that of his namesake Roger Bacon than to that of Galileo. For it was Roger Bacon who first conceived the idea of a total synthesis of scientific and philosophic knowledge which would enlarge the bounds of human life and give Christian civilization power to unite the world.

But with Roger Bacon we find ourselves back in the full

stream of medieval culture—a culture which was as completely dominated by religious beliefs and embodied in religious institutions as any of the great religious cultures of the Eastern world. And this medieval culture was the matrix in which the Western type was formed and the ultimate source of the new forces that have moved and transformed the world. The older school of "enlightened" rationalist historians dismissed the thousand years of medieval history as an age of intellectual darkness and social stagnation—an aimless wandering in the wilderness between the old world of classical culture and the Promised Land of modern Enlightenment and Liberty. But thanks to the disinterested work of the historians of the last century and a half, we have now come to understand that these centuries were ages of intense social and spiritual activity and often of violent conflict and revolutionary change. From Cassiodorus and Bede to Erasmus and Copernicus the tradition of thought was never completely interrupted; so that we can follow the sequence of culture without a break from the fall of the Roman Empire in the West to the age of the Renaissance.

No doubt it is easy to see how the Humanist or rationalist notion of the Dark Ages arose. From the economic point of view the early Middle Ages were indeed a period of retrogression and stagnation; there were long periods in which commercial activity was at a standstill and city life had almost disappeared.

From the political point of view there were times in which the state was reduced almost to vanishing point and the classical tradition of citizenship and public law seemed to be extinguished. Even from the intellectual point of view the scientific achievements of the ancient world were forgotten for centuries and the standard of literary culture was often rudimentary. Yet in spite of all this, Western culture preserved a spiritual energy which was independent of political power or economic prosperity. Even in the darkest periods of the Middle Ages this dynamic principle continued to operate. For what distinguishes Western culture from the other world civilizations is its *missionary character*—its transmission from one people to another in a continuous series of spiritual movements. Christianity first entered Western Europe as a missionary movement which originated in the Hellenistic cities of the Levant, and for centuries the men from the East—Paul, Irenaeus, Athanasius, Cassian, Theodore of Tarsus, and the Greek and Syrian Popes of the eighth century—played a leading part in laying the foundations of Western Christianity. In the age which followed the fall of the Empire, this process of transmission was continued, by the Christians of the Western provinces towards the barbarian peoples, as we see in St. Patrick's mission to Ireland, St. Amand's evangelization of Belgium and above all in the epoch-making work of Gregory the Great for the conversion of England.

Up to this point the spread of Christian culture in the West followed the normal course of expansion from East to West—from the old centres of higher culture towards the younger and less civilized peoples and lands. But from the sixth century this process is reversed by a new movement of missionary activity passing from the West to East, from the new Christian peoples of Ireland and England to the Continent—a movement which was not confined to the conversion of Dutch and German pagans, but which also led to the reform of the Frankish Church and the revival of education and classical learning. This marks a new departure in the history of civilization, since it involved a dualism between cultural leadership and political power which distinguishes Western culture from that of the Byzantine world where the political centre continued to be the centre of culture, as it was also for the most part in the older oriental societies.

This independence of cultural leadership and political power was one of the main factors that produced the freedom and the dynamic activity of Western culture. For European history is the history of a series of renaissances— of spiritual and intellectual revivals which arose independently, usually under religious influences, and were transmitted by a spontaneous process of free communication. In the earlier Middle Ages the chief organ of this process of transmission was the monastic order and its motive force was the quest for individual perfection or salvation. It was this motive which led Columba to Scotland and Columban to Burgundy and Boniface to Germany, and in each case the spiritual initiative of the individual became embodied in a corporate institution which in its turn became the centre of a new movement of transmission, like the movement from Iona to Lindisfarne and the creation of a new Christian culture in Northumbria, the reform of Gallic monasticism which proceeded from Columban's foundation at Luxeuil, and the influence of the Anglo-Saxon foundation of Fulda on Christian culture in Germany.

We find a similar process at work in later periods of the Middle Ages, e.g. in the influence of the monastic reformers of Burgundy and Lorraine on the reform of the Church in the tenth and eleventh centuries, or in the work of the Italians in Normandy, where a succession of monastic leaders from Northern Italy—William of Volpiano, John of Fecamp, Lanfranc of Bec and Anselm of Canterbury—raised Normandy from a semi-barbaric condition to a position of intellectual leadership in North-Western Europe. But during the later centuries of the Middle Ages the vital movement of culture was by no means confined to monastic life. It was represented in every field of social and intellectual activity, from the economic activity of commune and gild up to the abstract level of science and metaphysics. Everywhere we find the same rapid and spontaneous transmission of influences from one end of Western Europe to the other; everywhere we see the co-operation of men and movements of diverse national origins which tended towards the creation of a common but highly variegated pattern of culture throughout Western Christendom. Nor did this cease with the medieval period, for the Renaissance itself was a typical example of this free process of communication and creation which passed from one country to another, uniting men of different race and language in common cultural aims and a fellowship of ideas.

It may be objected that all this is in no way peculiar to Western culture, but is of the very nature of the process of cultural development and change everywhere and always. But though every culture produces elements of change and many of them have experienced religious or intellectual movements which have been generated and transmitted by the free spiritual activity of individuals, there has been none in which the movement of change has so transfused the whole life of the culture that the two have become identified. The ancient oriental cultures were all based on the conception of a sacred order which ruled every aspect of man's life and which must be preserved and handed on unchanged and complete, if society is to survive. The civilization of China is the most typical and successful of these cultures, and though China has owed much to the intrusion of independent spiritual movements, notably to that of Buddhist monasticism, it has always regarded such movements as foreign to the sacred order of Chinese life, whether they were condemned wholeheartedly as mortal enemies of the Confucian tradition, or tolerated halfheartedly as spiritual luxuries which could be added like an exotic ornament to the body of native tradition.

It is only in Western Europe that the whole pattern of the culture is to be found in a continuous succession and alternation of free spiritual movements; so that every century of Western history shows a change in the balance of cultural elements, and the appearance of some new spiritual force which creates new ideas and institutions and produces a further movement of social change.

Only once in the history of Western Europe do we see an attempt to create a unitary, all-embracing, sacred order, comparable to that of the Byzantine culture or to those of the oriental world. This was the Carolingian Empire which was conceived as the society of the whole Christian people under the control of a theocratic monarchy, and which attempted to regulate every detail of life and thought down to the method of ecclesiastical chant and the rules of the monastic order by legislative decrees and governmental inspection. But this was a brief and unsuccessful episode which stands out in sharp contrast to the general course of Western development, and, even so, its cultural achievement was largely dependent on the contribution of independent elements coming from outside the

Empire, like Alcuin from England, John Scotus from Ireland and Theodulf from Spain.

Apart from this single exceptional case, there has never been any unitary organization of Western culture apart from that of the Christian Church, which provided an effective principle of social unity. And even in the Middle Ages the religious unity imposed by the Church never constituted a true theocracy of the oriental type, since it involved a dualism between the spiritual and the temporal powers, which produced an internal tension in Western society and was a fertile source of criticism and change. Nevertheless throughout the whole history of Western Europe down to the last century the absence of unitary organization and of a single uniform source of culture did not destroy the spiritual continuity of the Western tradition. Behind the ever-changing pattern of Western culture there was a living faith which gave Europe a certain sense of spiritual community, in spite of all the conflicts and divisions and social schisms that marked its history. It is often difficult to trace the connection between this spirit of faith and the new movements of change which often seem to represent a radical denial of any common spiritual basis. Nevertheless, when we study these movements closely we shall usually find that such a connection does really exist.

In fact, nowhere is the dynamism of Western religion more strikingly manifested than in the indirect and unconscious influence it has exercised on the social and intellectual movements which were avowedly secular. It is easy to find examples of this in the history of the modern revolutionary and reformist movements, but by far the most important and the most interesting is to be found in the history of the rise of the modern scientific movement which has had such immeasurable importance in the history of the modern world.

But I do not propose to deal with this subject in my present lectures; only a man like Pierre Duhem, who was at once a scientist, an historian and a philosopher, is capable of undertaking such a task, and even he did not live to complete the task he had set himself. What I wish to do is to study the earlier phases of the Western development and to see how far the formation of the Western Europe culture complex was conditioned by religious factors.

At this stage of European history the relations between religion and culture are to be seen in their simplest form. No historian denies that the coming of Christianity to the peoples of the West had a profound effect on their culture; nevertheless this great spiritual revolution left the material conditions of Western life unchanged. There remained an immense gulf between the semi-barbarian society of Merovingian Gaul and Anglo-Saxon Britain and the mature religious culture of the Christian Empire—between the mind of a man like St. Augustine or Boethius and that of the warrior chiefs like Clovis or Chilperic who controlled the destinies of the West. The rise of the new Western European culture is dominated by this sharp dualism between two cultures, two social traditions and two spiritual worlds—the war society of the barbarian kingdom with its cult of heroism and aggression and the peace society of the Christian Church with its ideals of asceticism and renunciation and its high theological culture. Nor is its importance confined to the Dark Ages from A.D. 500–1000; it remains characteristic in some degree of medieval culture as a whole and its effects are still traceable in the later history of Western Europe. Indeed I believe that it is to be regarded as the principal source of that dynamic element which is of such decisive significance for Western culture.

But it is important to realize that this dualism was not simply a crude dualism of opposition and conflict. At a relatively early period it was sublimated on the higher level of culture and became an internal principle of polarity and tension. Thus already in the first century of Northumbrian Christianity the tradition of Latin patristic culture found its worthiest representative in the barbarous North in the person of the Venerable Bede, and it is no less significant that the last work of the last Roman philosopher—the *De Consolatione Philosophiae* of Boethius—should have been first translated into the vernacular by a warrior king in the interval of his heroic struggles with the Danes for the preservation of Western Christendom.

This creative process of cultural assimilation which finds

conscious expression in the literary tradition was also at work in the depth of the individual conscience and in the growth of new social institutions. We see it in the lives of the saints, in the laws of the kings, in the letters of missionaries and scholars, and in the songs of poets. No doubt all the evidence we possess sheds but a fitful and uncertain light on the vital realities of the social process. Yet even so our knowledge of the origins of Western culture is far more authentic and detailed than anything we possess in the case of the other great cultures of the ancient or the oriental world.

But there are other respects in which we are better equipped to understand the birth process of Western culture than our predecessors. The historians and philosophers whose minds were formed by the liberal enlightenment of the eighteenth century could feel little interest and no spiritual sympathy with ages in which the darkness of barbarism seemed only to be deepened by religious superstition and monastic asceticism; while in the nineteenth century the nationalist tendencies that were nowhere stronger than in the field of history reacted towards an uncritical idealization of Teutonic and Slavonic barbarians and caused the unity of Western culture to be ignored or depreciated.

But our generation has been forced to realize how fragile and unsubstantial are the barriers that separate civilization from the forces of destruction. We have learnt that barbarism is not a picturesque myth or a half-forgotten memory of a long-passed stage of history, but an ugly underlying reality which may erupt with shattering force whenever the moral authority of a civilization loses its control.

For us, therefore, the history of the Dark Ages and the first beginnings of a new culture in the West fourteen hundred years ago have acquired, or ought to acquire, a new significance. We can understand better than Gibbon the desperate struggle of the later Empire to maintain its higher standards of urban culture and civilized order under the weight of a top-heavy bureaucracy against the constant pressure of war and invasion, and we can realize in a more intimate way than the nineteenth-century historians what were the feelings of the Roman provincials when the dikes at last broke and the tide of barbarism spread ever more widely over the land.

Above all, we are in a better position to appreciate the vital function of religion both as a principle of continuity and conservation and as the source of new spiritual life. In that age religion was the only power that remained unaffected by the collapse of civilization, by the loss of faith in social institutions and cultural traditions and by the loss of hope in life. Wherever genuine religion exists it must always possess this quality, since it is of the essence of religion to bring man into relation with transcendent and eternal realities. Therefore it is natural that the Dark Ages of history—the hour of human failure and impotence— should also be the hour when the power of eternity is manifested. Inevitably these ages of the death and birth of cultures are furthest withdrawn from the light of history. But where, as in the case of the origins of our own culture, we are able in some degree to penetrate the darkness, it is possible to see something of the creative process at work in the depths of the social consciousness; and however incomplete this knowledge may be, it is of very high value for the student of religion and the student of culture.

Chapter II

The Religious Origins of Western Culture: The Church and the Barbarians

THE BEGINNINGS of Western culture are to be found in the new spiritual community which arose from the ruins of the Roman Empire owing to the conversion of the Northern barbarians to the Christian faith. The Christian Church inherited the traditions of the Empire. It came to the barbarians as the bearer of a higher civilization, endowed with the prestige of Roman law and the authority of the Roman name. The breakdown of the political organization of the Roman Empire had left a great void which no barbarian king or general could fill, and this void was filled by the Church as the teacher and law-giver of the new peoples. The Latin Fathers—Ambrose, Augustine, Leo and Gregory —were in a real sense the fathers of Western culture, since it was only in so far as the different peoples of the West were incorporated in the spiritual community of Christendom that they acquired a common culture. It is this, above all, that distinguishes the Western development from that of the other world civilizations. The great cultures of the ancient East, like China and India, were autochthonous growths which represent a continuous process of development in which religion and culture grew together from the same sociological roots and the same natural environment. But in the West it was not so. Primitive Europe outside the Mediterranean lands preserved no common centre and no unified tradition of spiritual culture. The people of the

North possessed no written literature, no cities, no stone architecture. They were, in short, "barbarians"; and it was only by Christianity and the elements of a higher culture transmitted to them by the Church that Western Europe acquired unity and form.

This missionary aspect of Western culture, of which I have already spoken in the Introduction, is older than Christianity, since it goes back to the remote past beyond the beginnings of recorded history. Even the Romans in the midst of their ruthless conquest of empire were not unconscious of it, and when the greatest of Latin poets set himself to create a national epic, he chose for his hero not the typical heroic warrior but a kind of pilgrim father, the pious long-suffering Aeneas who was charged with the providential mission to found a new city and bring the gods to Latium:

> *genus unde Latinum*
> *Albanique patres atque alta moenia Romae.*

Now the Virgilian myth became the Christian reality. When St. Paul, in obedience to the warning of a dream, set sail from Troy in A.D. 49 and came to Philippi in Macedonia he did more to change the course of history than the great battle that had decided the fate of the Roman Empire on the same spot nearly a century earlier, for he brought to Europe the seed of a new life which was ultimately destined to create a new world. All this took place underneath the surface of history, so that it was unrecognized by the leaders of contemporary culture, like Gallio the brother of Seneca, who actually saw it taking place beneath their eyes. But it is impossible to read the contemporary account of these journeys and the letters that St. Paul wrote to the first Christian communities of Europe and Asia Minor without realizing that a new principle had been introduced into the static civilization of the Roman world that contained infinite possibilities of change. As the mob at Salonika protested: these men have turned the world upside down, proclaiming another king than Caesar —Jesus. And so indeed they did, and this act of creative revolution marks the beginning of a new era in world his-

tory, and, above all, in the history of the West. Up to this
point Europe had been divided between the Roman world
and the outer world of barbarians. Now the Roman world
was itself divided between the servants of Caesar and the
servants of Christ. In the course of centuries this latter division was finally overcome by the conversion of the Empire,
so that Roman and Christian became almost synonymous
terms. But by that time the power of the Empire in the
West was broken. Rome was no longer the capital of
Caesar, it had become the Apostolic See. To St. Leo and
his contemporaries the Roman Empire was an instrument
in the hands of providence to bring the nations together to
receive the Gospel of Christ. St. Peter and St. Paul had
taken the place of Romulus and Remus as the founders of
the second Rome, the *Urbs sacerdotalis et regalis*, which
was the centre of the Christian world:

> *En omne sub regnum Remi*
> *mortale concessit genus*
> *idem loquuntur dissoni*
> *ritus, idipsum sentiunt.*
> *Hoc destinatum, quo magis*
> *jus Christiani nominis,*
> *quodcunque terrarum jacet,*
> *uno inligaret vinculo.*[1]

Thus the conversion of the Roman Empire, the process
by which the state of Augustus and Nero became the state
of Constantine and Theodosius, has a vital relation to the
rise of the new culture. This has never been adequately
recognized by the historians, owing to the curious divorce
between ancient and modern history which has caused the
study of the transitional age of the third and fourth centuries to be so neglected in English education, which in
this respect was still influenced by the ideals and prejudices
of the Italian humanists. And these prejudices, in turn, re-

[1] Prudentius, *Peristephanon*, II, 429; cp. Leonis M., sermo 82.
Translation: "Lo, the whole race of man has been bowed to the
Kingdom of Remus, different rites say the same and think the
same. So it is destined that the Christian law should bind all the
earth in one bond."

flected the cultural disunity of the age in question. The higher culture of the ancient world continued to shut its eyes to the existence of the new faith, even after Christianity had become the official religion of the Empire. And this obstinate conservatism was strongest in the West, where it was strengthened by the traditions of Roman patriotism and the resentment of the senatorial aristocracy against the new capital on the Bosphorus with its eunuch consul and its Greek senators. To these defenders of a lost cause, like Quintus Aurelius Symmachus, Claudian and Rutilius Namatianus, Christianity was an alien interloper which undermined the moral resistance of the state at the time when the barbarians were attacking it from without. It was against these opinions that St. Augustine and Orosius wrote in the fifth century, so that it was not until after the fall of Rome that the dualism between the old culture and the new religion was finally overcome.

In the East, however, conditions were very different, and for centuries to come the Eastern Empire was to remain the centre of the development of Christian thought and culture.

The new religion had had its origins in the semi-oriental underworld of the great Hellenistic cities, bringing new life and hope to classes and individuals spiritually estranged from the soulless materialistic culture of the Roman world-state. By degrees it permeated the whole society, until in the fourth century it became the official religion of the Empire and inspired the new type of Byzantine culture which had its centre in the New Rome founded by the first Christian Emperor at Constantinople. This culture was Asiatic Greek in origin. For we must remember that at the time of the fall of the Roman Empire in the West the main centres of Christian culture and the majority of the Christian population were still non-European. The mother tongue of the Church was Greek and its theological development was mainly due to Asiatic Greek councils and Asiatic Greek theologians, at a time when in the Latin West paganism was still strong, and the ruling classes, and, far more, the rural population, were still largely non-Christian in culture and tradition.

It is interesting to speculate on what might have been

the result if the Western development had followed the Eastern pattern—if a kind of Latin Byzantine culture had arisen in the fifth and sixth centuries with its capital at Rome or Milan or Treves, as might well have happened, if external forces had not intervened. In fact, however, the imperial system in the West had broken down under the pressure of the barbarian invasion, before the new religion had had time to permeate the culture and social life of the Western provinces.

Only in Africa were conditions comparable to those in the Eastern provinces, and Africa was not destined to remain a part of Western Christendom for very long. There were indeed a few Western European cities, such as Rome and Lyons, which had an important share in the first movement of Christian expansion, but even at Rome the pagan resistance was more stubborn and long continued than in the East. In the predominantly rural areas of Central and Western Europe the social elements which contributed most to the rapid diffusion of Christianity were non-existent, and these regions remained pagan in culture, if not in name, down to the last days of the Western Empire and beyond.

Thus, unlike Christian Byzantium, Christian Rome represents only a brief interlude between paganism and barbarism. There were only eighteen years between Theodosius' closing of the temples and the first sack of the Eternal City by the barbarians. The great age of the Western Fathers from Ambrose to Augustine was crammed into a single generation, and St. Augustine died with the Vandals at the gate.

There were, of course, very wide differences in the conditions that prevailed in the different provinces and the different strata of society. An aristocrat like Sidonius Apollinaris, who lived under the relatively tolerant rule of the Visigothic kings, could continue to lead the life of a cultured and wealthy landowner while his contemporaries of the same class in less favoured regions were being slaughtered or reduced to beggary. Roughly speaking, we may say that all along the Northern frontiers of the Empire from York to Belgrade the structure of civilized life had collapsed, the cities and villas had been destroyed and society relapsed into a state of pagan barbarism. But in the South, round the shores of the Mediterranean, there was as yet no break in the continuity of culture, and the barbarian conquerors were a small alien element, which existed as a parasitic growth upon a Latin-speaking population that vastly outnumbered them and continued to live its own life with its own laws and institutions.

Nevertheless the development of Western Christianity did not always correspond with this pattern. In the Mediterranean lands the conquerors were Arians, who sometimes, as in Africa, subjected the Church to intense persecution; while in the North, though the conquerors were far more barbarous in culture and pagan in religion, they were more accessible to the missionary action of the Church, which was also the representative of the higher culture.

Hence the barbarian kingdoms of the South were short-lived and had little influence on the future of Western culture, except negatively in so far as they prepared the way for the Moslem conquest of Africa and Spain in the eighth century. It was the baptism of Clovis in 496 and that of Ethelbert of Kent in 597 that mark the real beginnings of a new age in Western Europe.

Thus it was in those parts of the West where the material destruction of the barbarian invasions had been greatest that the new development took place. The spiritual resources of the Church had not been seriously impaired by the fall of the Empire. Indeed in certain respects they were strengthened, since the Church now united the social traditions of Roman culture with its own spiritual traditions and thus fulfilled a double function in a society which needed social as well as religious leadership. The new barbarian kingdoms had taken over the military and political functions of the Empire—they held the sword, they levied the taxes, they administered justice—of a sort—but everything else belonged to the Church—moral authority, learning and culture, the prestige of the Roman name and the care of the people. A man's real citizenship was not to be found in his subjection to the barbarian state, but in his membership of the Christian Church, and it was to the bishop rather than to the king that he looked as the leader of Christian society.

But all the time a process of assimilation was going on which tended to create a new social unity. As the barbarians were converted to Christianity, they also acquired elements of the higher culture, while on the other hand the Christian society was gradually losing touch with the traditions of Roman culture and was itself becoming positively barbarized. We find a good illustration of this double process in the picture which St. Gregory of Tours gives us of the conditions in the kingdom of the Franks during the second half of the sixth century. He was himself a man of aristocratic Gallic lineage, a descendant of Roman officials and a member of a dynasty of bishops. But the society in which he lived and which he describes is already profoundly barbarous and his own writings show little sign of classical culture, as he himself admits in the prefaces to his History and to his hagiographical works. But he was a true Roman in his unflinching realism, his loyalty to the past and his sense of social responsibility which he maintained in a society equally oblivious of the Roman order and the Christian spirit. He still represents the Roman-Christian ideal of the bishop as *Defensor Civitatis* and the ultimate guardian and champion of the civic tradition in its new Christian form—the tradition which had been so nobly maintained in the age of the invasions by St. Germanus of Auxerre, St. Avitus of Vienna, St. Anianus of Orléans and St. Sidonius Apollinaris (431/2–487).

But in the age of Gregory of Tours the barbarism which had destroyed the Empire had also invaded the Church. The Merovingian kings had not ceased to be barbarians by becoming Christians. Indeed, in proportion as they became detached from the tribal background of the old Germanic kingship they seemed to become more ferocious, more treacherous and more corrupt. And it was on these savages that the Church was increasingly dependent, since with the breakdown of the old Roman organization the king inevitably intervened more and more in the appointment of bishops and in the government of the Church. And consequently the outward decline in the condition of culture was accompanied by a deterioration of moral standards which also affected the bishops and the monasteries.

The world which Gregory of Tours describes is a world of violence and corruption in which rulers set an example of injustice and contempt for the law, and even the barbaric virtues of loyalty and military honour were no longer preserved. In such a world religion was able to maintain its power only by the awe inspired by its supernatural prestige and the spiritual violence it opposed to the physical violence of barbarism. The fear of the wrath of God and the vengeance of the saints was the only power capable of intimidating the lawless ruffians who were so common among the new ruling class in the semi-barbarous Frankish state.

In the Dark Ages the saints were not merely patterns of moral perfection, whose prayers were invoked by the Church. They were supernatural powers who inhabited their sanctuaries and continued to watch over the welfare of their land and their people. Such were St. Julian of Brioude, St. Caesarius of Arles, St. Germanus of Auxerre —such, above all, was St. Martin, whose shrine at Tours was a fountain of grace and miraculous healing, to which the sick resorted from all parts of Gaul; an asylum where all the oppressed—the fugitive slave, the escaped criminal and even those on whom the vengeance of the king had fallen—could find refuge and supernatural protection. It is difficult to exaggerate the importance of the cult of the saints in the period that followed the fall of the Empire in the West, for its influence was felt equally at both ends of the social scale—among the leaders of culture like Gregory of Tours and St. Gregory the Great and among the common people, especially the peasants who, as "pagani", had hitherto been unaffected by the new religion of the cities. In many cases the local pagan cult was displaced only by the deliberate substitution of the cult of a local saint, as we see in Gregory of Tours' description of how the Bishop of Javols put an end to the annual pagan festival of the peasants at Lake Helanus by building a church to St. Hilary of Poitiers on the spot to which they could bring the offerings which had formerly been thrown into the waters of the sacred lake.

Thus the early centuries of the Middle Ages saw the rise of a new Christian mythology—the legends of the saints —to which Gregory of Tours himself contributed so much by his hagiographical writings—the two books on the Miracles of St. Martin, the Life of the Fathers, the book of the Miracles of St. Julian of Brioude and the books of the Glory of the Blessed Martyrs and the Glory of the Confessors. This literature and the cult to which it corresponds represent the other side of the dark picture of contemporary society which he presents in his History of the Franks. On the one side we see a world of violence and injustice which is sinking to destruction by its own weight. But on the other side there is the world of divine power and mystery in which the harsh necessities of daily experience no longer dominate man's life—where nothing is impossible and every human suffering and misfortune may find a remedy.

It is very difficult for the modern mind to enter this world of popular Christian imagination which finds expression in the early medieval legends of the saints, since it is farther removed from us than the mysticism of the late Middle Ages, or the metaphysical religion of the age of the Fathers. Yet it is genuinely Christian in spirit, though it is the Christianity of a society striving against the all-pervading influence of a barbaric environment. In this twilight world it was inevitable that the Christian ascetic and saint should acquire some of the features of the pagan shaman and demigod: that his prestige should depend upon his power as a wonder-worker and that men should seek his decision in the same way as they had formerly resorted to the shrine of a pagan oracle.

Nevertheless it was only in this world of Christian mythology—in the cult of the saints and their relics and their miracles—that the vital transfusion of the Christian faith and ethics with the barbaric tradition of the new peoples of the West could be achieved. It was obviously impossible for peoples without any tradition of philosophy or written literature to assimilate directly the subtle and profound theological metaphysics of a St. Augustine or the great teachers of the Byzantine world. The barbarians could understand and accept the spirit of the new religion only when it was manifested to them visibly in the lives and acts of men who seemed endowed with supernatural qualities. The conversion of Western Europe was achieved not so much by the teaching of a new doctrine as by the manifestation of a new power, which invaded and subdued the barbarians of the West, as it had already subdued the civilized lands of the Mediterranean. And as the martyrs had been the heroes and witnesses of the conquest of the Empire, so it was the hermits and the monks who were the confessors and apostles of the faith among the barbarians.

Here the relation between religion and culture is not that of assimilation and permeation, but rather one of contradiction and contrast. The lives of the saints and ascetics impressed the mind of the barbarians because they were the manifestation of a way of life and a scale of values entirely opposed to all they had hitherto known and accepted. But the contrast was not between the higher civilization of the Christian Roman world and the barbarism of the pagans, but a contrast between two spiritual worlds or two planes of reality. For behind the ethical contrast between the life of the saint and the barbarism of society there lies the eschatological dualism of the present world and the world to come which was the background of the medieval Christian view of life.

The Western Church did not come to the barbarians with a civilizing mission or any conscious hopes of social progress, but with a tremendous message of divine judgment and divine salvation. Humanity was born under a curse, enslaved by the dark powers of cosmic evil and sinking ever deeper under the burden of its own guilt. Only by the way of the Cross and by the grace of the crucified Redeemer was it possible for men to extricate themselves from the *massa damnata* of unregenerate humanity and escape from the wreckage of a doomed world.

This stern doctrine came with peculiar force to the declining civilization of the post-Roman world—a world in which war and famine and slavery and torture were the unavoidable facts of daily experience, where the weak could hardly survive, and the strong died young in battle.

No doubt it is easy for us to see the other side of the picture. Indeed, modern nationalism has tended to idealize the native cultures of the Western barbarians, and to see the Germans, the Celts, the Slavs and the rest as young peoples full of creative powers who were bringing new life to an exhausted and decadent civilization. But though this view found its ultimate justification in the course of history, it was not possible for the men who actually had to deal with the barbarians to recognize it. To the Christian world during the Dark Ages the forces of barbarism were inevitably seen in their negative aspects—as a formless power of war and destruction which brought ruin to the cities and slavery to the peoples. This is the view which finds expression so often in the Christian liturgy, which prays that God may come to the aid of the Christian people and subdue the barbarian peoples who put their trust in their own savagery. Nor were the barbarian princes who were nominally Christian much better, as we see from St. Gildas' strictures on the tyrants of Britain, St. Patrick's letter to Coroticus or Gregory of Tours' picture of Merovingian society.

We see from the letters and homilies of St. Gregory the Great that the Christian conscience was by no means indifferent to the social injustice and physical suffering of the time—the prisoners "tied by the neck like dogs and led away to slavery", the mutilated peasants, the depopulated and starving cities. But these things were past the aid of man to cure. "What is there," asks St. Gregory, "to please us in this world? Everywhere we see sorrow and lamentation. The cities and towns are destroyed, the fields are laid waste and the land returns to solitude. No peasant is left to till the fields, there are few inhabitants left in the cities, and yet even these scanty remnants of humanity are still subject to ceaseless sufferings. . . . Some are led away captive, others are mutilated and still more slain before our eyes. What is there then to please us in this world? If we still love such a world as this, it is plain that we love not pleasure but misery."[2]

These things, St. Columban wrote a few years later in his letter to Pope Boniface, were signs of the end. The world was visibly falling to pieces and the Shepherd of Shepherds was about to come for the last time. And therefore it was natural that Christians should turn their eyes to the other world—to the Eternal City, of which they were already citizens by adoption and which was steadily extending its frontiers against the transitory and fading visible world.

But though the religion of that age was intensely other-worldly, its other-worldliness had a very different character from much that we have come to associate with the word in its modern pietist form. It was collective rather than individualist, objective rather than subjective, realist rather than idealist. Although the world to come lay outside history and beyond time, it was the fixed limit towards which time and history were carrying the world. The ocean of eternity surrounded the sinking island of human existence on every side. In the past, the world of men had been confident and secure. As the waters of the sea retreated, they had pushed the limit of culture further and further under the protection of the dikes they had built. But now the waters were advancing, the dikes were down and soon there would be no more land. Only the Church remained as an ark of refuge, and it was a better investment to spend one's time and money on the building of an ark than to waste it in vain attempts to mend the broken dikes or reclaim the ruined fields and saltings.

This is a crude picture of the other-worldly attitude of early Christendom. But the reality was no less crude. St. Gregory the Great represents the highest surviving traditions of Roman society and stands head and shoulders above the average level of Lombard or Merovingian culture. He had applied the strong practical intelligence and statesmanship of ancient Rome to the service of the Church and at the same time he was a great Christian teacher in

[2] S. Greg. Mag., Homil. in Ezech. II, Epistle vi, 22.

the spirit of St. Ambrose and St. Leo. Yet when he records in his Dialogues the lives and deeds of the holy men who were his immediate predecessors he introduces us into a wonderland of supernatural marvels which equal or surpass anything to be found in the legends of the martyrs or the lives of the Fathers of the Desert.

To that age the saints and ascetics were living and visible witnesses to the power of the world to come. And they were not the only witnesses. Even more important was the corporate experience of and communion with the eternal world which the Church already possessed in the Sacred Mysteries. I pointed out last year how the religion cultures of the ancient world found their centre in the ritual order of prayer and sacrifice around which the whole life of the community revolved. In the religion cultures of the Byzantine and medieval world the Christian liturgy held a similar position. The centuries which followed the fall of the Empire in the West, in spite of the impoverishment of their material culture, were from the liturgical point of view a great creative age, and it is remarkable that this is no less true of the semi-barbaric West than of the stable and comparatively prosperous Byzantine world. All these ages possessed of poetry, music and art found expression in the liturgy—an expression which no later age has been able to surpass.

Nothing indeed could be more striking than the contrast between the secular and the liturgical poetry of this age. In Byzantium we have, on the one side, the dying echoes of the classical Hellenic tradition in the last poets of the Palatine Anthology, while, on the other, there is the greatest of the liturgical poets, Romanus the Melodist, who endowed the new spirit of the new Christian culture with a new music and a new rhythm.

But in the West the contrast is even more striking since it can be seen not in two distinct schools of poetry but in the work of the same writer. Venantius Fortunatus (c. 530–601) seems at first sight the typical representative of a decadent culture, a literary parasite who makes his living by composing laborious compliments and panegyrics to flatter his barbarian patrons. But the moment he is touched by the liturgical spirit his tired rhetoric is miraculously transformed into the mighty music of the *Vexilla Regis* and the *Pange lingua gloriosi*.

It is impossible to insist too strongly on the importance of this transformation of literary style and aesthetic feeling, for nothing gives us a clearer insight into the nature of the spiritual changes that were producing a new type of culture. It began long before the fall of the Empire, since its origins go back to the New Testament and the first beginnings of Gentile Christianity. But it was not until the fifth century that its influence was strongly felt on the higher levels of Roman culture. And it is remarkable that it was the most Roman in temperament of all the fathers, St. Ambrose of Milan, who took the first and most decisive step towards the creation of a new liturgical poetry. We possess a most vivid account of the impression that it produced on a contemporary in the *Confessions* of St. Augustine, in which he describes his wonder and delight at the new spiritual world that was opened to him by St. Ambrose at Milan at the dawn of his conversion:

The days were not long enough as I meditated, and found wonderful delight in meditating, upon the depth of Your design for the salvation of the human race. I wept at the beauty of Your hymns and canticles, and was powerfully moved at the sweet sound of Your Church's singing. These sounds flowed into my ears, and the truth streamed into my heart; so that my feeling of devotion overflowed, and the tears ran from my eyes, and I was happy in them.

It was only a little while before that the church of Milan had begun to practise this kind of consolation and exultation, to the great joy of the brethren singing together with heart and voice. For it was only about a year since Justina, the mother of the boy emperor Valentinian, was persecuting Your servant Ambrose in the interests of her own heresy: for she had been seduced by the Arians. The devoted people had stayed night and day in the church, ready to die with their bishop. And my mother, Your handmaid, bearing a great part of the trouble and vigil, had lived in prayer. I also, though still not warmed by the fire of Your

Spirit, was stirred to excitement by the disturbed and wrought-up state of the city.

It was at this time that the practice was instituted of singing hymns and psalms after the manner of the Eastern churches, to keep the people from being altogether worn out with anxiety and want of sleep. The custom has been retained from that day to this, and has been imitated by many, indeed in almost all congregations throughout the world.[3]

This new liturgical poetry of the West differs from that of the East in its sobriety and simplicity which are nevertheless not without their own beauty. It was created by a man, trained in classical traditions, who was careful not to transgress the rules of classical prosody. But since he subordinated his art to the new requirements of the liturgy and wrote for the Church and the people, he produced something entirely new which has lived on for seventeen hundred years in the hymnaries of Western Christendom and the liturgy of the Western Church.

In this he succeeded better than Prudentius, a greater poet, but one who was too individual to subordinate his genius to the needs of the congregation. On the other hand, St. Ambrose's great disciple St. Augustine went further (in his rhythmic "psalm against the Donatists") and abandoned the whole tradition of classical poetry in a direct appeal to the popular audience—*volens etiam causam Donatistorum ad ipsius humillimi vulgi et omnino imperitorum atque idiotarum notitiam pervenire.*[4]

This curious work bears a close resemblance to the new religious poetry which had arisen in Syria and found its greatest representation in St. Ephrem, "the Harp of the Holy Spirit".

It is constructed in regular strophes of twelve verses of sixteen syllables. Each strophe begins with a successive letter of the alphabet and ends with a recurrent refrain, and each verse of the strophe ends in the same vowel. All these

[3] Saint Augustine, *Confessions*, IX, vi–vii. F. J. Sheed's translation.

[4] Translation: Wishing to bring the affair of the Donatists to the knowledge of the lowest class, the ignorant and illiterate.

features are characteristic of the new Syriac religious poetry, so that everything points to the oriental origin of the new style. Nevertheless, in spite of the great influence of St. Augustine, his experiment in the new style of rhythmic verse found no immediate imitators. It was not intended for liturgical use, but for popular propaganda, and the liturgical poets continued to follow the tradition of St. Ambrose. It is only in the furthest West in the new Celtic Churches that the use of rhythmical and, above all, rimed poetry was fully developed in the service of the liturgy as well as for private prayer.

Meanwhile throughout the West the liturgy was becoming more and more the centre of Christian culture. Although Prudentius and Paulinus of Nola do not compare with St. Ambrose as liturgical poets, they reflect the growing importance of the liturgy in the intellectual and spiritual life of the time. Even Sidonius Apollinaris, who seems at first sight a typical representative of the old secular culture, devoted his talents to the composition of liturgies and the improvisation of prayers, as Gregory of Tours relates (H.F. II, xxii).

Whatever else might be lost, and however dark might be the prospects of Western society, the sacred order of the liturgy remained intact and, in it, the whole Christian world, Roman, Byzantine and barbarian, found an inner principle of unity. Moreover the liturgy was not only the bond of Christian unity. It was also the means by which the mind of the gentiles and the barbarians was attuned to a new view of life and a new concept of history. It displayed in a visible, almost dramatic form what had happened and was to happen to the human race—the sacred history of man's creation and redemption and the providential dispensation that governed the course of history, the great theme which is so majestically unfolded in the prophecies and prayers of the Paschal liturgy. For while the liturgy had the same key significance in the culture of ancient Christendom which it had possessed in the archaic cultures, its spiritual content was entirely different. As we have seen,[5] the archaic ritual order was conceived as the

[5] Cf. *Religion and Culture*, ch. vii.

pattern of the cosmic order, and consequently its typical mysteries were the mysteries of nature itself represented and manifested in the dramatic action of a sacred myth. Such were the mysteries of Eleusis, such were the still older and more venerable mysteries of Sumerian and Egyptian religion, like the myth of Tammuz and Ninanna or Isis and Osiris—all of which centre in the mystery of the life of the earth and the cycle of the agricultural year. The Christian mystery, on the other hand, was essentially the mystery of eternal life. It was not concerned with the life of nature or with culture as a part of the order of nature, but with the redemption and regeneration of humanity by the Incarnation of the Divine Word.

But since the Incarnation and the whole redemptive process were historically situated, the Christian mystery was also an historical mystery—the revelation of the divine purpose manifested on earth and in time, as the fulfilment of the ages. Thus instead of the nature myth which was the key to the ritual order of the archaic civilization, the Christian mystery is based on a *sacred history*, and liturgy develops into an historical cycle in which the whole story of human creation and redemption is progressively unfolded. And at the same time an element of historical and social continuity was provided by the commemoration of the feasts of the saints, by which every age and every people and indeed every city found its liturgical representative and patron.

It is almost impossible to convey to the modern mind the realism and objectivity with which the Christians of those ages viewed this liturgical participation in the mysteries of salvation. The commemoration and mystical representation of the sacred history was at the same time the initiation and rebirth of the creature into an eternal existence. On this plane the old order had already passed away and the eternal world invaded and transfused the world of time, so that creation was brought back to its spiritual source and mankind was united with the angelic hierarchies in a common spiritual action. The theological and metaphysical aspects of this conception of the liturgy were worked out most fully during this period in the Byzantine

Church by writers like the Pseudo-Dionysius and Saint Maximus the Confessor. But there was no real divergence between East and West in this matter, since in the sixth and seventh centuries all the different liturgical traditions shared the same liturgical spirit and *theoria* which was the common inheritance of Eastern and Western Christendom.

Thus in the West, after the fall of the Empire, the Church possessed in the liturgy a rich tradition of Christian culture as an order of worship, a structure of thought and a principle of life. And in spite of the general decline in culture this tradition continued to develop spontaneously and to bear fruit in different forms according to the complicated evolution of the different Western Rites. There were the rich and colourful liturgies of Visigothic Spain and Merovingian Gaul. There was the Northern Italian tradition, represented by the Ambrosian Rite. And finally there was the ancient and conservative Roman tradition, which from the time of St. Gregory the Great came to exercise a far-reaching normative influence on all the Western Churches.

The preservation and development of this liturgical tradition was one of the main preoccupations of the Church in the dark age that followed the barbarian conquest, since it was in this way that the vitality and continuity of the inner life of Christendom which was the seed of the new order were preserved. But this demanded a concentration of religious and intellectual energy which could not be found in the dying culture of the ancient city and in the tradition of the schools as represented by men of letters like Venantius Fortunatus or Ennodius.

The problem was solved by the rise of a new institution which became the guardian of the liturgical tradition and the social organ of a new Christian culture. As the darkness deepened over Western Europe it was in the monasteries rather than in the cities that the tradition of Latin culture and the patterns of Christian life were preserved. The monks were the apostles of the West and the founders of medieval culture.

Chapter III

The Monks of the West and the Formation of the Western Tradition

ANY STUDY of the origins of medieval culture must inevitably give an important place to the history of Western monasticism, since the monastery was the most typical cultural institution throughout the whole period that extends from the decline of classical civilization to the rise of the European universities in the twelfth century—upwards of seven hundred years. And it is even more important for the subject with which I am particularly concerned—the relation of religion and culture, for it was through monasticism that religion exercised a direct formative influence on the whole cultural development of these centuries.

No doubt, as I said in *Religion and Culture*, there have been other cultures—Tibet, Burma and Ceylon, for example—in which a non-Christian monasticism played a somewhat similar role. But these were secondary or marginal cultures which have had little influence on the course of world history. The situation in China is more comparable, since there we have an example of a great world culture which was influenced by the coming of Buddhist monasticism at the very period when Western and Byzantine culture were being moulded by Christian monasticism. But, in China, the old tradition of Confucian learning remained intact and the Buddhist monks never took the place of the Confucian scholars. In the West, on the other hand, the educational institutions of the Roman Empire were swept away by the barbarian invasion or declined and died with the declining city culture of the Latin world. It was only by the Church and, particularly, by the monks that the tradition of classical culture and the writings of classical authors, "the Latin classics", were preserved. And already in the sixth century we have an outstanding example in the case of Cassiodorus (496–575) of the way in which the old tradition of learning found a refuge in the monastery, and the monastic schools and libraries and scriptoria became the chief organs of higher intellectual culture in Western Europe.

Nevertheless, this was not the primary task of monasticism. In fact, nothing could be further removed from the original spirit of the institution. It was born in the African desert as a protest against the whole tradition of the classical culture of the Greek and the Roman world. It stood for the absolute renunciation of everything the ancient world had prized—not only pleasure and wealth and honour, but family life and citizenship and society. Its founders and models were the terrible ascetics of Nitria and the Thebaid who passed their lives in ceaseless prayer and fasting and in an almost physical struggle with the powers of darkness.

After the peace of the Church when the supreme test of martyrdom was no longer demanded, the ascetics had come in the eyes of the Christian world to hold the position the martyrs had formerly occupied as the living witnesses of the faith and the reality of the supernatural world. They were men who "had tasted the powers of the World to come" and, as we see in the Lausiac History and the other documents of primitive monasticism, they were regarded as the watchmen or guardians who "kept the walls" of the Christian City and repelled the attacks of its spiritual enemies. The fame and influence of the new movement reached their height at the very moment when Rome, the earthly city, was falling a victim to the barbarians. It was in that generation that leaders of Roman society, like Paula and Melania, and leaders of Western Christian thought like Jerome and Rufinus and Cassian made their pilgrimages to the Egyptian and Syrian deserts and initiated a literary propaganda in favour of the new movement which had enormous success throughout the Latin West and the Byzantine East.

The writings of John Cassian—the Institutes and the Collations—are particularly important, since they sum up the whole spirit and practice of Egyptian monasticism in a form acceptable to Western Latin culture and became the authoritative standard of monastic spirituality for all the subsequent generations of Western monasticism from St. Benedict and Caesarius of Arles to the Brethren of the Common Life and the early Jesuits.

And, at the same time, men like St. Martin and St. Honoratus and Cassian himself were introducing the monastic way of life in the Western provinces. The movement spread with amazing rapidity, since it reached Spain and Britain at the same time as Gaul, and extended into Ireland from the moment of its conversion to Christianity by St. Patrick.

In its main features this early Western monasticism was indistinguishable from that of the East and its most important centre, which was situated on the Riviera at Lerins and Marseilles and in the islands of the Ligurian Sea, was a stronghold of oriental influences. But, from the beginning, we can trace signs of another influence which was destined to socialize the ideal of the monastic life, and transform it into a great cultural institution. There was much in oriental monasticism that was repugnant to the disciplined and practical ethos of the Roman tradition, and St. Augustine's work on monasticism—*de Opere Monachorum*—is outspoken in its condemnation of the hypocrisy of the long-haired false ascetics and the wandering monks who lived in idleness and exploited popular superstition. Yet St. Augustine was himself a monk as well as a bishop, and one of the creators of the Western monastic tradition. For it was he more than anyone else who was responsible for that combination of the monastic life with the priesthood which ultimately became one of the distinctive features of Western monasticism.[1]

---

[1] Fr. Hertling has written, "The union of the monastic ideal with sacerdotal activity is the deliberate personal creation of St. Augustine, a creation which still remains alive and fruitful"

The Augustinian conception of monasticism, as described, for example, in his Sermons (e.g. 355 and 356) is inspired by the ideal of the common life of the primitive Church rather than by the intense asceticism of the monks of the desert. And the same is true to a great extent of the ideal of St. Basil, which became the classical standard of Byzantine monasticism in Europe and Asia Minor. For St. Basil the social nature of man and the Christian doctrine of the common life of the Mystical Body prove that the life of a community is necessary to perfection and therefore superior in principle to the solitary asceticism of the hermit.

The monastic community was a self-contained society which was completely Christian in so far as it existed only for spiritual ends and was regulated down to the most minute detail by a rule of life which took the place of social custom and secular law. Thus it was a free society, independent of external control and based on voluntary membership. In the East this independence was less complete owing to the monastic legislation of Justinian, which acquired canonical authority. And it was partly for this reason that, in spite of St. Basil, the extreme individualism of the solitary ascetics of the desert continued to enjoy such a high prestige and that the great centres of the ascetic tradition in Egypt and in North-West Mesopotamia (especially in the region of Tur Abdin) became the leaders of the resistance to the Imperial Church and were consequently lost to Orthodoxy.

In the West, however, the state was too weak and too barbarous to attempt to control the monasteries. Here the great legislators of monasticism were not Justinian, but St. Benedict and St. Gregory the Great. The Rule of St. Benedict marks the final assimilation of the monastic institution by the Roman spirit and the tradition of the Western Church. Its conception of the monastic life is essentially social and co-operative—as a discipline of the common life;

(*Zeitschrift für Christliche Theologie*, 1930, p. 359).

But we must remember that the idea of an episcopal monastery goes back to St. Eusebius at Vercelli, c. 360.

"the school of the service of the Lord". It differs from the older rules in its strongly practical character, its regulation of the details of common life and common work and its concern with the monastic economy. The Rule lays down that "the monastery should be so arranged that all necessary things such as water-mill, gardens, and workshops should be within the enclosure". In fact the Benedictine Abbey was a self-contained economic organism, like the villa of a Roman landowner, save that the monks were themselves the workers and the old classical contrast between servile work and free leisure no longer obtained. The primary task of the monk, however, was still the performance of the divine liturgy of prayer and psalmody which is minutely regulated by St. Benedict. This is the work of God—*Opus Dei*—with which nothing must interfere and which is the true end and justification of the monastic life.

Thus, in an age of insecurity and disorder and barbarism, the Benedictine Rule embodied an ideal of spiritual order and disciplined moral activity which made the monastery an oasis of peace in the world of war. It is true that the forces of barbarism were often too strong for it. Monte Cassino itself was destroyed by the Lombards about 581, and the monks were forced to take refuge in Rome. But such catastrophes did not weaken the spirit of the Rule; on the contrary, they brought the Benedictines into closer relation with Rome, and with St. Gregory, through whom St. Benedict and his Rule acquired their worldwide fame and their new apostolic mission to the barbarians in the far West. For it was at Rome that the Benedictine tradition became combined with the Augustinian tradition of a clerical monasticism and with the liturgical traditions of the Roman monasteries which were responsible for the performance of the liturgical offices and the music of the great basilicas.

Thus in the age of St. Gregory, and largely owing to his personal influence, the foundations were laid for a synthesis of the various elements of Western monasticism according to the spirit of the Benedictine rule under the guidance and control of the Papacy. St. Gregory had himself been a monk, and he did more than any of his predecessors to promote and protect the cause of monasticism, even against the authority of the episcopate, when circumstances rendered this necessary. Above all, he realized clearly that the monastic institution had become an essential organ of the Church, and the chief hope for the future of Christian culture. It is remarkable that St. Gregory, who was certainly not lacking in a sense of social responsibility, deliberately dissuaded his friends from entering the public service on the ground that the world was nearing its end and that it was better to seek the peace of the cloister in which a man becomes already a partaker in eternity, than to become involved in the temporal anxieties and ambitions that are inseparable from the service of the state.[2]

But while in the Mediterranean the monks were retreating from the dying culture of the ancient world, in the North monasticism was becoming the creator of a new Christian culture and a school of the Christian life for the new peoples of the West.

It was among the Celtic peoples that this aspect of monasticism was first developed. We know, indeed, practically nothing of monastic origins in Britain, apart from the foundation by St. Ninian of the monastery of Candida Casa in Galloway in 397, which became a centre of Christian influence first among the Picts and later in Ireland. But in the fourth and fifth centuries the famous Pelagius was a monk from Britain, while his chief disciple Caelestius was, apparently, of Irish origin. Moreover Faustus of Riez, the greatest and most learned of the early abbots of Lerins, was himself a Briton, and there is little doubt that it was from Lerins that the main tradition of Celtic monasticism and liturgy was derived.

With the collapse of civic life in Britain and the disappearance of the old Roman sees, the monks became the leading element in the Church, while in Ireland the monastic element was predominant from the first, and was the characteristic feature of the new Irish Christian culture. If St. Patrick himself was not a monk, he was under strong monastic influence and had a direct contact with the great

[2] Cf. especially S. Greg. Mag., Epist. vii, 26.

centre of Gallic monasticism at Lerins. He himself when he was an old man tells in his Confession how he longed to return to Gaul to "visit the brethren and to behold the faces of the Saints of the Lord". And there is no doubt that monasticism in Ireland is as old as the time of St. Patrick, since he writes of "the countless sons of the Scots and the daughters of chieftains, who had become monks and virgins of Christ".

In Ireland the Roman tradition of city life and the city episcopate were non-existent, and so it was natural that the Irish Church should have found its natural centres in the monasteries which rapidly became very numerous and very populous. A medieval tradition states that St. Patrick demanded from his converts a tithe of the population and the land of Ireland for the religious life. And, although this is no more than a legend, there is no doubt that early Irish monasticism was a great mass movement led by the sons and daughters of the ruling families who founded the monasteries and were followed by their fellow tribesmen and dependants. Although the monastic community, which was a society of peace, represents the opposite pole of thought and action to the tribal community, which was a society of warriors, there was a certain parallelism between them. On the one side we have the chieftain and his company of warriors who are bound to follow him to the death; on the other, we have the abbot and his community which is sworn to obedience to eternal life. On the one hand there is the ethos of honour and fidelity and the cult of the hero; on the other, the ethos of sacrifice and sanctity and the cult of the saint and the martyr. Again, on the one side, there is the oral tradition of heroic poetry and, on the other, the literary tradition of the Sacred Scriptures and the legends of the saints.

This correspondence between the patterns of pagan and monastic culture made it possible for men to pass from the one to the other by a profound change in their beliefs and their system of moral values without losing vital contact with their old social tradition, which was sublimated and transformed, but not destroyed or lost. Thus, family and regional loyalties came to centre in the hereditary monastery and the hereditary saints of the clan or kingdom, and the abbot became a spiritual chieftain whose dignity was usually transmitted to a member of the founder's kin.[3]

All this helps to explain the appeal the monastic institution made to the barbarian society, and especially to its ruling elements, and why so many men and women of royal blood entered the cloister and took a leading part in the conversion of their kinsfolk. Men of this kind, like St. Illtyd and St. Cadoc and St. David in Wales, St. Columba and St. Enda and St. Finnian of Clonard in Ireland, and SS. Wilfrid and Benedict Biscop, Willebrord and Boniface, Aldhelm and Bede in England, played a decisive part in the creation of the new Christian culture which first arose in these islands and gradually influenced the whole of Western Europe by its monastic foundations and its missionary and educational activity.

In this new environment monasticism inevitably tended to assume a role of cultural leadership foreign to the original spirit of the institution. The monks had to instruct their converts not only in Christian doctrine but in the Latin tongue, which was the sacred language of scripture and liturgy. They had to teach reading and writing and those arts and sciences which were necessary for the maintenance of the Church and the liturgy, such as calligraphy, painting, music and, above all, chronology and the knowledge of the calendar which had a similar importance for the liturgical culture of the early Middle Ages to that which they had possessed in the archaic ritual cultures.

Thus there arose an autonomous Christian culture centring in the monasteries and permeating the Church and the life of the people by educational and religious influence. It was no longer a question of the conquering barbarians being affected by the religion and culture of the conquered, as with the Franks and Goths; it was a new creation produced by the grafting of Latin Christian traditions on the native barbarian stock, so that it became in-

---

[3] Cf. Levison, *England and the Continent in the Eighth Century* (1946), pp. 27–29, for similar conditions in Northumbria, especially the custom of queens becoming abbesses of royal convents after the death of their consorts.

ternally assimilated by the new peoples. And it found original intellectual expression in the new vernacular literatures which make their first appearance in Ireland and England. Here the old oral heroic tradition achieved form and expression as in the songs of Beowulf and Widsith, while the new Christian poetry makes use of the traditional heroic imagery, as we see, for example, in poems like *The Dream of the Rood* or *Andreas*.

But the strength of the new Western monastic movement was due not only to its appeal to the kings and the nobles of the barbarian kingdom, it was also a power with the peasants which brought Christian culture to the heart of the rural society. For the monastery was an institution which was separable from the urban order of the Later Empire and capable of becoming the spiritual and economic centre of a purely rural society. By its sanctification of work and poverty it revolutionized both the order of social values which had dominated the slave-owning society of the Empire and that which was expressed in the aristocratic warrior ethos of the barbarian conquerors, so that the peasant, who for so long had been the forgotten bearer of the whole social structure, found his way of life recognized and honoured by the highest spiritual authority of the age. Even St. Gregory, who himself represented the traditions of the Senatorial aristocracy and the great Roman landowners, gives in his Dialogues a most sympathetic picture of the peasant life of contemporary Italian monasticism, as in his description of Abbot Equitius who used to travel throughout the country teaching and preaching and who, when summoned to give an account of his mission, presented himself before the Pope's messengers in peasant dress and hobnail shoes carrying the scythe with which he had been mowing the hay.[4]

These Italian monks were often themselves peasants by birth like St. Honoratus, who founded the great monastery at Fondi with its two hundred monks, although he was of servile origin. In Northern Europe social conditions were different, since, as I have said, the leaders of Celtic and Saxon monasticism were drawn from the ruling class of

[4] S. Greg. *Dialog*. I, iv.

barbarian society. But there was no less insistence on simplicity of life and the value of manual labour. To the modern mind the most striking feature of Celtic monasticism is its extreme asceticism, which is nearer to the Egyptian than the Benedictine pattern of life. Nevertheless, agriculture was far from being neglected. Indeed, nothing could be simpler and more functional than St. Molua's statement of the economic basis of the monastic life. "My dearest Brethren," he said, "till the earth well and work hard, so that you may have a sufficiency of food and drink and clothing. For, where there is sufficiency among the servants of God, then there will be stability, and when there is stability in service, then there will be the religious life. And the end of religious life is life eternal!"[5]

It was the disciplined and tireless labour of the monks which turned the tide of barbarism in Western Europe and brought back into cultivation the lands which had been deserted and depopulated in the age of the invasions. As Newman writes in a well-known passage on the Mission of St. Benedict: "St. Benedict found the world, physical and social, in ruins, and his mission was to restore it in the way not of science, but of nature, not as if setting about to do it, not professing to do it by any set time, or by any rare specific, or by any series of strokes, but so quietly, patiently, gradually, that often till the work was done, it was not known to be doing. It was a restoration rather than a visitation, correction or conversion. The new work which he helped to create was a growth rather than a structure. Silent men were observed about the country, or discovered in the forest, digging, clearing and building; and other silent men, not seen, were sitting in the cold cloister, tiring their eyes and keeping their attention on the stretch, while they painfully copied and recopied the manuscripts which they had saved. There was no one who contended or cried out, or drew attention to what was going on, but by degrees the woody swamp became a hermitage, a religious house, a

[5] Plumner, *Vitae Sanctorum Hiberniae*, II, 223 (1910). St. Molua or Laisren was the founder of Clonfertmulloe or Kyle in the sixth century.

farm, an abbey, a village, a seminary, a school of learning and a city."[6]

All this is no less true of Celtic monasticism than of the Benedictines. In some respects it was even more true, since it was the Irish monks who contributed most to create the tradition of monastic learning and educational activity during the dark period which followed the decline of the Byzantine Empire after the death of Justinian (565). The causes of this new development in the far West are complex. The most important of them, as I have already mentioned, was undoubtedly the exotic character of the new Christian culture in Ireland. Latin was the sacred language of the liturgy and the Scriptures, which every monk had to acquire, and which could be acquired only by books and the careful study of texts and grammar. But this new learning had to compete in Ireland with a very ancient and elaborate system of vernacular culture and education, which had been handed down for centuries by the sacred order of seers and poets (filid) who held a very important place in Irish society. The representatives of the new culture could only triumph by meeting their rivals on their own ground, as men of learning and masters of the word of power, and therefore it was natural and inevitable that Irish monasticism should acquire many of the features of the old learned class and that the monasteries should become not only abodes of prayer and asceticism but also schools and centres of learning.

Thus the Latin culture of Gallic monasticism transplanted to Wales and Ireland soon gave birth to a new literary tradition. It is often difficult to distinguish between the continental and insular elements in the new culture, since there is a certain affinity between the baroque eccentricities of later Gallic rhetoricians, like Virgilius Maro of Toulouse, and the fantastic verbosity of the "Hisperic" Latinity, which was so much admired in the British and Irish monasteries. At first sight, the laborious conceits of these monkish schoolmasters contrast very unfavourably with the "lucidity and discretion" of St. Benedict, or even

[6] Newman, *Historical Studies*, II.

with the honest bad Latin of Gregory of Tours. But it was a sign of the exuberance of a youthful culture rather than the pedantry of decadence, and it even produced works of real power and imagination, like the remarkable poem "Altus Prosator", which is ascribed to St. Columba. Since this has a reasonably good claim to be the oldest existing monument of Scottish literary culture, it is astonishing that it is not more famous. For, in spite of its barbaric Latin, it is a work of genius, which strikes a new note in European literature. The poet is inspired by the apocalyptic vision of the approaching end of all things which, as I said in the last chapter, is characteristic of the age; and the passages which deal directly with this theme use all the new resources of rhythm and assonance and alliteration and repetition to intensify the sense of urgency and doom in an extraordinarily impressive way:

> *Regis regum rectissimi prope est dies domini,*
> *dies irae et vindictae tenebrarum et nebulae,*
> *diesque mirabilium tonitruorum fortium,*
> *dies quoque angustiae meroris ac tristitae,*
> *in quo cessabit mulierum amor ac desiderium,*
> *hominumque contentio mundi huius et cupido.*[7]

This poem helps one to understand the austere and uncompromising spirit of Celtic monasticism. The leaders of that movement, like St. Columban and St. Columba himself, conceived their mission in the spirit of the prophets of the Old Testament, who were set over the nations and the kingdoms to pluck up and break down, and to build and to plant. For the principle of spiritual authority in Celtic Christianity was found in the numinous character of the saint rather than in the jurisdiction of an ecclesiastical hierarchy. A great saint and wonder worker like St. Columba attracted disciples and created a centre of spiritual

[7] The *Irish Liber Hymnorum*, ed. Bernard and Atkinson (1891), Vol. I, 66. *Translation:* "The day of the Lord, the all just King of Kings is at hand, a day of wrath and vengeance and the cloud of darkness, of marvellous strong thunder, of bitter grief and woe, on which love and the desire of women shall cease and the strife of men and the lust of this world."

power which radiated through his monastic foundations, which retained their loyalty to him after his death. These formed the *familia* or *paroechia* of the saint, and to a great extent took the place of the territorial diocese of the Latin and Byzantine world.

Thus, in Ireland, it was the abbot and not the bishop who was the real source of authority, and the latter was often a subordinate member of the monastic community who possessed the power of ordination, but no territorial jurisdiction or hierarchical authority. These great monastic *familiae* with their thousands of monks and dependants, their far-flung settlements and their complete independence of any external authority, have more resemblance to the later medieval religious orders than to the older type of Benedictine monastery, and, as we see from the attractive *Versiculi Familie Benchuir*, they already possessed a strong sense of corporate loyalty and devotion to the rule of their founder.

> *Bencuir bona regula*
> *Recta atque divina,*
> *Stricta, sancta, sedula*
> *Summa, justa et mira.*
>
> *Navis nunquam turbata*
> *Quamvis fluctibus tonsa,*
> *Nuptiis quoque parata*
> *   regi domino sponsa.*
>
> . . . . . .
>
> *Certe civitas firma,*
> *   fortis atque munita,*
> *Gloriosa ac digna,*
> *   Supra montem posita.*[8]

This change in the social basis of Christian culture shows itself in many different ways, some of which were destined

[8] *The Antiphonary of Bangor*, ed. F. E. Warren, II, 28. Translation: "the rule of Bangor is good, righteous, divine, severe, holy, zealous, just and wondrous.

"A ship that is never troubled though tossed by the waves: a bride adorned for the marriage of her lord and king.

"Truly it is a stronghold, secure and well defended—the city set on a hill, glorious and comely."

to leave a permanent mark on the life and discipline of the whole Western Church. Perhaps the most remarkable instance of this was the change in the system of moral discipline which substituted the practice of private penance and confession for the ancient canonical tradition of public penitence, which had been characteristic of the Latin Church. The old system rested on the principle that public sins demanded public satisfaction to the Church, which involved a temporary suspension of the privileges of membership of the Christian community, followed by the public reconciliation of the penitent by the bishop. In the Celtic Churches, on the other hand, the practice of penance followed the pattern of the monastic discipline where any infraction of the Rule or the moral law was expiated by an appropriate penance determined by the authority of the abbot or the confessor. Thus there arose the elaborate codes of penalties known as the Penitentials, in which the precise penance for every possible sin is minutely prescribed. These penitentials have a remarkable analogy to the barbaric legal codes which lay down an exact tariff of payments and punishments for the different classes of men and the different crimes, just as the old system of canonical discipline has an analogy to the civic traditions of the classical Roman world. It is, therefore, not surprising that the Celtic penitentials found ready acceptance in communities which followed barbarian law, both in Anglo-Saxon Britain and on the Continent. And the famous penitentials attributed to Theodore of Canterbury and Egbert of York represent the adoption of the Celtic system and its adaptation to the general situation of the Western Church in the newly converted countries of the North.

But the greatest service of the Irish monks to Western Christendom was the new movement of missionary expansion which did so much to spread Christianity and restore the monastic life throughout Western Europe in the seventh and eighth centuries. The driving force in this movement was primarily the ascetic ideal of pilgrimage—*peregrinandi pro Christo*—which peopled the islands of the northern seas, as far as the Faroes, and even to Iceland, with monks and hermits. But those who were led eastward

to Britain and the Continent combined this motive with a
spirit of active missionary enterprise. In this way the monastery of St. Columba at Iona became the centre from which
the evangelization of Scotland and Northern Britain proceeded, while the journey of St. Columban to the Continent became the starting point of a movement of monastic
reform which extended from Annegray and Luxeuil in
Burgundy to Lake Constance and finally to Bobbio near
Piacenza in Italy. St. Columban was perhaps the most dynamic personality the Celtic Church produced, and it was
through him and his disciples that Irish monasticism first
became a force in continental culture. He brought new life
to the decadent monasticism of the later Merovingian age,
and almost all the great monastic founders and missionaries of the seventh century, with the exception of St.
Amand, were his disciples, or the heirs of his tradition and
his Rule; such were St. Gall (–640), St. Wandrille
(–668), St. Ouen (610–684), St. Philibert (608–684),
St. Fara (–657), St. Omer (c. 670), St. Bertin (c. 709),
St. Valery (–622), St. Romaric (–653), men and
women whose names are still written across the map of
Europe, like the German princes of the eighteenth century
and the Russian commissars of our own time.

The resultant monasticism was not, however, of a purely
Celtic type. The Rule of St. Columban was too severe to
become the normal standard of religious life in continental
Europe. It was gradually tempered by the influence of the
Rule of St. Benedict, so that the use of both Rules as co-
ordinate authorities became characteristic of the Hiberno-
Gallican monasticism of the seventh century. It was in this
way that the Benedictine Rule first became widely known
and followed in Gaul, since it provided the ideal *via media*
between the superhuman asceticism of Celtic monasticism
and the chaotic multiplication of independent rules and observances that prevailed in Merovingian Gaul.

But it was in Anglo-Saxon England during the same period that the meeting of these two monastic traditions
produced the deepest and most lasting influence on Western culture. Here, as in Ireland, a new Christian culture

was planted in barbarian soil by the work of the monastic missionaries and the monastic schools. But it was not, as in Ireland, the direct product of the native society, nor was it a case, as in Gaul, of scattered Celtic and Benedictine influences that mingled with the existing traditions of an old-established Christian society. The conversion of the Anglo-Saxons was due to the direct initiative of St. Gregory the Great, who sent St. Augustine and his companions from the centre of Latin Christendom and of Benedictine monasticism to the Jutish kingdom of Kent (596–97), while, on the other hand, Northumbria was converted mainly by the Celtic monks from Iona, who founded the island monastery of Lindisfarne in 634. Thus both elements were represented in a pure undiluted form, so that a collision between them was unavoidable.

The battle was fought out in Northumbria where the Roman tradition found enthusiastic support among a group of young Northumbrians led by St. Wilfrid (634–709) and St. Benedict Biscop (628–90), while the Celtic tradition was supported by Lindisfarne and the Northumbrian court. St. Wilfrid was a man of boundless energy and imperious will, whose long life was passed in a series of conflicts and exiles. But though he succeeded in his main object of inducing the Northumbrians to accept the discipline and authority of Rome and abandon the cause of Iona and the Celtic observance, he failed in his further attempt to reorganize the Northumbrian dioceses on strict canonical principles. This was first accomplished from Canterbury by the second Roman mission in 668, led by Theodore of Tarsus, a refugee from the eastern territories of the Byzantine Empire, which had been recently occupied by the Moslems. In the course of his long episcopate (669–90) Theodore entirely reorganized the Anglo-Saxon Church, establishing the canonical Western system of territorial dioceses, annual synods and episcopal jurisdiction without any serious conflict with the existing bishops and monasteries of the Celtic tradition. He was, moreover, a man of high culture, and, assisted by Hadrian, an Italian abbot of African origin, he made Canterbury a centre of learning which rivalled the great monastic schools of Ireland. We possess a contemporary witness to the prestige of the new school in the letter written by St. Aldhelm—himself trained in both traditions—to Eahfrid, a monk who had just returned from six years' study in Ireland.[9]

But, at the same time, another centre of the higher culture was being established in Northumbria, which was even more important than the school at Canterbury. This was the creation of Wilfrid and Benedict Biscop, who established their monasteries at Ripon and Hexham and Wearmouth and Jarrow, as colonies of Latin culture among the Northern barbarians and fortresses of Roman order against Celtic particularism. Benedict Biscop, above all, devoted himself to the development of religious art and learning. He had served his novitiate at Lerins, the ancient capital of Western monasticism, and on his repeated journeys to Rome and Gaul he brought back to England a wealth of manuscripts, paintings, relics and vestments, as well as masons and glaziers and singers for the adornment and service of the Church. Finally, in 678, he brought with him from Rome the arch-chanter of St. Peter's, and the abbot of one of the Basilican monasteries at Rome who acted as Papal legate at the Council of Heathfield in 680, and who spent two or three years instructing the monks of Northumbria in the music of the Roman chant and the annual order of the Roman liturgy.[10]

The rise of this centre of intensive Latin monastic culture in Northumbria was the more important because it was in direct contact with Lindisfarne, the chief centre of Celtic monastic culture in Britain, so that the two traditions influenced and stimulated one another. Hence it was in Northumbria that Anglo-Saxon culture, and perhaps the whole culture of Western monasticism in the Dark Ages, achieved their climax at the beginning of the eighth cen-

[9] Perhaps identifiable with Eadfrid, abbot of Lindisfarne, 698–721, to whom the Lindisfarne Gospels are ascribed.

[10] The chapter which Bede devotes to this mission of Abbot John shows the immense importance that the liturgical chant possessed in the monastic culture. Here again early medieval Christendom follows the pattern of the archaic ritual cultures and the doctrine of sacred music which is expressed in the Chinese Book of Rites and in Plato's Laws.

tury. The immense literary and patristic learning of the Venerable Bede testifies to the strength of the Latin element, while the art of the Anglian stone crosses shows Syrian or East Mediterranean influences. On the other hand the calligraphy of the Lindisfarne Gospels and the evolution of the Insular Script represent a blending of Celtic and Latin influences; while the vernacular literature, which made its first appearance and reached its highest achievement during this period, shows how the new literary culture was able to assimilate and preserve the epic traditions of the old heroic poetry of the Teutonic barbarians.

This rich and many-sided Northumbrian culture came to an untimely end, like the parallel monastic culture of early Christian Ireland, owing to the Viking invasions of the ninth century. But before it perished it had succeeded in implanting the seeds of a great revival of religious life and Christian culture on the Continent. This was the work, above all, of two Anglo-Saxon monks: St. Boniface of Crediton, the Apostle of Germany (675–753), and Alcuin of York, the adviser of Charlemagne (730–804), the spiritual fathers of Carolingian culture. When Boniface embarked on his mission, religion and culture in the Frankish kingdom were at a low ebb, and the victorious tide of Moslem invasion was sweeping over the Christian lands of the Western Mediterranean and Northern Africa. By 720 the Saracens had penetrated as far as Narbonne; and in the following years all the old centres of monastic culture in Southern Gaul, such as Lerins, were sacked, and even Luxeuil, the centre of the tradition of St. Columban in Burgundy, fell a victim to Arab raiders. At the same time Charles Martel, the leader who checked the Moslem advance at Poitiers in 732, was hardly less of a danger to the Church, owing to his wholesale exploitation and expropriation of bishoprics and monasteries to provide benefices or fiefs for his warriors.

But the creation by St. Boniface and his Anglo-Saxon companions of a new province of Christian culture on the northern flank of Christendom had an importance that far exceeded its material results. At first sight it might seem

that the conversion of a few tribes of German barbarians—
Hessians, Saxons and Frisians—was a very small gain in comparison with the loss to Christendom of the old civilized
territories of North Africa and Spain, whose Churches had
hitherto played the leading part in the development of
Christian life and thought in the West. Nevertheless, the
work of St. Boniface did more than any other factor to
lay the foundations of medieval Christendom. His mission
to Germany was not an isolated spiritual adventure like the
achievements of his Celtic predecessors; it was part of a far-
sighted programme of construction and reform planned
with all the method and statesmanship of the Roman tradition. It involved a triple alliance between the Anglo-
Saxon missionaries, the Papacy, and the family of Charles
Martel, the *de facto* rulers of the Frankish kingdom, out
of which the Carolingian Empire and the Carolingian culture ultimately emerged. St. Boniface's direct personal relation with Rome as apostolic legate for Germany enabled
him to overcome the centrifugal tendencies of the Celtic
tradition which was still strong on the Continent, and to
prevent any interference with his work by the local Gallican
episcopate. At the same time his extension of Christian
culture in Germany secured the support of the sons of
Charles Martel—Pepin and Carloman—and he made use of
it to carry through a far-reaching programme of ecclesiastical reform for the Frankish Church itself in a series of
councils held between 740 and 747.

This alliance between the reforming party and the new
monarchy was sealed by the solemn religious consecration
of Pepin as king of the Franks by St. Boniface himself at
Soissons in 752, a ceremony which was repeated by Pope
Stephen II at St. Denis in 754, as though to accentuate the
importance of the act, which indeed marks a new era in
Western history. Yet none of this could have been accomplished without the help of the Anglo-Saxon monks and
missionaries. For St. Boniface's work depended on his
monastic foundations, above all on Fulda (744), which
were the centres of Christian culture and missionary action
in the newly converted territories. It was in these Anglo-
Saxon colonies that the new type of Christian culture, which

had been developed in Northumbria in the seventh century, was adapted and transmitted to the Germanic peoples of the Continent, and a new generation was trained which provided the personnel for the re-education and spiritual leadership of the Frankish Church. New foundations followed one another rapidly during the next fifty or hundred years: St. Gall in Switzerland (c. 750), Hersfeld, founded by St. Boniface's successor St. Lull in 769, Benedictbeuern and Tegernsee in Bavaria (740 and 757), Kremsmünster in Austria (777), Lorsch in Hesse (764), New Corvey in Saxony (822), were all of them, like Fulda, sources of missionary activity and centres of intellectual culture and material civilization, not only for Germany, but also for the neighbouring lands to the north and east. We can get an idea of the immense scale of these monastic foundations from the well-known plan of an abbey produced at St. Gall about 820. It is no longer the simple religious community envisaged by the old monastic rules, but a vast complex of buildings, churches, workshops, store-houses, offices, schools and alms-houses, housing a whole population of dependants, workers and servants like the temple cities of antiquity. The monastery had, in fact, taken the place of the moribund city, and was to remain the centre of medieval culture until the rise of the new type of city commune in the eleventh and twelfth centuries.

Under these circumstances it is not surprising that the whole Carolingian culture should have a monastic character. Indeed it was the Carolingian age which finally established the Benedictine Rule as the universal standard of the religious life in the West. The great monasteries were the cultural centres of the Carolingian Empire, and it was by their alliance with the monastic culture that Charles and his son, Louis the Pious, were able to carry out their ambitious plans for ecclesiastical and liturgical reform which contributed so much to the spiritual and formal unification of Western Christendom. Although the political structure of the Empire endured for less than a century, its work of cultural and religious unification remained the permanent foundation of all the later medieval developments. The extent to which the Carolingian age defined the terms of medieval culture is to be seen very clearly in the case of the liturgy, since the liturgical reform imposed by Charles the Great led to the introduction of a common rite throughout Western Europe. For the Roman rite, as known to the Middle Ages, was, in fact, the officially authorized rite of the Carolingian Empire and represents the fusion of Roman and Gallican elements resulting from the revision of the liturgical books carried out by Alcuin and his fellow workers.

Here, as in so many other ways, the monastic culture of the Carolingian Empire followed the pattern laid down by the short-lived flowering of Christian culture in Northumbria between 650 and 750, of which Boniface and Alcuin were the heirs and transmitters. But on the Continent the revival of culture found in Charles the Great a patron who had the vision to appreciate its possibilities and the power to realize them. Not only did he gather at his court the most learned men of his time from every part of Western Europe, from Italy and Spain to Britain and Ireland, but he carried out a systematic programme for the reform of clerical education. Few rulers have possessed a clearer sense of the importance of education and a greater concern for the diffusion of letters than is shown in the legislation and correspondence of Charles the Great. Finally, in the school of the palace directed by Alcuin, the last great representative of the Northumbrian culture, and in his immediate court circle, he established a centre of higher study, where for the first time in the Middle Ages scholars and nobles, laymen and ecclesiastics met on the common ground of humane letters and rational discussion.

In all this there was a deliberate purpose to create or restore a Latin Christian culture which should be the common spiritual possession of the new Western Christian empire. No doubt the new learning was elementary and lacking in originality. Its main achievements were educational rather than literary or philosophical, and consisted of text-books like the *De Institutione Clericorum* of Rabanus Maurus (776–856); dictionaries and commentaries like the *Liber Glossarum* and the *Glossa ordinaris*; the reform of the script, and the reform of the liturgy for which Alcuin himself was largely responsible, and most of all the collection and copying of manuscripts. But in comparison with the debased culture of seventh-century Gaul, traditionalism itself was a progressive force, for it secured the survival of the classical inheritance of Western culture. The words of Alcuin's teacher, Aelbert of York—that it would be disgraceful to allow the knowledge which had been discovered by the wise men of old to perish in our generation—show a sense of responsibility to the past which is the mark of genuine humanism rather than of a blind adherence to traditionalism. The spirit of Christian humanism finds expression in Alcuin's own letters to Charles the Great: "If your intentions are carried out," he writes, "it may be that a new Athens will arise in France, and an Athens fairer than of old, for our Athens, ennobled by the teaching of Christ, will surpass the wisdom of the Academy. The old Athens had only the teachings of Plato to instruct it, yet even so it flourished by the seven liberal arts. But our Athens will be enriched by the sevenfold gift of the Holy Spirit and will, therefore, surpass all the dignity of earthly wisdom."[11]

It may seem to us pathetic, or even absurd, that a monkish schoolmaster like Alcuin, and an illiterate barbarian like Charlemagne, should dream of building a new Athens in a world which possessed only the rudiments of civilization and was about to be overwhelmed by a fresh tide of barbarism. Nevertheless, their ideal of a Christian culture which would restore and preserve the inheritance of ancient civilization and classical literature was never lost and ultimately found its progressive realization in the development of Western culture.

In this sense the achievement of the Carolingian age was a true renaissance and the starting point of Western culture as a conscious unity. The pupils of Alcuin, Rabanus Maurus, Einhard, Angilbert of St. Riquier, Adalard of Corbie, and Amalarius of Metz, handed on the tradition to their pupils in turn, to Servatus Lupus and Walafrid Strabo, the disciples of Rabanus Maurus at Fulda, and to Heiric of

[11] Ep. 170.

Auxerre, the pupil of Servatus Lupus at Ferrières. In this way the Carolingian revival was carried on by the great Carolingian abbeys, each of which preserved the tradition established by the Palace School of Charlemagne and Alcuin's later teaching at Tours. And after the fall of the Empire it was the great monasteries, especially those of Southern Germany, St. Gall, Reichenau and Tegernsee, that were the only remaining islands of intellectual life amidst the returning flood of barbarism which once again threatened to submerge Western Christendom. For, though monasticism seems at first sight ill-adapted to withstand the material destructiveness of an age of lawlessness and war, it was an institution which possessed extraordinary recuperative power. Ninety-nine out of a hundred monasteries could be burnt and the monks killed or driven out, and yet the whole tradition could be reconstituted from the one survivor, and the desolate sites could be repeopled by fresh supplies of monks who would take up again the broken tradition, following the same rule, singing the same liturgy, reading the same books and thinking the same thoughts as their predecessors. In this way monasticism and the monastic culture came back to England and Normandy in the age of St. Dunstan from Fleury and Ghent after more than a century of utter destruction; with the result that a century later the Norman and English monasteries were again among the leaders of Western culture.

It is true that there was a limit to this power of recuperation. Irish and Scottish monasticism never fully recovered from the effects of the Viking invasion, and the breach in the continuity of Anglo-Saxon monastic tradition was hardly less serious. However resistant monasticism might be to external disaster and insecurity, it was, nevertheless, ultimately dependent on the existence of Christian society and its temporal institutions. Therefore in order to understand the relations between religion and culture in Western Europe, it is also necessary to study the evolution of the great external organ of Christian Society, the institution of kingship, and its relation to the Church and to Christendom as an inclusive political religious unity.

Chapter IV

The Barbarians and the Christian Kingdom

THE EVOLUTION of monarchical institutions and the idea of kingship during the Dark Ages from 400 to 1000 provides one of the most instructive examples in history of the complex process by which different social and religious elements become interwoven in the formation of a culture. For the fully developed Christian monarchy of the Middle Ages, which possessed such a remarkable uniformity of type throughout the European world, represents the ultimate fusion of a whole series of traditions that had their origin in remote ages and possessed extremely different cultural backgrounds.

When the barbarian tribes broke into the Roman Empire in the fifth century, they came into a world which was in the midst of a process of social and religious change. The classical Mediterranean tradition of citizenship and civic magistracy was already overshadowed by the oriental conception of divine monarchy, and the Roman Imperator was being transformed into a Byzantine Basileus secluded in the eunuch-guarded recesses of the Sacred Palace. But this tradition of oriental theocracy was not altogether in harmony with the spirit of the new religion, which was also of oriental origin but which still retained the memory of centuries of persecution and passive resistance to the imperial power.

As we have already seen, the Christian tradition was essentially dualistic, accepting a fundamental opposition between the Church and the world: the kingdom of God and the kingdom of Caesar. And, though this opposition was weakened in the East by the gradual incorporation of the Orthodox Church in the monarchical order of the Byzantine Empire, in the West it was being reinterpreted and reinforced by the Augustinian philosophy of history. For St. Augustine's *City of God*, one of the books which did most to form the mind of Western Christendom, sees all history as a struggle between two dynamic spiritual principles manifested through the ages in the never-ending conflict between two societies—the City of God, and Babylon, the City of Confusion, which remain eternally divided, although in the present world they mix and interpenetrate one another in every form of human society.[1]

Yet in spite of this underlying religious dualism, the Christians of the Latin world, with the exception of Salvian, show a loyalty to the Roman Empire which lasted down to the time of St. Gregory the Great and beyond. But it was loyalty to a tradition and to a civilization—to the idea of the *pax Romana* and the *Romana fides*—rather than to the person and the authority of the Emperor which had become shadowy and remote. In practice the Roman bishops and nobles, like Sidonius Apollinaris and Cassiodorus and St. Isidore, found no difficulty in accepting the *de facto* authority of the barbarian kings as "powers ordained by God", very much in the same way as the oriental Christians like St. John of Damascus accepted the sovereignty of the khalifs, and the East Syrian bishops acknowledged the authority of the kings of Persia. Indeed, the Christian view of the world actually favoured a realistic attitude in politics, owing to its spiritual dualism which treated all temporal conditions and institutions as transitory and provisional. The Christian people was the Second Israel dwelling in exile and captivity, and Christians could accept the oppression and arbitrary rule of the barbarians as the Hebrew prophets had accepted the rule of the Gentiles who were the unconscious instruments of the divine purpose in history.

But to the barbarians themselves kingship had a very different significance. It was their one vital social institution, and it possessed a psychological appeal to all that was

[1] *De Civitate Dei*, I, c. 35.

deepest in their cultural and moral tradition. The barbarian king was neither a despot like the oriental monarch nor a magistrate like the Roman Emperor; he was a war leader who enjoyed the prestige and *mana* of divine ancestry and heroic tradition. The barbarian peoples were, in fact, no less king-conscious than the Homeric Achaeans, and, though they never produced a Homer, they possessed the same type of heroic epic traditions which they preserved for centuries and which formed a link between later medieval culture and the age of the barbarian invasions, just as the Greek epic linked the classical world with the age of the Trojan War and the fall of the Mycenean Culture. So, too, the relation between the barbarian kingship and the sacred monarchy of the Roman Byzantine Basileus is parallel to that between the Achaean warrior kings and the Egyptian Pharaoh, or the great king of the Hittites. But whereas the details of this relation are lost in the mists of myth and legend, we are able to follow the history of medieval kingship in detail on both sides of its pedigree.

For the new barbarian kingdoms had a double origin. On the one side they inherited the tradition of some heroic god-descended royal race like the Amals, the Balts, the Asdings, or the Merovingians; while, on the other, they were allies and deputies of the Roman Empire, and inherited the political and administrative traditions of a highly organized state. This dual character appears most strikingly in the case of Theodoric, the Ostrogoth. Theodoric was an Amal, the heir of the heroic traditions of the race of Eormanric, and himself the hero of the medieval epic of Dietrich of Berne. Yet, at the same time, he was a man of Roman education, a patron of Roman art and literature, and a ruler who carried on the Roman tradition of law and government. Procopius, who was no friend of the Goths, wrote of him that "his manner of ruling over his subjects was worthy of a great Emperor; for he maintained justice, made good laws, protected his country from invasion and gave proof of extraordinary prudence and valour".[2] Barbarian rulers of this type recognized clearly enough that their native tradition of warrior kingship was not enough.

[2] Procopius, de Bello Gothico, I, 1.

As King Athaulf the Visigoth declared, Gothic barbarism could not submit to the reign of law, but without the laws there could be no state. Therefore he had abandoned his blind hatred of everything Roman and had made up his mind to use the Gothic power in the service of civilization for the honour and exaltation of the name of Rome.[3]

Nevertheless, it was just those peoples like the Goths, who went furthest to accept the high civilization of Rome, that failed to survive. The kingdoms of the Ostrogoths and the Vandals in Italy and Africa were destroyed by Justinian and that of the Visigoths in Spain, in spite of its much longer history, was swept away by Musa ibn Nusair and his general Tariq in 711–13. It is, therefore, to Northern Europe—to the Merovingian kingdom between the Rhine and the Seine, the Anglo-Saxon kingdoms of Britain and the Scandinavian kingdoms of the remote Baltic world— that we must look for the origins of the traditions of barbarian kingship inherited by the kingdoms of the West and finally incorporated into the order of medieval Christendom. It is in these lands that we can best discern the original features of the institutions that underlie the historic forms of kingship. In this country, above all, the earliest Anglo-Saxon literature has preserved the heroic tradition of the warrior kings of the migration period, and at a much later date the old Norse poetry and sagas carried the same tradition on into the world of medieval culture. Both these traditions show a remarkable agreement in their independent versions of the Northern tradition. The Scandinavian literature which is derived from the kingless aristocratic society of medieval Iceland is no less concerned with the heroic ideal of kingship than the Anglo-Saxon epics, which are, presumably, the work of court poets dependent on some royal or princely patron.[4]

In comparison with the new barbarian kingdoms that had

[3] Orosius, vii, 48, 1.

[4] It is true, however, that from the beginning Icelandic poets and saga makers took service with the kings of Norway and Denmark, so that Icelandic literature was also influenced directly by royal patrons and the tradition of court poetry.

arisen with a civilized Roman basis, the ancient barbarian kingship of the North was a social and religious, rather than a political institution. The king was not primarily a governor and a law-giver, but the head and the symbolic representative of his people.

It is very difficult for us to enter into the spirit of the old Germanic polity, as represented by the earliest laws like those of Kent, especially as these laws were mainly intended as a Christian revision or modernization of an existing body of law and tradition which is unknown to us. We have the impression of a complex stratified or hierarchical society which was, however, quite different from the feudal or class hierarchies with which we are familiar.

As Professor Jolliffe has shown so well in his *Constitutional History of Medieval England*,[5] this archaic type of tribal kingdom derived its stability not from the power and authority of the ruler but from its own specific gravity and from the complex network of kinship and inherited status which held the people together in a community the structure of which was consecrated by religion and sacred tradition. And the king was the natural centre in which all these traditions and loyalties were concentrated. He was the embodiment of the life of the nation and the life of the land. He was the representative of the people to the gods as high priest, who presided at the sacrifices, and he represented the gods to the people by virtue of his divine ancestry and the sacred prestige of his blood and his office.

But it is hardly necessary to say that the people or "folk" of which we speak is not a nation in the modern sense of the word. Kings and kingdoms were as plentiful in the pagan North as in the Homeric world or in ancient Canaan. The Runic verses of the Rök Stone in Sweden speaks of "twenty kings of four names, sons of four brothers who for four winters dwelt in Seeland"; and even in historic times, at the beginning of the eleventh century, the Norwegian province of Uppland was subdivided among five different kingdoms. The rise of the greater kingdoms, above all that of

[5] J. E. A. Jolliffe, *Constitutional History of Medieval England* (1937), pp. 44–47. Cf. also his earlier work, *Pre-feudal England: The Jutes* (1933).

the Franks, was a consequence of the period of the barbarian invasions and the conquest of alien peoples; but in proportion as these new kingdoms increased in size, they lost their "national" bond with the people and their link with the primitive tradition of racial kingship. These elements survived most fully in the Scandinavian North, which had been least affected by alien influence. In Sweden, especially, the monarchy preserved its archaic religious character down to the twelfth century; and the institution of kingship remained inseparably connected with the great sanctuary of Yngvi Frey at Old Upsala, of whom the king was at once the high priest and the human counterpart. It is from the Swedish tradition that we derive through Norwegian and Icelandic sources the fullest evidence concerning the priest king, whose chief function was to offer sacrifice on behalf of the people for good harvests and victory in battle and who was himself liable to be sacrificed if his offerings proved unacceptable to the gods.

The historical circumstances of Anglo-Saxon England placed it midway between the two developments. Its kingdoms were the creation of successful warrior leaders, all of whom ultimately claimed divine descent, although few were the direct representatives of a known continental dynasty, save for the royal house of Mercia, which was descended from Offa of Angle, one of the heroes of the old epic traditions and a ruler of the continental Angles. But, unlike the other barbarian states which had established themselves on Roman soil, the Anglo-Saxon kingdoms had not taken over the Roman traditions of centralized political authority. They remained socially and spiritually akin to the barbarian kingdoms of the North. Even at a later date their literature shows how deeply their traditions were rooted in the Northern world—the lands of the Danes and the Geats and the Frisians. The great ship burial of an East Anglian king of the early seventh century which was discovered at Sutton Hoo on the River Deben in Suffolk in 1939 gives us a remarkable sidelight on this world and on the great warrior kings, "Sackers of Cities" and "Treasurers of Heroes" of whom we read in Beowulf[6] and Widsith.

[6] Cf. the ship burial of King Scyld in *Beowulf*, 34–35.

The coming of Christianity to this Homeric world inevitably produced a social as well as a religious revolution. King Raedwald attempted to reconcile the old and the new worlds by maintaining the sacrifices in the same temple which he dedicated to Christian worship, but such compromises are rare. From the time of St. Augustine the royal families were the primary targets of missionary activities, and the royal courts were the centres from which the conversion of England was achieved. However small was the political power of the king, he was the keystone of the social structure, and his conversion to Christianity was the symbol and pledge of the conversion of his people. Thus, though the kingship lost its old divine prerogatives and much of its traditional magical associations with good harvests and victory in war by becoming merged in the wider unity of Christendom, it gained new prestige by its close association with the Church, from which it gradually acquired a new form of sacredness. The cult of St. Oswald the Martyr, the second Christian king of Northumbria, and of many lesser figures in the reigning houses, like St. Oswin and St. Hilda, St. Sigebert of East Anglia, St. Sebbi of Essex, St. Ethelburga, St. Sexburga and St. Edith, provided Anglo-Saxon royalty with a Christian substitute for the divine ancestry of pagan tradition.

Yet, at the same time, it may be doubted whether these gains were not outweighed by the loss of the heroic ethos of pagan kingship. The royal saints of Anglo-Saxon England were, for the most part, men who were defeated in battle by the pagans, like St. Oswald and St. Edwin, or men who resigned their crowns to become monks, like St. Sebbi, of whom it was said he ought to have been a bishop rather than a king. It was hard for warlike barbarians to accept the Christian ethic of renunciation and forgiveness in their rulers who had been the living embodiment of their pride of blood, as we see from St. Bede's story of King Sigebert of Essex who was killed "because he was wont to spare his enemies and forgive them the wrongs they had done as soon as they asked him". Moreover, even Bede himself was conscious of the dangers arising from the weakening of the ties of personal loyalty and of the military virtues which

accompanied the rise of the new Christian culture, as he
shows in the last sentences of his history and in the epistle
to Archbishop Egbert of York where he criticizes the
abuse of monastic endowments as a threat to the military
security of Northumbria.

A similar weakening of royalty and of the social order
took place in all the barbarian kingdoms of the West as a
result of the transition from pagan to Christian culture. We
see a striking example of it in the Visigothic kingdom of
Spain, in many respects the most advanced and powerful
of all these kingdoms. Ever since the Visigoths ceased to be
Arians and accepted Catholicism as the state religion (in
589), the relations between state and Church had been so
close that they formed practically a single organism, governed by the king and the great councils held at Toledo,
which were legislative assemblies as well as ecclesiastical
synods. But although the Church was so closely associated
with the monarchy and used all its resources to support the
royal power and anathematize sedition and rebellion, it was
powerless to prevent what a contemporary calls the "de-
testable Spanish custom of killing their kings". The history
of Visigothic Spain after the extinction of the ancient royal
dynasty in 531 is a long series of rebellions, assassinations
and palace revolutions. It may be that the new religious
sanctions were not strong enough to compensate for the
loss of the instinctive pagan loyalty to the ancient god-
descended royal line of the Balts, which had come to an
end in 531. In any case, although the alliance of the Church
and the monarchy produced a characteristically Spanish
fusion of religion and politics, and a remarkable code of
ecclesiastical and civil legislation, it failed to overcome the
indiscipline and social disunity which proved fatal to the
existence of Christian Spain.

No doubt the same elements of weakness existed in the
Frankish kingdom, which, in the well-known words of
Fustel de Coulanges, was "a régime of despotism tempered by assassination". Indeed, the history of the Merovingian dynasty presents a darker picture of lawlessness, crime
and sheer incapacity than that of any of the barbarian

kingdoms. Yet, in spite of this, the Franks remained loyal for centuries to the family of Clovis if not to its individual representatives for the sake of the hereditary sacred prestige of the royal blood, and this conservatism allowed the Frankish state to maintain its continuity during the formative period in which the conquerors and the conquered became fused into a new social unity. The process of assimilation was favoured by two important factors. In the first place there was no religious barrier between the Franks and their Gallo-Roman subjects, since the Franks were not Arians like the Goths and Vandals and Lombards, but had become Catholic in the reign of Clovis (496); and, secondly, they were not, like the Goths, isolated in the midst of an alien population, but still remained in contact with the other German peoples, so that they extended their dominions during the sixth century eastward to Thuringia and Bavaria, as well as southward to Burgundy and Aquitaine.

The result of this was that the kingdom of the Franks became the centre towards which all the living forces of Western culture converged: the meeting place of Latin and German elements, and of Mediterranean and Atlantic influences. In "France", as it may now be called, Irish and Anglo-Saxon monks met those from Italy and Spain, and Syrian traders met the Frisian merchants who traded with England and the Baltic. The Frankish monarchy was the only institution which provided a principle of organization for this development, but it was incapable of assuming the role of cultural leadership until its whole character and spiritual purpose had been drastically transformed.

Hence the internal revolution which substituted the family of Charles Martel and Pepin for the old royal house meant far more than a mere change of dynasties. It was the birth of a new ideal of kingship and a new conception of the nature of the Frankish state. The tradition of loyalty to the Merovingians, decadent and impotent though they were, was too strong to be set aside by purely political methods, and it was only after gaining the approval of Pope Zachary that Pepin ventured to supersede the old dynasty and accept the royal crown by a solemn act of religious consecration which was performed by St. Boniface at Soissons in 751.

This was the first introduction among the Franks of the religious ceremony by which the king was crowned and anointed by the Church, and the importance of the new rite was accentuated by its repetition three years later by the hands of the Pope himself when he visited Pepin to seek his aid against the Lombards. Henceforward it was to be a characteristic feature of Western kingship, so that the chrism or oil of consecration was held to confer a new sacred character on the person of the ruler.[7] There has been much discussion by historians with regard to the origins of the ceremony. It was already in use in the seventh century in Visigothic Spain, where, as I have said, the kingship was exceptionally dependent on the support of the Church, and it is probable that it was practised even earlier among the Celtic peoples, whence it was no doubt transmitted to the Anglo-Saxons. But there can be no question that its ultimate origin is to be found in the Old Testament where it embodies the theocratic principle and the dependence of the secular power on the spiritual power of the prophet, as we see in the case of Samuel anointing David in place of Saul, and in the even more dramatic story of Eliseus' mission to anoint Jehu as king to destroy the house of Ahab. In both of these cases the prophet as the representative of God intervenes to change the course of history by transferring the kingship to a new line, and we can hardly doubt that these precedents were in the minds of the Pope and St. Boniface and the advisers of King Pepin when the new rite was introduced.

Thus from the beginning the new monarchy was associated with the Church and was regarded as the divinely appointed organ of Christendom. No doubt Charles Martel and his son Pepin, "le petit poïngeur," were tough and ruthless soldiers who did not "carry the sword in vain", and the former in particular used the wealth of the Church and the lands of the monasteries to provide fiefs or "benefices" for

---

[7] Cf. the words of the German tenth-century rite: "The grace of God has this day changed thee into another man and has made thee by the rite of unction partaker in His divinity."

his warriors. But this secularization of Church property took place at the very moment when St. Bede was criticizing the excessive multiplication of monastic foundations as a source of the military weakness of Northumbria, and it is possible that Charles Martel's ruthless cutting out of dead wood was not altogether a misfortune for the Frankish Church.

In any case, there is no doubt that the Carolingian house as a whole was traditionally friendly to the party of ecclesiastical reform. St. Boniface, the noblest representative of that party, admitted that without the support of Charles Martel his missionary work would have been impossible. But it was under Charles's sons, Pepin and Carloman, that the Carolingians became most fully identified with the reforming movement and gave their support to St. Boniface not only in his missionary activity but in his reform of the Frankish Church, carried out in the series of great councils that accompanied the formal inauguration of the Carolingian monarchy in 751.

In this work the primary agent was the apostle of Germany himself, who, for all his unworldliness, possessed a remarkable talent for construction and organization, and he found an invaluable ally in Carloman, the most religious of all the Carolingians, who was responsible for summoning the first council of the Frankish Church to assemble after an interval of eighty years, thus putting an end to the ecclesiastical anarchy which had characterized the later Merovingian period.

Nevertheless, St. Boniface's programme of reform was not fully realized. He had hoped to use his power as Legate of the Holy See to restore the complete hierarchical order of bishops and metropolitans and, finally, of archbishops, who were to be invested by the Pope with the pallium as a mark of their delegated authority. But the resistance of the profoundly secularized episcopate, and the traditional authority of the secular power, rendered such a sweeping reform impossible. The patron of St. Boniface, Carloman, the ruler of Germany and North-West France, resigned his power in 747 and became a monk, first at Mount Soracte and afterwards at Monte Cassino. Pepin, who now united the whole Frankish realm and set about the conquest of Aquitaine, was not a man to accept any diminution of his authority, although he was ready to use his power in an enlightened way and to forward the work of reform. Therefore, instead of bringing the Frankish Church under the immediate jurisdiction of Rome, the reformers were obliged to seek an alternative solution in a close association between the Frankish monarchy and the Papacy.

St. Boniface accepted this solution in so far as he presided at the ceremony which consecrated the new monarchy, but he ceased to take any further share in the affairs of the Frankish Church. He withdrew to the monastery he had founded at Fulda to be the centre of missionary activity in central Germany, and soon afterwards returned to Frisia, which had been the starting point of his missionary activities, to offer his life as the crown of his apostolate (754). One of his last acts was to write to St. Fulrad of St. Denis, King Pepin's confidential adviser, on behalf of his missionaries and monks, "almost all strangers; some of them priests stationed in many places to minister to the Church and the people; some monks placed in our cells to teach children their letters; and some old men who have long lived and laboured with me. I am anxious about all these, that after my death they may have your counsel and the royal protection, and that they may not be scattered like sheep without a shepherd and that the peoples who dwell on the pagan marches may not lose the law of Christ".[8]

In fact his disciple, St. Lull, who succeeded him as Archbishop of Mainz, was out of touch with the men who controlled the destinies of the Frankish kingdom. Some years later he complained to an English archbishop (Ethelbert of York) that "the Church is daily oppressed and harassed because new princes follow new ways and make new laws according to their desires"—*quia moderni principes novos mores novosque leges secundum sua desideria condunt.*[9] And thus, in spite of the influence of St. Boniface and the Anglo-Saxon missionaries on the reforming policy of the Carolingians, they were not responsible for the vital deci-

[8] S. Bonifatü et Julli, Ep. 93, ed. Dümmler M.G.H.
[9] Ibid., Ep. 125.

sions which transformed the character of the Frankish monarchy. They were due to the initiative of the Papacy and to the Frankish advisers of Pepin and his successor, Charles the Great, such as St. Fulrad of St. Denis, St. Chrodegang of Metz, and Wilichair of Sens. The appeals of Popes Stephen II and Paul I to King Pepin and that of Hadrian I to Charlemagne created a new political bond between the Papacy and the Frankish monarchy and ultimately led to the destruction of the Lombard kingdom, the abolition of the Byzantine sovereignty over Rome and Ravenna and the recognition of the king of the Franks as the patron and protector of the Holy See. In return, the Pope accepted the control of the Carolingian monarchy over the property and personnel of the Church, and the way was prepared for the establishment of the new Western Empire, which gave constitutional form and ritual consecration to the new relation between the Papacy and the Frankish kingdom.

For the new Empire was an essentially theocratic institution. "It expressed both the new conception of Christendom as the ultimate social unity, and the sacred character of the ruler as the divinely appointed leader of the Christian people. The traditional expressions that convey the sacred or numinous nature of the imperial power—*sacrum imperium, sancta majestas, divus Augustus,* and the like, which had been preserved in the Byzantine Empire—acquired a new significance in the West, for, as we see from Alcuin's correspondence,[10] the conception of the theocratic mission of the Frankish monarchy preceded Charles's assumption of the imperial title and was psychologically its cause rather than its consequence. In fact the fusion of the temporal and spiritual powers was far more complete in the Carolingian state than it had been in the Christian barbarian kingdoms, or even in the Byzantine Empire. The legislation of Charles the Great, which was of such importance for the development of Western culture, is the supreme expression of this theocratic conception of au-

[10] Cf. especially Ep. 174, in which Alcuin writes of the three supreme powers of the world: the Roman Papacy, the Roman Empire and the Frankish kingdom.

thority. It is the legislation of a unitary Church-state and
covers every aspect of the common life of the Christian
people from economics and police to liturgy and higher
education and preaching. In the same way the administration of the Carolingian state was equally unitary, since the
bishop, no less than the count, was appointed and controlled by the emperor and acted with the count as joint
representative of the imperial authority. So, too, the *missi*,
the imperial delegates who carried out periodical tours of
inspection through the provinces, were always composed of
lay and ecclesiastical members in equal numbers—usually a
count and a bishop or abbot. For the immense expansion
of the Carolingian state in consequence of the conquest of
Saxony and Hungary and the Spanish March and the annexation of Italy, Bavaria and Frisia had rendered religion
the only real bond of union between the different peoples
and languages of the Empire, and it was not as the princes
of the Franks, but as the rulers and leaders of the whole
Christian people, that Charles and his successor, Louis the
Pious, governed their dominions.

No doubt Charles himself, like his father and grand-
father, was a mighty warrior before the Lord, and it was
his sword rather than his religious prerogative which had
created the new Empire. Nevertheless he was inspired to
an even greater extent than his predecessors by the ideals
of the monks and scholars whom he had gathered at his
court and from whom his counsellors and ministers and
officials were recruited.

I have already written in the previous chapter of this
aspect of Charles the Great's work—his promotion of education and literature, and his far-reaching plans for ecclesiastical and liturgical reform, which did so much to increase the
cultural unity of Western Europe. But apart from these
cultural results, the Carolingian legislation in itself marks
the emergence of the new social consciousness of Western
Christendom. Hitherto the legislation of the Western kingdoms had been of the nature of a Christian appendix to
the old barbarian tribal codes. Now, for the first time, a
complete break was made with the past, and Christendom
enacted its own laws, which covered the whole field of social

activity in Church and state, and referred all things to the single standard of the Christian ethos. This was inspired neither by Germanic nor Roman precedent. The Carolingian emperors gave the law to the whole Christian people in the spirit of the kings and judges of the Old Testament, declaring the law of God to the people of God. In the letter which Cathaulf addressed to Charles at the beginning of his reign, the writer speaks of the king as the earthly representative of God, and he counsels Charles to use the Book of Divine Law as his manual of government, according to the precept of Deuteronomy xvii. 18–20, which commands the king to make a copy of the law from the books of the priests, to keep it always with him and to read it constantly so that he may learn to fear the Lord and keep His laws, lest his heart be lifted up in pride above his brethren and he turn aside to the right hand or to the left.

So, too, Alcuin writes again and again of Charles as the second David, the chosen leader of the people of God, who not only guards the frontiers of Christendom against the pagan barbarian, but also guides and protects the Church herself and guards the Catholic faith against heresy and theological error. It would be a mistake to regard these utterances either as mere courtly flattery, or as a proof that the Church had become entirely subordinated to political interests and the supremacy of the state. What they show is rather a unitary conception of the Christian community in which the distinction of Church and state, which is so obvious to modern lawyers and political theorists, had become blurred and unimportant. This is shown very clearly in the passage with which Jonas of Orléans begins his treatise on the royal office—*De Institutione Regia*—in the reign of Louis the Pious. "All the faithful must know," he writes, "that the universal Church is the body of Christ who is its Head, and in it there are two figures which stand out supreme—the priest and the king"—*in ea duae principaliter existant eximie personae, sacerdotalis videlicet et regalis.* But, above all, it is in the coronation rite itself that the new Carolingian Christian kingship achieved its classical expression, which was transmitted from the Carolingian liturgy, on the one hand, to the West Frankish realm and the Anglo-

Saxon kingdom, and on the other to East Frankish king-doms and to the medieval empire.

It is unnecessary for me to say much about this, be-cause we still possess this rite without substantial change in our own coronation service, and the evolution of the English coronation rite takes us back with hardly any seri-ous gaps to its Carolingian origins. This is one of the most remarkable examples in history of the continuity of the Western development, since here it is not a question of un-conscious influence or of the vestigial survival of ancient tradition in popular custom, but of a solemn public act which holds a central place in the political order of a great modern state. And all the elaborate ritual and symbolism which make up the ceremony have their origin in the an-cient conception of the king as a sacred representative figure, the head of the Christian society, standing between God and the people, bound by reciprocal bonds of loyalty and fidelity to one and the other, since the royal charisma, the grace conferred by unction, was manifested and justified only in so far as the king was the servant of God, the guardian of justice and the protector of the rights of his people. For if the people are bound to obey the king, the king himself is no less bound to keep his oath, which makes him a minister of God, as well as a sovereign.

Thus there is a kind of theocratic constitutionalism im-plicit in the coronation rite which was gradually worked out in the evolution of the medieval state. For both the priest and the king were members and ministers of the same Christian society; both alike were consecrated by God for their office, the one to teach and offer sacrifice, the other to rule and judge. Throughout the Middle Ages there was a continuous tension which often rose to a conflict between these two authorities. But both of them were regarded as functionaries of the same society, and no one questioned that each of them possessed a sacred character, although there were wide differences of opinion with regard to their mutual relations and the determination of their respective functions and prerogatives. Even during the Carolingian period the position which was secured by the exceptional achievement of Charles the Great was rapidly undermined and disintegrated by the weakness of his successor, so that the sense of unity of Christian society, which was the source of Charles the Great's unique authority, was equally responsible for the formal judgment and deposition of Louis the Pious in 834 by the bishops as the ultimate representatives of divine authority. For the divine right of the anointed king was counterbalanced throughout the greater part of the Middle Ages by its conditional and revocable character; and this was not a mere concession to theological theory; it was enforced by the very real authority of the Church. Here again the influence of the Old Testament tradition of theocracy was paramount, so that the medieval monarchy, and most of all the medieval empire, possessed a theocratic character in a different sense from that which is to be seen in the Byzantine Empire, or in the absolute monarchies of Europe after the Renaissance and the Reformation. Nevertheless even in these later periods it is not difficult to find examples of the older view of the limited and essentially dependent nature of divine right. Throughout these periods, both in Catholic and Protestant Europe, there was a large body of opinion which acknowledged the Divine right of kings without admitting that this involved the principle of Passive Obedience, so that there is an historic connection between the modern idea of constitutional monarchy and the medieval tradition of kingship.

Chapter V

The Second Dark Age and the
Conversion of the North

THE CAROLINGIAN EMPIRE was an attempt to realize a vast programme of social and cultural reconstruction with slender material forces and no technical equipment. The remarkable thing is not that it was a material and political failure, but that the ideal of unity and the tradition of Christian culture which inspired it were able to survive so long in the adverse conditions of the ninth century.

For from the moment that its founder died, the Empire was involved in a mounting tide of difficulties and disasters against which emperors and bishops maintained an heroic but ineffectual struggle. It was not merely that the disappearance of the dominant personality of Charlemagne allowed the fundamental contradiction between the barbaric Frankish tradition of patrimonial tribal monarchy and the specifically Carolingian ideal of a unitary Christian Church-state to become explicit. The crisis was due still more to the fact that for the next century and a half Western Christendom was exposed to a new storm of barbarian invasion even more destructive than those of the fifth century. For not only was the Carolingian Empire far weaker and smaller than the Roman world, it was open to attack simultaneously from every side: from the Scandinavian pirates of the North, from Saracen raiders in the Western Mediterranean and finally by a new horde from the eastern steppes—the Magyars—whose raids extended from the Lower Danube over the whole of Central Europe and Northern Italy. Thus by the tenth century Western Christendom had become surrounded by a rising flood of barbarism and the leadership of Western culture had passed to Islamic Spain which was then at the height of its prosperity under the independent Khalifate of Cordova.

The threat to Christian civilization was rendered more serious by the fact that the monasteries which had hitherto been the centres of Western culture were particularly exposed to barbarian attacks. Long before the Carolingian Empire was seriously threatened, the great monastic centres of Northumbrian and Celtic culture had been destroyed—Lindisfarne in 793, Jarrow in 794 and Iona in 802 and 806. Thenceforward the shrines and monasteries of Ireland were devastated year by year until by 830 a powerful Scandinavian kingdom was established in Eastern Ireland which became the base for further raids on Western Britain and the Atlantic coasts of France and Spain. Thus the movement of destruction followed the same path as the Irish and Anglo-Saxon missionaries, who had contributed so much to the formation of the Carolingian culture; and as the new monastic foundations had been the characteristic feature of the earlier movement, so now the destruction of the monasteries was no less characteristic of the new outburst of barbarism.

The monastic culture of Ireland and Northumbria never recovered from this assault, and even in the Carolingian Empire it caused a setback to the monastic movement which had far-reaching effects on religion and culture.

But the main threat to Western Christendom came not from this sporadic raiding but from the massive threat of an organized invasion from Denmark by way of Frisia and South-East England. This danger had been staved off for half a century by the co-ordinated action of Carolingian diplomacy and missionary activity. Indeed it was during the reign of Charlemagne's successor, Louis the Pious, that Christianity first penetrated into Scandinavia through the work of St. Anskar, the first archbishop of the new see of Hamburg, formed in 831. It was only after the fall of Louis the Pious, and still more after the outbreak of civil war between his sons, that the attacks upon the Carolingian kingdoms became serious. In 845 the Danish king sailed up the Weser and destroyed Hamburg, the northern outpost of Christian civilization; in the same year Paris was sacked and Charles the Bald paid a heavy ransom to the Danes, while at the same time in the Mediterranean Rome was attacked by the Saracens, who plundered the tombs of the Apostles, the sacred centre of Western Christendom.

But these disasters were only the prelude to the main attack on the West, which began about 850 and continued without intermission for the next fifty years. During these years it was no longer a question of isolated pirate raids, but of skilfully planned invasion by highly organized professional armies bent on conquest and settlement. Year after year they established their winter quarters in strategic positions on the coast of the Atlantic and the English Channel from which they launched their annual campaigns on Frisia, Eastern England or Western France. From 855 to 862 they were established on the Loire and the Lower Seine. In 865 the main attack on England began, which led to the rapid conquest and settlement of Northumbria and Mercia and to the long struggle with Wessex from 871–78, in which the stubborn and heroic resistance of King Alfred ultimately decided the issue. But this was followed in 879 by an even more formidable onslaught on all the Western Carolingian lands from the Elbe to the Garonne. On Candlemas Day 880 the whole northern army of the German kingdom, led by Bruno the Duke of Saxony, two bishops and twelve counts, was destroyed by the Danes in a great battle in the snow and ice at Ebersdorf on the Luneberg Heath. The two young kings of Germany and West Francia did gain temporary successes at Saucourt and Thiméon, but both of them died almost immediately afterwards, and Charles the Fat, who temporarily reunited all the Carolingian kingdoms, proved completely incapable of dealing with the situation. The great army which had come from England established itself in the very heart of the Carolingian Empire and proceeded to devastate methodically the lands between the Rhine and the Seine, burning Cologne and Treves and Metz, and sacking the imperial palace and the tomb of Charlemagne at Aachen. In 882 the army was at Condé on the Scheldt, in 883 it was at Amiens, while in 885–86 it was concentrating its efforts on the siege of Paris, where the forces of Christendom made a last desperate stand.

It is of these dark years that the chronicler of St. Vedast writes, "The Northmen cease not to slay and carry into captivity the Christian people, to destroy the churches and to burn the towns. Everywhere there is nothing but dead bodies—clergy and laymen, nobles and common people, women and children. There is no road or place where the ground is not covered with corpses. We live in distress and anguish before this spectacle of the destruction of the Christian people."[1]

These years witnessed the final collapse of the Carolingian Empire. The failure of the last attempt to rally the united forces of the West round the surviving representative of the house of Charlemagne was followed by a new alignment of power round the local leaders of national resistance—Eudes, the Count of Paris, in France, Arnulf in Germany, Rudolf in Burgundy, and Guy of Spoleto in Italy. These new kings derived their authority from their military leadership and their power to protect their country from the inroads of the barbarians. Nor were they altogether unsuccessful, for the victory of Eudes at Montfaucon in 888, and the still more important success of Arnulf in 891 when he stormed the camp of the main Viking army at Louvain, marked the turn of the tide. The Vikings once more diverted their efforts against King Alfred in the great invasion of 892–96, which is so fully described in the Anglo-Saxon chronicle, from which Wessex finally emerged battered but undefeated. Much suffering was still in store for the West, and the worst of the Magyar invasions was still to come. But the climax of the storm had passed and the survival of Christendom was secured.

I have dealt in some detail with the events of these years, because they were of such decisive importance in the history of the West. There has never been a war which so directly threatened the existence of Western Christendom as a whole; indeed the Christian resistance has more right to

[1] Annal. Vedast. ann. 884.

the name of a crusade than the Crusades themselves.[2] It subjected the inchoate order of Western Christendom to a terrible test which burnt away anything that was weak and superfluous and left only the hardest and most resistant elements which were inured to insecurity and violence. Thus these years saw the complete destruction of the monastic culture of Northumbria and East Anglia which had produced such rich fruits in the previous century. They marked the end of the great age of Celtic Christian culture, which survived only in a weakened and impoverished condition. They destroyed the Carolingian Empire itself and ended the intellectual revival when it was just reaching its creative period in the lifetime of John Scotus and Servatus Lupus.

Above all, this age destroyed the hope of a pacific development of culture which had inspired the leaders of the Church and the missionary movement and reasserted the warlike character of Western society which it had inherited from its barbarian past. Henceforward the warrior ethos, the practice of private war and the blood feud were as prevalent in Christian society as among its pagan neighbours. The reign of law which Charlemagne and the ecclesiastical statesmen of the Carolingian Empire had attempted to impose was forgotten, and the personal relation of fidelity between lord and vassal became the only basis of social organization.

But in so far as these changes lessened the distance between the Christians and the barbarians, they made it easier for the latter to become assimilated by Christian society. The Viking conquerors on Christian soil in England, Normandy and Ireland often became Christian from the moment of their settlement, thus forming an intermediate zone between Christendom and the pagan world through which Christian influence gradually penetrated back to the homelands of the conquerors and prepared the way for the conversion of Scandinavia.

England and Ireland were the chief centres of this process of cultural and religious interpenetration during the

[2] The whole army that fell at Ebersdorf in 880 was canonized collectively by the German Church as the Martyrs of Ebersdorf.

tenth century and it was also in England that the first of
the new national kingdoms arose as an organized centre of
resistance against the heathen invader. No Christian land
had suffered more severely than England from the disaster
of the ninth century; nowhere were the centres of the old
monastic culture so completely destroyed. Yet King Alfred,
unlike his contemporaries on the Continent, such as Eudes
in France, Arnulf in Germany and Boso in Provence, was
not content to organize a successful military resistance.
Alone among the rulers of his time, he realized the vital
importance of the spiritual issue and devoted no less energy
to the recovery of the tradition of Christian culture than
to the defence of national existence.

It is impossible to be in any doubt about King Alfred's
sense of the urgency of the problem, since he himself
summed up the whole situation in the preface to his translation of St. Gregory's treatise on Pastoral Care which is
one of the most remarkable documents of medieval culture
and the earliest monument of English prose.

He describes in moving words how the tradition of the
golden age of Christian culture had been lost until only
the name of Christendom was left. "The name alone we
loved that we were Christians, and very few of the virtues."

*When I remember all this then I remember also how I
saw before it was all ravaged and burned, how the churches
stood around all England, filled with treasures and books
and a great company of God's servants, and how little they
felt the profit of books for they could not understand them
because they were not written in our tongue. As if they
said our elders who held these places before us loved wisdom and through it they got wealth and left it to us. Here
we may see their traces but we cannot follow after them,
and for that have lost both the wealth and the wisdom because we were not willing to bend our minds to the pursuit
of learning.*

The remedy for this state of things Alfred found in the
development of the vernacular culture.

For it seems well to me that we also change into the

*tongue that we all know the books that are most needful
to be known by all men; and we will bring it about as we
very well may, if we have peace, that all the youth of free
men of England, those that have the opportunity to give
themselves to it, should be bound to learning, while they
can be bound to no other usefulness, until the time when
they all know how to read English writing. Let them further learn the Latin tongue who desire to learn it and to
rise to a higher state.*[3]

It was with this aim that King Alfred, with the help of
Archbishop St. Plegmund, Asser the Welshman, St. Grim-
bald the Fleming and John the monk of Corvey in Saxony,
began his library of translations which he carried on during
the last twelve years of his reign in the midst of the "various and manifold troubles of the Kingdom". And all his
achievements as a warrior king (like Arnulf and Eudes and
his ancestors) are perhaps less heroic than the determination with which he set himself in his later years to acquire
learning in order to restore to his people the lost tradition
of Christian culture.

It is interesting to compare the work of Alfred with that
of Charlemagne. He was attempting to do for England
what Charlemagne had attempted to do for Western
Christendom as a whole. He was working in far more un-
favourable circumstances with insufficient resources and
inadequate intellectual help. Nevertheless his modest plan
for the diffusion of a vernacular Christian culture was perhaps more suited to the real needs of the age than the
theocratic universalism of the Carolingian Empire.

The Empire was not strong enough to withstand the dis-
integrating effects of the barbarian attacks, but its tradition
was still powerful enough to prevent the new kingdoms
from basing themselves on the foundation of autonomous
national traditions of culture. In the West the fall of the
Empire was followed by the dissolution of the authority of
the state itself. It was not the national kingdom but the
local centres of military control—the county and feudal
principality—which became the vital political realities. The

[3] Preface to *Cura Pastoralis*, translated by M. Williams.

new kingdoms of Burgundy, Italy, Provence and Lorraine possessed only a shadowy and fitful existence, and though the kingdom of France or Western Francia retained something of its ancient prestige, the actual position of the king in the tenth century was no more than that of honorary president of a committee of feudal magnates who were their own masters and ruled as kings in their own principalities.

In the East, however, the political development followed a different course. Christian Germany was so largely a Carolingian creation, and the German Church had been so closely associated with the Empire in the work of government and in the extension of Christian culture to the Elbe and the Danubian lands that the Carolingian tradition survived the fall of the Empire and determined the whole character of the subsequent development. The centrifugal tendency which showed itself in the rise of the five great duchies—Saxony, Bavaria, Thuringia, Franconia and Swabia —was checked by the loyalty of the episcopate to the monarchical principle which was solemnly reasserted as a principle of Christian faith by the great synod of Hohenaltheim in 916.

This alliance of Church and king became the corner stone of the new political order established by Otto the Great (936–73)—an order which was consummated by Otto's coronation at Rome in 963 and the restoration of the Western Empire. The new Empire was thoroughly Carolingian in tradition and ideals. Indeed, Otto I went even further than Charlemagne in his reliance on the Church in the practical administration of the Empire, so that the bishops acquired the functions of the Carolingian court and became the main instruments of government. This conversion of the episcopate into a territorial and political power was to some extent common to all the lands that had formed part of the Carolingian Empire—to France and Italy as well as to Germany and Lorraine. It did not exist in Anglo-Saxon society, nor in the newly converted barbarian kingdoms of Scandinavia, Poland and Hungary. But nowhere did the process go so far, or have such serious political and religious consequences, as in the lands of the

Empire in Germany and Lorraine, where it was destined to condition the relations of Church and state for six hundred years. Even the Reformation did not exhaust the consequences of this anomalous situation, and the German episcopate remained inextricably entangled with the political order until the ecclesiastical principalities were finally liquidated in the age of Napoleon.

If the Germanic Empire had possessed the universal character of its Carolingian prototype as the political expression of the *respublica Christiana*, the situation might not have been so irremediable. But since, in spite of its theoretical claims, it was never conterminous with Western Christendom, and possessed its own national aims and interests, there was an inherent contradiction between the spiritual office and the political functions of the new type of count-bishop who was the central figure in the administration of the Empire. The leading minds in the Carolingian Church, like Rabanus Maurus, had always been conscious of the danger, and even in the tenth century St. Radbod of Utrecht was faithful to the tradition of St. Willebrord and St. Boniface and refused to accept secular office as inconsistent with the spiritual functions of the episcopate.

But in the age of Otto I this attitude was no longer tenable. The great leader of the Church in Germany, St. Bruno, the brother of the Emperor, accumulated every kind of ecclesiastical and secular dignity. He was Archbishop of Cologne, Abbot of Lorsch and Corvey, Arch-Chancellor of the Empire, Duke of Lorraine and, finally, Regent of the Empire during the absence of Otto in Italy.[4] Yet at the same time he was a great patron of learning, a student of Greek and a leader in the new movement of educational and cultural revival which accompanied the restoration of the Empire. It was, in fact, when the influence of these ecclesiastical statesmen was at its highest, during the minority of Otto III and under his brief reign, that the new Empire came nearest to realizing the Carolingian ideals of Christian universalism. No doubt this was partly due to the

[4] It is significant that it was in 1870 that his cultus was first confirmed by the Holy See.

personality of the young Emperor himself, who was half Byzantine in blood and was intensely alive to the appeal of Roman tradition and Byzantine religion. But no less important was the formative influence of the remarkable group of ecclesiastics who were his teachers and advisers, St. Bernward of Hildesheim, St. Heribert of Cologne, St. Notker of Liége and, above all, Gerbert of Aurillac, Pope Sylvester II, the most universal intelligence of his age.

Thus the close of the tenth century witnessed a brief spasmodic attempt to transform the Germanic national kingdom of the Saxon emperors into the universal and international empire of Christian Rome. Otto III made it his aim to revive the international prestige of Rome, free the city from the control of the local aristocratic factions and establish the closest possible unity with the Papacy. His favourite residence was at Rome in the "palace-monastery" on the Aventine, close to St. Alessio, and he took as his programme of government "the restoration of the republic and the renovation of the Roman Empire"—*Restitutio republicae et Renovatio Imperii Romanorum.*

And though his brief reign ended in failure and disappointment, it nevertheless had a greater influence on the future development of Western Christendom than many reigns that were more famous and more materially successful. In the first place, by the nomination of the first Northern European Popes—Gregory V and Sylvester II—it foreshadowed the internationalization of the Papacy which was to characterize the great age of the medieval Church. And in the second place, by the abandonment of the Saxon policy of German imperialist expansion which had identified the conversion of the pagans with their submission to the German Empire and the German Church, it led to the formation of the new Christian kingdoms of Eastern Europe.

Yet the age which saw the conversion of Hungary and Poland and Russia was also a time of triumph for Northern paganism. Again for the last time the Viking fleets were launched against the West, and a new age of barbarian conquest began. The causes of the new movement are obscured by the complicated struggle for power which divided the three Northern kingdoms against one another. But it is probable that the consolidation of German power by Otto I was felt as a threat to Northern independence, and the defeat of Otto II in Italy was the signal for the Danes, like the Wends east of the Elbe, to renounce Christianity and to invade the territory of Christendom.

It was, however, England rather than the Continent that was the chief victim of the new Viking attack. The restored Christian kingdom of the house of Alfred, which had attained its zenith under King Edgar (959-75), had now fallen on evil times, and under the pressure of invasion it collapsed in blood and ruin. For twenty-five years England was plundered from end to end and drained of immense sums of money, relics of which are still found in graves and hoards and in runic inscriptions from one end of Scandinavia to the other. Finally, in 1016, Canute, the son of the leader of the pagan reaction, was recognized as king of England, thus becoming the founder of an Anglo-Scandinavian empire.

But the victory of Canute was not a victory for paganism. As soon as he was in power he dismissed the Viking army and ruled England "under the laws of King Edgar" according to the traditions of Christian kingship. He became a great benefactor of the Church, building the tombs and adorning the sepulchres of the saints, like St. Alphege, whom his father had slain. Like Ine and Ethulwulf, he made a pilgrimage to Rome to visit the tombs of the Apostles and assist with the princes of Christendom at the coronation of the Emperor in 1027. He introduced English bishops and monks into Denmark and Norway and it seemed for a time as though Canterbury might replace Hamburg as the ecclesiastical capital of the North.

Thus the incorporation of Scandinavia into Western Christendom was due, not as in Central Europe to the power and prestige of the Western Empire, but to the conquest of Christian England by the barbarians who brought back Christianity to the North with the other spoils of invasion.

Hence the conversion of the Northern peoples did not mean the victory of an alien culture and the loss of national independence, as happened to the continental Saxons or the Slavs of Eastern Germany. The pagan North entered the society of Western Christendom at the very time when its social vitality was greatest and its culture most creative. It was the work of the greatest of their own rulers, kings like St. Vladimir in Russia, Canute the Mighty in Denmark and Olaf Trygvason and Olaf the Saint in Norway.

It was, in fact, only through the authority of a new universal religion that the national monarchy acquired the prestige necessary to overcome the conservatism of the old peasant culture and the independence of the old tribal kingdoms—"fylker" or folks.

In this way the victory of Christianity coincided with the attainment of national unity and was the culmination of the process of expansion and cultural interchange which had accompanied the Viking movement. The mixed culture of the Christian Viking states across the seas reacted on the culture of the Scandinavian homelands and led to the breaking down of local particularism alike in religion and politics. Indeed it seemed for a time as though the whole of the Nordic culture area from the British Isles to the Baltic would be united in a northern Christian empire under the sovereignty of the Danish king. Ruling from his court at Winchester, surrounded by English ecclesiastics, Scandinavian mercenaries and Icelandic poets, Canute brought the Northern lands for the first time into real contact with the international life of Western Christendom. The North had never before known a king so rich and so powerful. As Toraren the Icelander wrote:

> Canute rules the land
> As Christ, the shepherd of Greece, doth the heavens!

Nevertheless this empire of the North, like the contemporary Slavonic empire of Boleslav the Great in Poland (992–1025), was a fragile and transitory power, and the figure of Canute made little permanent impression on the Northern mind. It was not Canute, but his defeated rival and victim, Olaf the Saint, who became the type and representative of the new ideal of Christian kingship in the

Northern lands. For Canute, in spite of his Christian laws and his lavish generosity to the Church, made no appeal to the higher elements in the Nordic traditions. He was a successful warrior and statesman, but he was never a hero, for he owed his victories to his overwhelming power and to an unscrupulous use of his great financial resources. Olaf Haroldson, on the other hand, was an authentic representative of the Northern heroic tradition, like his predecessor Olaf Trygvason (995–1000). He completed the latter's work of Christianizing Norway, breaking the stubborn resistance of the pagan chiefs and countryfolk with fire and sword, and died like the other Olaf in an heroic battle against hopeless odds.

But the battle of Stiklestad (1030) differs from that of Svoldr (1000) in that it was a civil war against the king's faithless subjects who had been bought by Canute's English money. Thus it was an historical realization of the dominant motive of the old epic poetry—the tragedy of loyal heroism defeated by treachery and gold. As Olaf's friend the poet Sighvat wrote:

> There go the prince's foes,
> Bringing their open purses,
> Many bid dearly in metal
> For the head of our king.
>
> Every man knows that he who sells
> His own good lord for gold
> Will end in black hell
> And of such is he worthy.[5]

But in the case of Olaf this ancient tradition of Nordic heroism was united with a new spirit of religious faith. As Olaf's retainers kept their faith with their lord, so Olaf himself kept faith with the Lord of Heaven. And thus the new religion became the object of a deeper loyalty than the religion of the old gods had ever evoked.

The year after the battle, the body of St. Olaf was taken to Nidaros (Trondheim) and the defeated king became the patron and protector of the Christian North, and the fame

[5] *Heimskringla*, p. 403, ed. E. Monsen (Cambridge 1932).

of his virtues and miracles spread throughout the North with extraordinary rapidity.

Even his former enemies acknowledged his power and accepted him as the patron and guardian of the Norwegian monarchy, as we see in the fine poem called "The Song of the Sea Calm" which Canute's court poet Toraren wrote only a few years later. Although the poem is dedicated to King Swein, the Danish usurper, its real hero is the dead king who still rules the land from his shrine at Nidaros.

> There he lies
> Whole and pure
> The high praised king
>
> There the bells
> May ring aloud
> Of themselves,
> Above the shrine
> For every day
> The folk to hear
> The clanging bells
> Above the king.
>
> Hardly had Haroldson
> Got a home
> In the heavenly realm
> Ere he became
> A mighty man of peace.
>
> A host of men
> Where the holy king doth lie
> Kneel for help,
> Blind and dumb
> Seek the king,
> And home they go
> Their sickness healed.
>
> Pray thou to Olaf
> The man of God
> That he grant thee
> His holy spirit.
> With God himself

> *He seeks*
> *Success and peace*
> *For all men.*[6]

Thus the popular canonization of St. Olaf in 1031 is important not only as one of the first and most spontaneous instances of the way in which the new peoples consecrated their nationality by adopting a royal saint as their national patron, but still more because it marks the final reconciliation between the Nordic and the Christian traditions. St. Olaf quickly took the place of Thor as the patron of the farmers, their champion against trolls and witches, and the ideal type of the Northern warrior. The national code of law became known as the laws of St. Olaf, and the kings of Norway were regarded as the heirs and representatives of St. Olaf, almost in the same way as the kings of Sweden in the heathen time had been the successors and representatives of the God Frey.

The wholehearted acceptance of Christianity in Norway and Denmark gradually transformed the spirit of Scandinavian culture.

Adam of Bremen, who is a contemporary witness and was well informed of Northern affairs through his friendship with King Sweyn Estrithson of Denmark, has described the change in a remarkable passage. After speaking of their former piracy, he goes on:

> *But after their acceptance of Christianity, they have become imbued with better principles and have now learned to love peace and truth and to be content with their poverty; even to distribute what they have stored up and not as aforetime to gather up what was scattered. . . . Of all men they are the most temperate both in food and in their habits, loving above all things thrift and modesty. Yet so great is their veneration for priests and churches, that there is scarcely a Christian to be found who does not make an offering on every occasion that he hears Mass. . . . In many places of Norway and Sweden, the keepers of the flocks are men of noble rank, who after the manner of the pa-*

[6] Heimskringla, p. 469, trans. E. Monsen and A. H. Smith.

*triarchs live by the work of their hands. But all who dwell
in Norway are most Christian with the exception of those
who dwell far off beside the Arctic Seas.*[7]

He speaks in the same way of the habits of the Icelanders
who are forced to live in material poverty owing to the
severity of their climate:

*Blessed is the people, say I, of whose poverty no one is
envious, and most blessed in this—that they have now all
put on Christianity. There is much that is remarkable in
their manners, above all Charity, whence it comes that all
things are common among them not only for the native
population but also for the stranger. They treat their bishop
as it were a king, for the whole people pay regard to his
will, and whatever he ordains from God, from the scriptures and from the customs of other nations, they hold as
law.*[8]

However much Adam has idealized Scandinavian Christendom there is no doubt that a reaction was making itself
felt against the violence and cruelty of the Viking age, and
under the rule of kings like Olaf Kyrre—"the Peace King"
—of Norway, 1066–93, who was also called "the Farmer",
the new ideals of Christian kingship obtained general acceptance. The opening sentences of the Laws of St. Olaf,
though they date in their present form from a much later
period, seem to reflect the spirit of this period:

*This is the beginning of our law that we should bow to
the East and pray the Holy Christ for peace and good years,
that our land may be well peopled and that we may be
faithful to our king; may he be our friend and we his, and
may God be the friend of us all.*

The new Christian culture which spread over the North
in the eleventh and twelfth centuries was largely derived
from England whence came the majority of the early missionary bishops and the first monastic communities, and
on the other hand the annexation of the Norse earldoms

[7] Adam of Bremen, *Descriptio Insularum Aquilonis*, 30 and 31.
[8] Ibid., 35.

in Caithness and the Western Islands by Magnus, the successor of Olaf Kyrre, brought Norway into immediate relations with Scotland and Gaelic culture. Had it not been for the Norman conquest of England and Ireland, the British Isles and Scandinavia and Iceland might well have come to share a common culture and to form a distinct province of Western Christendom. But even the Norman conquest did not entirely break the connection. In some ways it strengthened it, as we see in the career of Turgot, who took refuge in Norway from the Normans and was the teacher of Olaf Kyrre, and afterwards became prior of Durham, archbishop of St. Andrews and the guide and biographer of St. Margaret of Scotland.

With the fall of Anglo-Saxon culture, the Scandinavian world became the great representative of vernacular culture in Northern Europe. And it was, above all, in Iceland that the scholars of the twelfth and thirteenth centuries took up the tradition of King Alfred and founded the great school of vernacular historiography and archaeology to which we owe so much of our knowledge of the past. We are apt to regard medieval culture as intolerant of everything that lay outside the tradition of Latin Christendom. But we must not forget that the Northern Sagas are as much the creation of medieval Christendom as the *chansons de geste* and that it is to the priests and the schools of Christian Iceland that we are indebted for the preservation of the rich tradition of Northern mythology and poetry and saga.

Chapter VI

The Byzantine Tradition and the Conversion of Eastern Europe

THE CONVERSION of the Scandinavian peoples was an event of peculiar importance for the West since it was these peoples who during the Viking age had constituted the most serious and immediate threat to the existence of Western Christendom. But it was not an isolated event, for it was during the same period that the peoples of Eastern Europe entered the society of Christian peoples, and formed a second European Christendom which extended from the Baltic to the Black Sea and from the Elbe to the Don and the Upper Volga. The formation of this second Christendom was organically related to the conversion of Scandinavia in so far as its expansion followed the lines of the Viking trade routes to the East, and found one of its most important centres of diffusion in the new Russian states which were organized and controlled by Scandinavian adventures. Further west, on the Danube and the Elbe and the Morava, the Eastern expansion of Christendom goes back to an earlier period and had its origins in the efforts of Charles the Great and his successors to extend the frontiers of their empire and Christendom in Central Europe.

But these efforts met only with partial success, and it was not until the tenth and eleventh centuries that Christian culture finally took root in Eastern Europe—in Bohemia and Hungary and Poland, as well as in Scandinavia and Russia.

At first sight this is a surprising fact, since the Byzantine Empire maintained its cultural and religious leadership throughout this whole period and its capital at Constantinople was in an admirable position to be the headquarters of a movement of missionary expansion across the Danube and the Black Sea. Already in the fourth century the Goths in South Russia had been converted and their bishop had been present at the Council of Nicaea, while in the Balkans St. Nicetas of Remesiana had carried on a successful apostolate among the pagan peoples on the Danube. But after the death of Justinian the Eastern Empire underwent a profound transformation. It turned its back upon Europe and became an oriental state, which was increasingly absorbed in the struggle for existence, first with the Persian Empire and after 640 with the Moslem Khalifate which had conquered Syria and Egypt. The Illyrian provinces which had been the backbone of the Empire from before the reign of Diocletian to that of Justinian—from the third to the sixth centuries—were devastated by the barbarians and occupied by Slavonic tribes, and when the Empire reestablished its position in the eighth century it owed its recovery to the Isaurian emperors who were Asiatic in origin and based their power on Asia Minor rather than on the European provinces.

Under these conditions it is not surprising that Byzantine cultural and religious influence expanded eastwards to Armenia and Georgia rather than northwards into Eastern Europe.

The only outstanding exception to this tendency is to be found in the strange career of Justinian II (685–95 and 705–11), who resembled Ivan the Terrible in his ruthless cruelty, his mental instability and his sudden outbursts of demonic energy.

Justinian II spent ten years in exile in the Crimea, where he married the sister of the Khagan of the Khazars, and he allied himself with the Bulgarians in order to recover his throne, rewarding the Bulgarian ruler with the purple mantle and the title of Caesar. Yet in his age and under the great Isaurian emperors who succeeded him there was no Byzantine missionary activity in Eastern Europe, comparable to that of the Celtic and Anglo-Saxon monks in the West during the same period. This was no doubt mainly due to the tremendous gulf which separated the urban culture of the Byzantine Empire from the successive waves of barbarian peoples who came pouring in from the outer wilderness. In the West no such gap existed, since the Christian barbarian kingdoms which had arisen on the ruins of the Western Empire provided a natural transition between the Latin culture of the Western Mediterranean and the pagan culture of the Northern barbarians. But the history of Eastern Europe has always been dominated by the geographical fact that it has no natural eastern frontier. The great Eurasian steppe stretches illimitably from the Danube to the Altai mountains, and southward by the oases to the Great Wall of China and the Manchurian forests. This was the highway of the nations which opened the heart of Eastern Europe to the warrior peoples of Central Asia, and it was never closed until Munnich and Marshal Keith stormed the Lines of Perekop in 1737.

The whole of this vast area forms a unity far closer than that of the West, since the peoples of the steppes have been in contact with one another from time immemorial and any change in their relations might set the whole area in motion from the frontiers of China to those of the Byzantine and Carolingian Empires. For while the highest civilizations of the far East and the far West have always ignored one another's existence and lacked the means of communication and co-operation, the barbarians of the steppes have been equally aware of the existence of both worlds and have shown themselves able to organize vast military combinations which they directed impartially against East and West. Consequently the relation of the Byzantine Empire to its barbarian neighbours was not that of a unified civilization dealing with divided barbarous tribes. It was a relation of empire with empire. For though the peoples of the steppes were in many respects more barbarous than the pagan Germans and Slavs, they were, from a military or military-political point of view, highly organized, and formed part of a wider whole which reached far beyond the range of Byzantine statesmanship. This organized imperial type of Eurasian barbarism already existed in the fifth century when the Huns who had been driven westward from the heart of Central Asia established themselves in Hungary, whence they invaded the eastern and the western provinces impartially. But Attila and the Huns were but the first of a long series of nomad conquerors on the Danube, Kotrigurs, Avars, Bulgars and Magyars—not to mention the Khazars and the Patzinaks and the Cumans—all of whom successively occupied the steppes from the Volga to the Danube. The ephemeral character of these nomad empires only increased their destructiveness, since the moment that a people became sufficiently civilized to receive the seeds of Christian culture, it was replaced by a new horde from the outer steppes, and the whole process had to begin again. It was not until the last of the great conquering tribes—the Mongols—united the whole Eurasian world in an organized imperial state in the thirteenth century that the situation was stablized but this greatest of the nomad empires found its centre of gravity in Eastern Asia, far beyond the reach of Byzantine cultural and religious influence.

Thus the Byzantine Empire throughout its entire history of a thousand years was confronted on its northern European frontier by a series of Asiatic barbarian empires, which constituted a continual threat to the Balkan provinces and the capital itself. This extension of Asia westward into the heart of Central Europe separated Eastern Christendom from the native peoples of Eastern or North-Eastern Europe—from the Slavonic peasant peoples who lived north of the steppes and the still more remote Finnish tribes who occupied the vast forest region that stretched from the eastern Baltic to the Urals and onwards into Siberia. For Western and Northern Europe this barrier did not exist, since the Germans came into immediate contact with the northern Slavs by way of the Elbe and with the southern Slavs by way of the Danube, while the Scandinavian peoples from time immemorial had followed the chain of rivers and lakes south-eastward from the Baltic to the Volga and the Dnieper. Hence it is not surprising that the first challenge to the peoples of the steppes came from the West rather than from the Byzantine Empire. It was Charlemagne and his son Pepin, the king of Italy, who destroyed the centre of the Avar kingdom in Hungary and reopened the Danubian lands to Christian missionary activity. The new spirit which animated this first expansion of Western Christendom finds expression in the hymn of triumph composed by some anonymous Carolingian poet on the final subjugation of the Avars in 796.

Omnes gentes qui fecisti, tu Christe, dei suboles,
terras, fontes, rivos, montes et formasti hominem,
Avarosque convertisti ultimis temporibus.

Misit deus Petrum sanctum, principem apostolum,
In auxilium Pippini magni regis filium
Ut viam ejus comitaret et Francorum aciem.

Nos fideles christiani deo agamus gratiam,
qui regnum regis confirma vit super regnum Uniae,
et victoriam donavit de paganis gentibus.[1]

These rough forcible tetrameters have little in common with the laborious elegiacs of the contemporary court scholars. They are even more remote from the spirit of Byzantine culture—their ideal is that of the Crusades and the *chansons de geste—gesta Dei per Francos.*

We are, however, relatively well informed about the ecclesiastical aspect of this expansion of Western Christendom to the Avar kingdom, thanks to the letters of Alcuin and the council held by Paulinus of Aquileia in King Pepin's camp during this very campaign.[2] The fall of the Avar Empire, which had for centuries overshadowed the life of Eastern Europe, produced an enormous impression on the Slavonic peoples, the memory of which still survives in the early medieval Russian chronicles. Not only

[1] *Poet. Latin. Aevi Carolini*, I, 116 (M.G.H.). *Translation:* "Thou, O Christ, son of God, who hast made all peoples, who hast formed lands, fountains, streams, mountains and man, in these last days Thou hast converted the Avars. God has sent St. Peter, chief of apostles, to the aid of Pepin, son of the great king, to go with him on his way and with the army of the Franks. Let us faithful Christians give thanks to God, who has confirmed the King's rule over the Kingdom of Hungary and has given him victory over the pagans."

[2] Cf. Alcuin's letters, 99, 107, 110–13 and *Concilia Aevi Carolini*, I, no. 20, pp. 172–76 (M.G.H.).

did it open the Danubian and West Balkan lands to Carolingian influences, it also gave the Slavonic peoples further
north a breathing space during which they were able to
assert their political independence. In this way there arose
in the ninth century the Great Moravian state which was
the first Slav kingdom to become Christian and to play a
part in European history. For the Byzantine Empire the
development was less favourable, since the fall of the Avars
destroyed the balance of power which Byzantine diplomacy
always attempted to maintain on its northern frontiers, and
left the Bulgars for almost a century without a rival power
to distract their attention from the Byzantine frontiers.
The result was that the Bulgars, under their Khagans, Krum
and Omurtag, established themselves firmly in the Balkans
from Belgrade and Ochrida to the Dobrudja and inflicted
a terrible defeat on the Byzantines in 811, when the Emperor Nicephorus and his whole army were destroyed.

For the next two centuries Bulgaria constituted a most
serious threat to the Byzantine Empire, but its establishment in the civilized lands of the Eastern Balkans produced a profound change in its own state and culture. The
Bulgars ceased to be a horde of Turco-Finnish nomads from
the steppes like the Avars or the Huns and became a people
of Slavonic language and Christian Byzantine culture. Indeed it was in ninth- and tenth-century Bulgaria that the
foundations were laid of the Slavonic literature and culture
which were subsequently transmitted to the Russians and
the Serbs, and thus became the main source of the cultural tradition of the Orthodox Church in Eastern Europe,
outside Greece.

This development, however, was by no means a peaceful or harmonious one, for the political methods of Byzantine imperialism contradicted its cultural and religious aims
and hindered the rise of independent Christian states on
the borders of the Empire. It had always been the policy
of Byzantium to make trouble for the barbarians on their
own frontiers by calling in more remote barbarian peoples
to attack them in their rear, calling in Avars against Huns
and Turks against Avars. The fact that the Bulgars had

become Christians did not prevent the Byzantines from using the same technique against them and bringing in fresh barbarian hordes from the steppes. The result was that the spread of Christianity in Eastern Europe became involved in the complicated web of power politics. The fear of Byzantine imperialism made the Bulgars look towards the West, while the fear of German Carolingian imperialism turned the eyes of the Moravians towards Byzantium.

It was against this confusing political background that the religious activity of Pope Nicholas I, the Patriarch Photius and the apostles of the Slavs, SS. Cyril and Methodius, must be viewed. St. Cyril, who was originally known as Constantine the Philosopher, was a learned monk of Thessalonica and was first sent by the Emperor and the Patriarch Photius to the Khazars in South Russia on a mission that was probably political as well as religious. On his return to Constantinople in 862–63 he met the envoys whom Ratislav, the prince of Moravia, had sent to establish friendly relations with the Eastern Empire, in order to counter-balance the combined pressure of the Carolingian kingdom and the German Church. Now at the same time that Constantine and his brother Methodius began their work for the Moravian Church, in response to the request of Ratislav, Boris the Khagan of Bulgaria was making similar advances to Rome in order to safeguard his independence against the Byzantines. We still possess the long and detailed reply of Pope Nicholas I to the questionnaire of the Bulgarians on all kinds of moral, ritual and social problems. It is a document which ranks with St. Gregory's letter to St. Augustine of Canterbury as a primary authority for the attitude adopted by the Papacy in its dealings with the barbarians, and, like the latter, it is a monument of statesmanship and pastoral wisdom. It shows how the conversion of the barbarians inevitably involved changes in their social culture and how necessary it was to distinguish between the essentials of the Christian way of life and the accidents of Byzantine or Latin culture, which the missionaries were apt to regard as a necessary part of Christianity.[3] And the

[3] For example, it seems from this document that the question of wearing trousers preoccupied the minds of Byzantine mission-

same problem arose in Moravia, where the Carolingian bishops attacked Cyril and Methodius for their use of the vernacular for liturgical purposes.

If the policy of Nicholas I and his successors Hadrian and John VIII had been victorious, a new Slavonic province of Christendom might have arisen in the Balkan and Danubian lands, which would have been independent of the state Churches of the Byzantine and Carolingian Empires. But the decline of the Papacy after the assassination of John VIII and the unscrupulous power-politics of the two empires rendered this impossible. The work of Cyril and Methodius was undone by the Carolingian bishops, while the action of the Byzantines in calling the pagan Magyars to their aid against the Bulgars destroyed the nascent Christian culture of both Moravia and the Danubian lands. For the coming of the Magyars into Hungary, together with the occupation of their former home west of the Don by the Petcheneg Turks,[4] once more restored the barrier of the peoples of the steppes between the Byzantine Empire and Central and Eastern Europe. Indeed the new barbarian attack went further than its predecessors. The Magyars not only destroyed the Moravian Kingdom, they also destroyed the Austrian March of the Carolingian Empire and carried their raids into the very heart of Western Europe.

Nevertheless the work of the missionaries was not altogether lost, for when Svatopluk and the pro-German party in Moravia drove out the disciples of Cyril and Methodius, ten years or so before the coming of the Magyars, they found a refuge in Bulgaria where the Cyrillian ideal of a vernacular Slavonic Christianity coincided with the aim of Boris and his successors to create an autonomous Bulgarian Church. It was here that St. Clement at Ochrida and St.

---

aries in the ninth century no less than of English and American missionaries in the nineteenth. But whereas these modern missionaries encouraged the wearing of trousers as a part of Christian civilization, the Byzantines banned them as a pagan and barbarous custom.

[4] Known to the Byzantines as "Patzinaks". It is confusing that Byzantine writers habitually speak of the Magyars, who were Finno-Ugrians, as "Turks", while the Petchenegs, who were really a Turkish people, are described as "Scythians".

Naum at Preslav carried on the work of Cyril and Methodius for the creation of a Christian Slavonic script and liturgy and literature. Under the great Tsar Symeon (893–927), who established an independent Bulgarian patriarchate, the new vernacular culture reached a precocious maturity, comparable to that of Anglo-Saxon Northumbria two centuries earlier. It was, however, of even greater importance, since Old Slavonic, the language of the new Christian culture, was to become the sacred liturgical language of Eastern Europe, and, above all, of Russia.

But this sudden development of Christian culture in Bulgaria was even more short-lived than that of Christian Northumbria. The ambitious attempt of Symeon the Great to establish a Bulgarian empire and a Bulgarian patriarchate inevitably led to conflict with Byzantium, and the Byzantines followed their traditional policy of bringing down Magyars, Petchenegs and Russians upon them from the outer lands. The second half of the tenth century and the early part of the eleventh saw the end of Bulgarian independence and the Hellenization of the Bulgarian Church.

No doubt the conquest of Bulgaria, which reunited the old Balkan provinces to the Empire, was an external triumph for Byzantine imperialism, but, like the annexation of the independent Christian kingdom of Armenia which took place at the same period, it was disastrous to the cause of Eastern Christendom. For the destruction of national independence and the identification of the Orthodox Church with Byzantine domination produced a mood of spiritual revolt among the subject peoples which led them not only to oppose the dominant alien civilization but to turn away from the Christian view of life towards the fundamental world-refusal of oriental dualism.

Already in the eighth and ninth centuries similar conditions on the eastern frontiers of the Empire had produced the militant sect of the Paulicians in Armenia and Asia Minor, and in the tenth century a Bulgarian priest, Bogomil or Theophilus, founded a similar but independent sect in Europe which was destined to make the name of Bulgar a synonym for heretic throughout the medieval West. Like their predecessors, the Bogomils taught that the material creation was essentially evil and that salvation was to be found in the total rejection of all the works of the flesh, including marriage, war and all external activity. In this last point they differed from the Paulicians, who were an exceptionally warlike and active sect.[5]

The Bogomils, on the other hand, were pacifist, quietist and anti-political. They avoided open conflict and practised concealment, so that they were able to carry on a subterranean propaganda among the peasant population of the Balkans. Moreover, their ideas infiltrated into orthodox Slavonic literature through their influence on Bulgarian vernacular literature, which was the source of the numerous apocalypses and apocryphal legends which were so popular in Russia in medieval and even in modern times. The existence of this heretical underworld is of great importance in the history of medieval culture alike in the East and the West, although the wholesale destruction of heretical literature has deprived us of literary evidence. Nevertheless there is little doubt that the whole movement, not only in the Balkans, but in the rest of Europe, had its origin and centre of diffusion in Bulgaria in the tenth and eleventh centuries.

Meanwhile the fall of the Bulgarian state had opened the way for the rise of a new power beyond the Danube. To the East the Khazar Empire still dominated the lands between the Black Sea and the Volga, and owed its importance to its control of the trade routes between the Near East and Europe. These routes from the Lower Volga to the Lower Don and from the Baltic eastward to the Upper and Middle Volga had been important channels of communication between North and South from time immemorial. For Russia is not only open to Asia by way of the steppes, it is also open to North and South and East by way of its rivers; and as the steppes have been the highway

[5] Their relations to the latter may be compared with that of the Quakers to the Anabaptists in the seventeenth century, or with that of the Bohemian Brethren to the Taborites in the fifteenth century.

of war, the rivers have been the highway of trade and culture. It is true that in the Middle Ages the trader and the warrior were often indistinguishable, and this was especially true of the Vikings who in the East no less than the West devoted themselves impartially to piracy and trade, and colonization and conquest. Traders and adventurers from Scandinavia seem to have been active in the East long before the expansion of the Vikings in the West began, and Arabic historians give a vivid picture of the way of life of these predatory adventurers.

The Rus, writes Ibn Rusta, *make raids upon Saqlaba (the Slavs), sailing in ships in order to go out to them, and they take them prisoner and carry them off to Khazar and Bulkar (on the Volga) and trade with them there. . . .*

When a child is born to any man among them he takes a drawn sword to the new-born child and places it between his hands and says to him, "I shall bequeath to thee no wealth, and thou shalt have nought except what thou dost gain for thyself by this sword of thine."

They have no landed property nor villages nor cultivated land; their only occupation is trading in sable and grey squirrel and other furs, and in these they trade and take as the price gold and silver and secure it in their belts.[6]

This account, which dates from the beginning of the tenth century, no doubt refers to the Rus of the North who came from the Baltic by way of Lake Ilmen or Lake Ladoga by the Upper Volga to the great Moslem emporium of Bolghar, the capital of the Northern Bulgars, near Kazan. But they were also active on the southern route to the Sea of Azov, and the first Russian raid on Constantinople took place as early as 860. The essential unity of the Rus and the Western Vikings is shown by the interesting story in the Annals of St. Bertin of the Russian envoys to Constantinople in 838, who tried to return to their own country by way of the West in the company of the Byzantine embassy to Louis the Pious and who admitted that they were Swedes by birth.

[6] Translated by C. A. Macartney, *The Magyars in the Ninth Century*, pp. 213 ff. (1930).

In fact, the history of the establishment of the Kievan state and its attacks on the Khazars and the Byzantine Empire affords a remarkable parallel to that of the establishment of the Western Viking states at Dublin and York and in Normandy and their attacks on Wessex and the Carolingian Empire, nor is it impossible that the slackening of the Viking attacks on the West in the tenth century was due in part to their energies, having been diverted to the new sphere of adventure that had been opened in the South-East. For the establishment of the Rus at Kiev in the second half of the ninth century and their development of the Dnieper as the main trade route between the Baltic and the Black Sea took place at a time when the pressure of the steppe peoples on South Russia had relaxed, and when the Magyars were moving westward into Hungary.

From Kiev the Viking merchant princes were able to organize and exploit the Slav peoples of the Ukraine and push back the Khazars from the Black Sea. Under their early rulers, Oleg (Helgi), Igor and Svyatoslav, the forays and conquests of the Rus equalled and surpassed those of the Western Vikings in the ninth century. They were directed not only against the Byzantine Empire, but against the Bulgarians of the north and the south, the Khazars and the Moslems of Azerbaijan, and on at least two occasions in 913–14 and 943–44 expeditions were carried out on a very large scale across the Caspian Sea.[7]

If these ventures had been more successful, it is possible that the course of Russian development might have been deflected to the East and that Russia might have become a part of the Islamic world. Fortunately for Europe and the Byzantine Empire the triumphant career of Svyatoslav, the greatest of the early Kievan rulers, ended in disaster (963–72). In the course of a few years he had destroyed the Khazar Empire and conquered the Bulgarians of the Volga and the Bulgarians of the Danube. He even resolved to transfer his capital from Kiev to Pereyaslavets (Little Preslav) in Bulgaria, thus uniting Russia and Bulgaria in a

[7] Cf. N. K. Chadwick, *The Beginnings of Russian History*; and G. Vernadsky, *Kievan Russia*, 33–35.

new empire which would control all the inland trade routes from the Danube to the Volga. After four years of war he was defeated by the energetic resistance of the new Emperor John Zimisces, and in the following year he was killed by the Patzinaks on his way back to Kiev at the falls of the Dnieper—the series of rapids and portages which was the weak point of the Kievan trade route through the steppes.

It was Vladimir, the son of Svyatoslav, who took the historic decision which decided the future of Russia in 988. According to tradition it was not taken until he had made enquiries from the Moslems, the Jews, the Latins and the Greeks, and the decisive factor was the splendour of the Byzantine liturgy as the Russian envoys saw it at St. Sofia. But no doubt the Byzantine connection and the prestige of the Byzantine Empire were the decisive factors.

After the conversion of Vladimir there was a rapid expansion of Christian Byzantine culture in Russia. Here, as in eighth-century Northumbria and ninth-century Bulgaria, we see how rapidly the conversion of a pagan people may be followed by the sudden blossoming of a seemingly mature Christian culture. Already under the rule of Yaroslav the Wise, the son of St. Vladimir (1036–54), Kiev became one of the greatest cities of Eastern Europe, as Adam of Bremen describes it "the rival of Constantinople and most renowned glory of 'Greece'". It was a city of churches and monasteries, and the cathedral of St. Sofia with its Byzantine mosaics and frescoes, which date from the days of Yaroslav, remains with St. Mark's at Venice a witness of the high achievement of Eastern Christendom at the prime of its medieval development. The influence of this new Slavonic Byzantine culture extended far to the north-east to Riazan, Rostov and Vladimir, as well as northwards to the Gulf of Finland and Lake Ilmen where Novgorod the Great retained its importance as the gateway to the Baltic, as Kiev was the gate to the Black Sea and the south.

In the eleventh and twelfth centuries this eastern way to Byzantium was still a familiar way to Scandinavian travellers. Novgorod or Holmgard as they called it was itself almost a part of the Scandinavian world and the courts of the Russian princes were the natural refuge of Northern

princes in exile—of Olaf Trygvason and St. Olaf, of Harold
Hadrada and of the family of his rival, the other Harold,
the last Saxon King of England. Icelandic tradition records
that it was in Russia—"in St. John's Church, on a hill
above the Dnieper"—that the first man to bring Christianity
to Iceland, Thorwald Codranson, found rest after his long
journeying,[8] and many an unknown Northerner, like the
man whose runic gravestone was found at Berezan Island
at the mouth of the Dnieper, followed the same path, as
mercenaries, traders or pilgrims.

Thus the conversion of Russia opened a new channel by
which Christian culture could penetrate the pagan North,
so that the whole continent seemed about to become a
Christian *orbis terrarum*. For Eastern Europe was now the
meeting place of two independent currents of Christian
culture; and while Byzantine influences were spreading
northwards by way of the Black Sea and the Russian
riverways, Western Christendom was expanding eastwards
through Central Europe, and new Christian states were
arising in the valleys of the Elbe, the Vistula and the
Danube.

For the same age which saw the revival of the Byzantine
Empire and the expansion of the Byzantine Church also
saw the revival of the tradition of Carolingian imperialism
by the new Germanic Empire of Otto I and his successors
and a fresh expansion of Western Christendom towards the
East. As in the age of Charles the Great, it was the Western
Empire and not Byzantium which delivered Christendom
from the ravages of the pagan power which the Magyars,
like the Avars, had established in the heart of Europe. Once
again the life of the Eastern March revived. Abbeys and
bishoprics were restored and colonists from Western Germany repeopled the deserted lands of Eastern Austria. The
attitude of the emperors and prelates of the Western Empire towards the Slavs both on the Danube and the Elbe
was, however, the same as that of the Byzantine Empire
towards the Slavs of the Balkans. They took for granted
that the spread of Christianity meant the expansion of the

[8] *Cristne Saga*, ix, 1, in *Origines Islandicae*, I, 403–4.

Empire and that the conversion of the Slavs involved their subjection to German bishops and German counts and margraves. Ambitious prelates like Pilgrim of Passau attempted to extend their jurisdiction over the conquered territories and did not hesitate to buttress their claims by the wholesale forgery of documents and charters.[9]

This ruthless exploitation of conquered and converted Slavs by Germanic imperialism provoked a reaction in Northern Europe as Byzantine imperialism had done in Bulgaria, but here it found expression, not in the underground resistance of heretical movements like the Bogomils, but in an open return to paganism. The defeat of Otto II by the Saracens in Italy in 982 was followed by a general rising of the pagan Slavs which swept over the Eastern Marches and pushed the frontier of Christendom back from the Oder to the Elbe.

Fortunately this external disaster to the expansion of Western Christendom was followed by a radical transformation of policy which altered the whole history of Central and Eastern Europe. This change was primarily due to the passing of the leadership in the conversion of the new peoples from the Empire and the imperial clergy to the rulers of those peoples themselves, but it was rendered possible by Otto III's wider conception of the Empire as a society of Christian peoples, which made him welcome the formation of new Christian kingdoms and the creation of new Churches in direct dependence on Rome rather than on the German hierarchy. Otto III was, moreover, closely attached to the most remarkable representative of the new Slav Christianity, St. Adalbert or Voytech, the first Czech bishop of Prague who had taken refuge at Sant' Alessio on the Aventine when he had been driven from Bohemia by the pagan reaction of 983, and who subsequently carried on an apostolate in Hungary and Poland and Prussia, where he finally died as a martyr in 997.

St. Adalbert exercised an immense influence on the development of Christendom in Eastern Europe. His monastic foundation at Brzevnov near Prague, where he estab-

[9] E.g. Pilgrim of Passau's attempt to establish his claims to a mythical province of Lorch with seven suffragan sees in 973.

lished a colony of Benedictines from Rome, became the fountainhead of monastic influence for the neighbouring countries. It was the mother house of Meseritz, the first Benedictine foundation in Poland, which was established by Adalbert himself, and of the great Hungarian abbeys of Pannonhalma and Pecsvarad which were founded by his disciple St. Astrik or Anastasius. And in death he was even more powerful than in life. Boleslav, the warrior king of Poland, obtained his body from the heathen Prussians and enshrined it in the church of Gnesen. The Emperor Otto himself, St. Adalbert's friend, hastened across Europe to worship at his shrine, and it was in honour of the martyr that he established the new hierarchy which freed Poland from its dependence on the German Church and made it an independent member of Christendom.

In the same way, Otto III and Pope Sylvester created the new Christian kingdom and hierarchy of Hungary. Here also the influence of St. Adalbert was evident. For it was he who had baptized St. Stephen, and it was his disciple, the monk St. Astrik, who became the first head of the new hierarchy. Thus it was from the new Rome of Otto III and Sylvester II that St. Stephen received the Holy Crown, the sacred symbol of Hungarian royalty, which marks the transformation of the Magyar robber state into the "Apostolic Kingdom" that was to be the eastern bulwark of Christendom.

The little treatise known as the Instruction of St. Stephen[10] to his son St. Emeric (1007–31) professes to express the ideals of the founder, and, whatever may be its date, it is certainly true to the spirit of Otto III and his ecclesiastical advisers, above all in the striking passage (Ch. VI) which attributes the greatness of the Roman Empire to its freedom from national prejudices and counsels the prince to welcome strangers and foreigners who bring more languages and customs into the kingdom: "for weak and fragile is a kingdom with one language and custom"—*nam unius linguae, uniusque moris regnum imbecille et fragilum*

[10] *Libellus de Institutione Morum ac Decretum S. Stepheni*, ed. *Scriptores Regum Hungaricarum*, Vol. II, 611–27 (Budapest 1938).

—a sentiment which seems strangely enlightened in comparison with the nationalism and xenophobia of modern Europe and which was equally in conflict with the traditions of a barbaric tribal society like that of the early Magyars.

In fact the conversion of Hungary even more than that of Poland opened the way to Christian culture in Eastern Europe, since the Middle Danube has always been the chief gateway between East and West. It was immediately used as an opportunity for further missionary activity by another of Otto III's familiar friends, St. Bruno of Querfurt (c. 970–1009), the disciple of St. Romuald and the biographer of St. Adalbert. He attempted to make Hungary the starting point of a mission to the East—to the nomads of the Russian steppe and to the pagan kinsmen of the Magyars on the Volga, a mission which brought him into friendly relations with the new Christian state of St. Vladimir at Kiev.

Thus by the beginning of the eleventh century a new society of Christian peoples was arising in Eastern Europe from Scandinavia to the Crimea and from the Danube to the Upper Volga. This new Christendom was still an island in a sea of paganism and barbarism between the Turkish nomads of the steppes and the Finnish tribes of the vast northern forests. Even on the Baltic and in East Germany, in Lithuania and Prussia, and as far west as Mecklenburg, there remained a hard core of pagan resistance, which was not to be overcome for centuries, since it owed its strength to the national resistance of the Baltic peoples against German colonial expansion and exploitation; and where this factor was absent, as in Hungary and Russia, the progress of evangelization was relatively rapid. The peoples of this new Christian society were in geographical and cultural contact with one another and their ruling families were closely related. Nor was the division between the Latin and Byzantine provinces of Christendom as yet so sharply defined as to destroy the sense of religious and cultural community. Traces of the work of Cyril and Methodius still lingered in the West, in Croatia and perhaps in Bohemia, where the abbey of Sarzarva maintained the Eastern Rite in the eleventh century, while in Russia, so long as the traditional relations with Scandinavia were still preserved, the close personal bond of the Russian princes with the North tended to keep Russia in an intermediate position between East and West.

Even in the twelfth century Helmold, the German priest, who had considerable knowledge of Eastern Europe, does not clearly distinguish the frontiers of the two Christendoms. "All these peoples, except the Prussians," he wrote, "claim to be Christians. But I have never discovered who were the teachers from whom they received their faith, save that in all their observances they seem to follow the Greeks rather than the Latins. For it is easy to travel by sea from Russia to Greece."[11]

The course of history, however, gradually increased the divergence between the Russian development and that of the Western Slav and Scandinavian peoples. The advent of a new horde of nomads—the Cumans—interfered with the great trade route from the Baltic to the Black Sea in the twelfth century, and finally in the thirteenth century the last and most tremendous eruption of the peoples of the steppes created a vast Eurasian empire which tore Russia violently away from the rest of Europe and practically ended its intercourse with the other Eastern European peoples.

Thus the Mongol conquest produced a cataclysmic interruption in the development of Eastern Christendom which divides the earlier from the later Middle Ages. During the earlier period—in the eleventh and twelfth centuries—the Christian peoples of Eastern Europe occupied an intermediate position between the Latin West and the Byzantine East; and though they were divided by their religious and cultural sympathies, the division was not an exclusive one. A Western ruler like Bela III of Hungary might look towards Byzantium while a Russian like Iziaslav I of Kiev might look towards Rome, while the relations between the ruling families were as close as they were in the eight-

[11] *Helmoldi Chronica Slavorum*, XXI, II (M.G.H.).

eenth and nineteenth centuries. During this earlier period the Christian culture of Eastern Europe was most advanced in Kievan Russia, owing to the high development of the Russian towns and their autonomous economic and political life, while the culture of Poland and Hungary was relatively backward.

In the later Middle Ages all this was changed. Hungary, Bohemia and Poland became closely integrated in the common life of Western Christendom and developed flourishing national cultures. While the Russian princes had become the vassals and taxgatherers of the Mongol Khans, Hungary and Poland shared in the political order of the Western kingdoms and developed advanced forms of aristocratic parliamentarism and constitutional liberties. Moreover, the union of Poland with the Lithuanian state led to an immense Eastern expansion of Polish and Latin-Christian culture, so that it came to include all the Western Russian principalities, which were not under the Mongol yoke, apart from Novgorod, including Kiev itself. Even Novgorod, the great and ancient city-state which retained its independence throughout the Middle Ages, was hard pressed in the thirteenth century by the militant expansion of the German crusading orders on the Baltic. This conflict, which acquired the character of a religious war, was responsible for the growing anti-Latin and anti-Western tendency in Russian national tradition.

But the same process was also taking place in the South at the centre of the Byzantine world. Here, too, the militant spirit of the crusading movement, allied with the economic imperialism of the Italian city-states, aroused a spirit of intense religious and patriotic resistance in the Byzantine world. Thus the foundation of the Latin Empire of Constantinople which seemed to mark the climax of the victorious advance of Western Christendom was a fatal blow to the cause of Christian unity and the cultural unity of Eastern Europe. It was the Ottoman sultans, not the Latins or the Russians or the Orthodox peoples of the Balkans, who entered into the inheritance of Justinian and the Byzantine emperors.

Chapter VII

The Reform of the Church in the Eleventh Century and the Medieval Papacy

THE BREAKDOWN of the Carolingian Empire and the disintegration of the authority of the state under the combined influence of barbarian invasion and feudal anarchy led to a similar crisis in the life of the Church. It was not merely that the monasteries and churches were sacked by Vikings and Saracens and Magyars, and that bishops and abbots died in battle with the heathen. Even more serious was the internal disintegration due to the exploitation and secularization of the Church by the leaders of the new feudal society. Abbeys and bishoprics were treated in the same way as lay fiefs. They were appropriated by violence; they were bought and sold or used as rewards for successful military adventures.

The despair of the representatives of the Carolingian tradition may be seen in the dark picture of the state of the Church which was drawn up by the prelates of the province of Rheims at Troslé in 909.

The cities are depopulated, the monasteries ruined and burned, the land is reduced to a solitude. As the first men lived without law or constraint, abandoned to their passions, so now every man does what pleases him, despising the laws of God and man and the ordinances of the Church. The powerful oppress the weak, the land is full of violence against the poor and the plunder of the goods of the Church. Men devour one another like the fishes in the

sea. In the case of the monasteries some have been de-
stroyed by the heathen, others have been deprived of their
property and reduced to nothing. In those that remain
there is no longer any observance of the rule. They no
longer have legitimate superiors, owing to the abuse of sub-
mitting to secular domination. We see in the monasteries
lay abbots with their wives and their children, their soldiers
and their dogs.

Nor does the council spare the bishops themselves:

God's flock perishes through our charge. It has come
about by our negligence, our ignorance and that of our
brethren, that there is in the Church an innumerable multi-
tude of both sexes and every condition who reach old age
without instruction, so that they are ignorant even of the
words of the Creed and the Lord's Prayer.[1]

When the leaders of any society realize the gravity of the
situation and admit their own responsibility like this the
situation is never desperate, and in fact at the very time
when the bishops of the Belgic province were composing
this jeremiad the first steps of reform were being taken in
neighbouring provinces. Once again, as in the fifth and
sixth centuries, Christianity showed its independence of external conditions and its power to create new organs of
spiritual regeneration. A new movement arose from the
midst of the feudal society to meet the new danger of the
feudal secularization of the Church.

This movement was at first purely monastic and ascetic.
It took the form of a flight from the world and public life
to the desert and the cloister, a repetition in different circumstances of the first great movement of Western monasticism which I described in earlier chapters.

For while the ecclesiastical hierarchy and the territorial
Church in general were so much a part of contemporary
society that they were almost at the mercy of the predominant social forces, the monastic institution represented the
principle of an autonomous Christian order which proved
to be the seed of a new life for the whole Church. It is

[1] *Mansi Concilia*, Vol. XVIII.

true that the old Carolingian monasteries had been exploited and secularized in the same way as the bishoprics, but every monastery was an independent organism, and thus each new foundation provided the opportunity for a fresh start and a return to the observance of the Benedictine Rule which remained the consecrated norm of monastic life.

Hence it was in the new monasteries founded by feudal princes or converted nobles, like Cluny in Burgundy (910), Brogne and Gorze in Lorraine and Camaldoli in Tuscany (1009), that the foundations were laid of the new movement of spiritual reform that was to transform the medieval Church.

No doubt the monk was concerned primarily with the salvation of his own soul rather than with any programme of ecclesiastical reform. But as we have seen,[2] Western monasticism always possessed a strong consciousness of its social responsibility and its missionary functions. If on the one hand it was based on the tradition of the Fathers of the Desert, it was inspired still more by the ideals of St. Augustine and St. Gregory. The Augustinian theology and philosophy of history with their intense realization of the burden of inherited evil under which the human race laboured and their conception of divine grace as a continually renewed source of supernatural energy which transforms human nature and changes the course of history—all this had become part of the spiritual patrimony of the Western Church and, above all, of Western monasticism, and Christendom had only to return to this tradition to recover its dynamic energy.

Thus although the efforts of the reformers of the tenth century were primarily devoted to the cause of monastic reform, they involved far wider issues. These men were not mere self-centred ascetics, but prophets of righteousness who defended the weak and the oppressed and spoke boldly against evil in high places. We see this, above all, in the writings of St. Odo, the second Abbot of Cluny (927–942), who was one of the greatest of the early leaders in the re-

[2] Cf. Ch. II, p. 26 ff.

forming movement. His chief work, the *Collationes*, is based on the Augustinian conception of the Two Cities or rather of the two races, the children of Abel and the children of Cain whose warfare must endure to the end of time. But while St. Augustine conceives this opposition primarily as a conflict between the Christian Church and the heathen world, St. Odo is concerned, above all, with the forces of evil that flourish *within* the Church.

Nothing could be darker than the picture St. Odo draws of the state of the Church, the decay of monasticism and the immorality and materialism of the clergy. Yet he is far from confining his criticism, as one might perhaps have expected, to strictly ecclesiastical abuses. The most striking feature of his teaching is its bold and almost revolutionary criticism of social injustice. The great evil of the age in his eyes is the oppression of the poor and he denounces the misdeeds of the ruling classes of his time in the spirit and the words of the Hebrew prophets: "Woe to you that are wealthy in Sion: you great men, heads of the people that go in with state into the house of Israel." The robber nobles who plunder the poor and their accomplices, the worldly prelates who fail to protect their people from injustice, are the true seed of Cain, the persecutors of God.

How then are these robbers Christians, or what do they deserve who slay their brothers for whom they are commanded to lay down their lives?

You have only to study the books of antiquity to see that the most powerful are always the worst. Worldly nobility is due not to nature but to pride and ambition. If we judged by realities we should give honour not to the rich for the fine clothes they wear but to the poor who are the makers of such things—nam sudoribus pauperum praeparatur unde potentiores saginantur.[3]

But St. Odo realizes that this reign of injustice has its roots deep in human nature and cannot be abolished by reliance on external means—on "the arm of the flesh". From

[3] *Collationes*, III, 26–30: "for the banquets of the powerful are cooked in the sweat of the poor."

the days of Abel, the first of the just, down to the last of the elect, suffering and defeat have been the portion of the children of God. The only remedy is to be found in that spiritual force by which the humility of God conquers the pride of the evil one. Hence the spiritual reformer cannot expect to have the majority on his side. He must be prepared to stand alone like Ezekiel and Jeremy. He must take as his example St. Augustine besieged by the Vandals at Hippo, or St. Gregory preaching at Rome with the Lombards at the gates. For the true helpers of the world are the poor in spirit, the men who bear the sign of the cross on their foreheads, who refuse to be overcome by the triumph of injustice and put their sole trust in the salvation of God.

To the modern this may appear an unpractical conclusion. Nevertheless it undoubtedly gave spiritual force to the movement of reform which the Carolingian Church had looked for in vain from councils and kings. However good were the intentions of the latter, they seldom had the power to give effect to their resolutions. The monastic reform, on the other hand, was an autonomous movement which derived its power from its internal spiritual resources. It was assisted rather than hindered by the decentralization and local particularism of feudal society, for these conditions made it possible for a founder to establish his new religious foundation without the interference of king or bishop. The classical example of this is Cluny itself, which was founded by Count William of Auvergne in 910 as the property of the apostles in immediate dependence on the Holy See, formally excluding any intervention whatsoever by king, bishop or court—a privilege which became the pattern and ideal for the other reformed monasteries. Thus from the beginning a kind of alliance was established between the Papacy and the monastic reformers, an alliance which was already confirmed by St. Odo's relations with Alberic, the Roman prince, and Leo VII in the first half of the tenth century.

Morever the loose and shapeless organization of the feudal state made it possible for the reformed congregations to extend their influence by patronage and recommendation in the same way as a great feudal estate, so that a reformer like St. Abbo of Fleury could even say in jest that he was more powerful than the king of the Franks since his abbey possessed dependencies in lands where the king had no authority.[4]

But though the influence of Cluny extended from Southern Italy to Eastern England it was by no means the only centre of reform. A similar movement was arising about the same time in the Low Countries where St. Gerard of Brogne (d. 959) was the reformer of the chief monasteries of Flanders, St. Peter and St. Bavo at Ghent, St. Omer, St. Bertin and St. Ghislain, and somewhat later a group of clerks from Metz established an equally important centre at Gorze in Lorraine under St. John of Vandières. In Italy the tradition of the monks of the desert and the oriental anchorites was revived by the action of ascetics like St. Nilus, the Byzantine monk, who founded the great Basilian monastery of Grottaferrata south of Rome, St. Romuald, the founder of Camaldoli, and St. John Gualbert, the founder of Vallombrosa.

These various movements often crossed and blended their influence with one another. Thus the reform of the Anglo-Saxon monasteries in the age of St. Dunstan was connected with the Flemish movement through St. Peter's at Ghent and with the Cluniac movement through the great monastery of Fleury, which had itself become a secondary centre of reform. In the same way St. William of Volpiano (962–1031), the Abbot of St. Benigne at Dijon, introduced the Cluniac reform into Normandy, while Richard of St. Vannes of Verdun brought the independent movement of reform in Lorraine into contact with that of Cluny, and his disciple, St. Poppo (978–1048), the Abbot of Stavelot and the friend and counsellor of the Emperors Henry II and Conrad II, became the reformer of the monasteries of Western Germany.

Thus all over Western Europe new centres of monastic reform were arising like islands of peace and spiritual order

[4] Vita Abbonis, Migne, CXXXIX, 41.

in the sea of feudal anarchy. Monasticism had ceased to be a helpless spectator of the moral disorder of Christendom, and had become an independent power in Western society. In men such as St. Odo and St. Romuald and St. William of Volpiano the lawless feudal nobles, who cared nothing for morality or law, recognized the presence of something stronger than brute force—a numinous supernatural power they dared not ignore. St. Peter Damian records that Ranier, the Marquis of Tuscany, used to say that no emperor could put such fear into him as the mere glance of St. Romuald, and even after his death the saint was still regarded as the protector of the poor and the avenger of the oppressed.[5]

As we have already seen in the earlier history of the Dark Ages,[6] the saint was not just a good man who was dead; he was a living power, who took an active interest and share in human affairs, strong to protect his own, and terrible in anger. Every great abbey and pilgrimage church was the home of such a power, where he held his court and received the petitions of his clients; and the legal rights of immunity and asylum that such holy places enjoyed were but the external recognition which society yielded to such an authority.

In the same way it was the saint who was lord and master of all the lands and serfs of the abbey, and the abbot was but his servant and steward, so that it is not surprising to find free men voluntarily giving up their liberty to become "the saint's men": for such *homines sanctorum* or *sainteurs*, as they were called, possessed a higher status than the ordinary serf, and a more powerful protector than the ordinary freeman.

By the beginning of the eleventh century the movement of monastic reform had attained maturity and began to affect every aspect of Western culture. The great abbots who were the leaders of the movement, like St. Odilo of Cluny

---

[5] E.g. St. Peter Damian's story of the peasant woman who successfully invoked the aid of St. Romuald against the noble who had stolen her cow (Vit. S. Rom., c. 104).

[6] Cf. Ch. II, p. 33.

(994–1019), St. Abbo of Fleury (988–1004), St. Poppo of Stavelot (977–1048), and St. William of Volpiano (990–1031), were the dominant figures of the age and exercised immense influence on contemporary rulers. Never had the movement for the foundation and restoration of monasteries been more active than, for instance, in Normandy, where the foundations of this age, like Fécamp and Bec and St. Evroult, became the centres of a great revival of Christian culture.

Nevertheless the reformers had as yet no idea of any fundamental change in the relations between the spiritual and temporal power. They still accepted the traditional Carolingian conception of the divine right of kings and the duty of the prince to intervene in religious and ecclesiastical affairs. In so far as they were concerned with the state of the Church outside the monastery, it was to the royal power rather than to the bishops or the Papacy that they looked for support. We see this clearly in the writings of the leading canonists of the time, like St. Abbo of Fleury and Bishop Burchard of Worms. The work of the former is addressed expressly to the French king, Hugh Capet, and his successor Robert the Pious, whose power he regards as a sacred ministerial office for the rule and reform of the Church; while the latter in his great *Decretum* represents the tradition of the bishops of the Empire and accepts the authority of the Emperor in the government of the Church without any consciousness of the contradiction between this state of affairs and the traditional principles of Canon Law on which his work is based.[7]

However inconsistent this attitude might be, it corresponded with the facts of the situation. For the movement for the restoration of ecclesiastical discipline and canonical order during the early part of the eleventh century depended entirely on the sympathy and co-operation of the royal power. It was the Emperor rather than the Pope who took the initiative in the work of reform, and it was under the auspices of emperors like Henry II and kings of France like Robert the Pious that the first reforming councils and

---

[7] For Burchard's position see especially Hauck, *Kirchengeschichte Deutschlands*, III, 442.

synods were held in Germany, Italy and France (e.g. at Pavia in 1022 and at Bourges in 1031).

But the exercise of the royal supremacy in religious matters was not conceived in any hostile spirit towards Rome. The relations between the Empire and the Papacy had never been more friendly and intimate than they were in the time of Otto III and Sylvester II in 999, and of Henry II and Benedict VIII (1012–24).

So long, however, as the Papacy was under the control of the Roman nobility, its interests were limited by the feuds of local factions; and so far from taking the lead in the movement of reform, it was in dire need of reform itself. Throughout the tenth century the secularism and corruption of the rival cliques which exploited the Papacy were a flagrant denial of the ideals of the reforming movement, and the reaction of the Northern episcopate found most violent expression in the synods of St. Basle and Chelles in 991 and 995. The fact that the spokesman of this anti-Roman opposition, Gerbert, himself became Pope Sylvester II four years later provided an unexpected dénouement of the conflict; but after a generation, the worst scandals of the tenth century were revived by John XIX and Benedict IX. Finally the deposition of Benedict IX and the election of two rival candidates led to the decisive intervention of the Emperor Henry III, who at the Council of Sutri in 1046 set aside all three Popes and imposed a German bishop, Suiger of Bamberg, as his own nominee.

Henry III was an austere and devout man, a friend of saints and reformers, who took his theocratic responsibilities towards the Church very seriously. Consequently it is not surprising that his drastic action at Rome met with general approval from the reforming party, apart from one or two exceptions like Bishop Wazo of Liége. Even St. Peter Damian, the leader of the Italian reformers, accepts his control of the Papacy as a manifestation of divine Providence, and he compares his reforming action to that of Christ driving the money-changers from the temple![8]

The action of Henry III had a far-reaching effect on the

---

[8] *Liber Gratissimus ad fin.*

course of the reforming movement. At first sight it might seem that it would reduce the Papacy to complete dependence on the imperial power, for the three Popes whom he nominated in rapid succession—Clement II in 1046 and Damasus II and St. Leo IX in 1048—were loyal prelates of the Empire from Germany and Lorraine, who had no Italian connections and were consequently forced to rely on the material support of the Emperor. Nevertheless, the mere fact that the Papacy was taken out of the control of the Roman nobles and their factions and brought into intimate relations with Northern and Central Europe had an immediate effect on its international influence.

Still more important was the fact that the coming of Leo IX created an alliance between the Papacy and the movement of religious reform, which had its centre in Lorraine and Burgundy. As Bishop of Toul, Leo had been for twenty-two years one of the leading figures in the Church of Lorraine at a time when it was the scene of the reforming activity of abbots like St. Richard of Verdun, St. Poppo of Stavelot and St. Odilo of Cluny, and of bishops like Wazo of Liége—all of whom died about the time when he became Pope. And the men whom he brought to Rome as his chosen helpers were all drawn from the same milieu —Humbert, the Abbot of Moyenmoutier, Hugh the White, Abbot of Remiremont, and Frederick, the Archdeacon of Liége, who was brother of Duke Godfrey of Lorraine and was later to become Abbot of Monte Cassino and Pope Stephen IX.

The introduction of this foreign element into the Curia had a revolutionary effect on the Papacy, which became the hierarchical centre and organ of leadership for the reforming movement. The reform of the Church was no longer the aim of scattered groups of ascetics and idealists, it became the official policy of the Roman Church.

In his brief pontificate of less than five years St. Leo devoted himself to the work of reform with superhuman energy, crossing the Alps again and again to hold reforming councils in Germany and France as well as in Italy, and establish direct personal control over the Churches of Western Christendom. At the same time he took an important part in the political affairs of Christendom. He had to deal with the difficult problem of the Normans, who were establishing themselves in Southern Italy with no less ruthlessness and violence than that of the Danes in England. He attempted to meet this danger by direct military action, supported by both the German and the Byzantine Empires. But his well-planned political strategy met with military disaster. He was defeated and captured by the Normans, and at the same time his plan for union between Western Christendom and the Byzantine Empire was resisted by the ecclesiastical intransigence of the Byzantine patriarch Michael Cerularius. He did not survive these disasters, and two years later, in 1056, the Emperor Henry III died prematurely, leaving his five-year-old son to succeed him under the regency of his widow.

This event was fatal to the old order and put an end to the co-operation between the Empire and the Papacy on which the policy of the reformers had hitherto been based. During the minority of Henry IV, the party of reform asserted the independence of the Papacy, disregarded the concordat of Sutri and began to elect their own candidates to the Papacy in independence of the Empire. They allied themselves with the anti-imperial party in Italy, represented by Duke Godfrey of Lorraine and Tuscany whose brother Frederick of Lorraine became Pope Stephen IX in 1057. Finally they brought about the alliance between the Papacy and the Normans in Southern Italy, a reversal of alliances which had enormous consequences, since it was an open defiance, not only of the German Empire, but of the Byzantine Empire also, and did more than anything else to make the breach with the Eastern Church irremediable.

The moving spirit behind these events seems to have been Humbert of Moyenmoutier, Cardinal Bishop of Silva Candida, who was the dominant figure alike in the reforming movement and in the negotiations with Constantinople and the Normans during these critical years (1049–61). The ideas which inspired his activity are to be seen in his treatise *Against the Simonists* (*c.* 1058), which is at once the earliest, the ablest, and the most extreme statement of the programme of the reformers. To Humbert, simony was not merely a sin; it was the supreme heresy, since it denied the spiritual character of the Church and subordinated the gifts of the Spirit to money and worldly power. But since the Holy Ghost cannot be bought or sold, it followed, so he argued, that the Simonists had no share in His gifts. Their sacraments were null and void, and their church was the church of Anti-Christ. To meet these evils he called for a return to the old canonical principles of free election and the emancipation of the Church from the control of the secular power and from the custom of lay investiture. Since the spiritual power is as superior to that of the king as heaven is superior to earth, the Church should guide and rule the state as the soul rules the body; so only was it possible to ensure the reign of justice and the peace and union of the Christian people.

It is clear that these views are irreconcilable, not only with the current practice of eleventh-century Feudalism, but with the whole tradition of the imperial state Church which had inextricably confused spiritual and secular functions, and had regarded emperors and kings as the divinely appointed leaders of Christian society. It was a reversion to the uncompromising dualism and anti-secularism of the early Church.

The revolutionary consequences of these theories were not clear to the older generation of reformers, who were Humbert's contemporaries, like St. Leo IX and the great leader of the monastic reform in Italy, St. Peter Damian, who remained faithful to the ideal of the union of the two powers which had been temporarily realized in the time of Henry III. But after the death of Cardinal Humbert and Pope Nicholas II in 1061 the leadership of the movement passed to younger men who were prepared to carry the ideas of Humbert to their logical conclusion at whatever cost. Foremost among them was the archdeacon of the Roman Church, the Tuscan Hildebrand, who had held an important position at Rome since 1059 and was elected Pope in 1073 as Gregory VII.

Although the importance of his influence on the history of medieval Christendom has always been fully recognized, his personality and his work have been the subject of the most diverse judgments. On the one hand, he has been regarded as the prime author and inspirer of the whole reforming movement, and on the other as an ambitious ecclesiastical politician of the type of Boniface VIII. But it is now generally recognized that both these views are equally erroneous. He was not an original thinker, for it was not Hildebrand but Humbert of Moyenmoutier who was the theorist and ideologist of the reforming movement. But on the other hand he was no mere ecclesiastical power politician, but a man of intense spiritual convictions with a deep sense of his prophetic mission.

His view of the Church and the world was characterized by the same Augustinian dualism that we have seen in the case of St. Odo of Cluny, but this was the common tradition of the Church of his age, and there is much less trace of direct Augustinian influence in his writings than is to be found in the work of Cardinal Humbert. It is in the Bible and, above all, in the Prophets that the real source of Gregory VII's inspiration is to be found; and the primary scriptural doctrines of divine judgment, the divine law of justice and the prophetic mission provide the recurrent theme of all his thought and teaching. His sense of the urgency of his mission and the terrible predicament of the Christian world finds its most striking expression in the last appeal he addressed to the Christian people from his exile in Salerno before his death.

To me also, though unworthy and a sinner, that word of the Prophet has come, "Go up into the mountain and cry aloud: spare not", and so whether I will or no, setting aside all fear and all affection, I cry, I cry and I cry again. The Christian religion, the true faith taught to our fathers by the Son of God, has fallen so low that it is an object of scorn, not only to the Evil One, but even to the Jews, the Saracens and the pagans. These have laws that profit them not to salvation and yet they are faithful to them. But we, blinded by the love of the world, have forsaken the True Law.

Every day we see men who go to death in thousands for

*their lords or their fellows, but those who fear God, few as
they are, think only of their own souls and forget their
brethren.*

*Since the day when the Church has placed me on the
apostolic throne, my whole desire and the end of all my
striving has been that the Holy Church, the Bride of God,
our mistress and our mother, should recover her honour and
remain free and chaste and Catholic.*[9]

There is nothing political in this ideal of reformation.
But the uncompromising simplicity with which it was
formulated made it a revolutionary force in a world in
which the Church had become a part of the social order,
and ecclesiastical and political relations had become inextricably entangled. Above all, the old Byzantine and Carolingian ideal of the sacred monarchy was an obstacle to any
radical programme of reform, since it consecrated the status
quo and surrounded vested interests with the halo of sacred
tradition. Hence Gregory VII's uncompromising determination to free the Church from its feudal dependence on
the secular power meant the abandonment of the old Byzantine and Carolingian conception of the divine right of
kings and the passive obedience of their Christian subjects.
But since the reformers no less than the conservatives continued to accept the unitary character of Christian society,
the denial of the imperial theocracy involved the assertion
of the supremacy of the spiritual power in the social life
of Christendom, so that it was inevitable that the Pope
should take the place which the Emperor had hitherto occupied as the supreme leader and judge of the Christian
people.

This change, revolutionary as it was, was in harmony
with the changing conditions of the new age. The Empire
was no longer able to fulfil even formally the universal functions which the Empire of Charlemagne had represented.
It had become an archaic survival from the point of view of
Western Europe as a whole, where the new feudal states
had become the leaders of culture. Yet the sense of the

[9] *Monumenta Gregoriana, Ep. coll.* 46, pp. 572–74.

unity of Christendom was stronger than ever and demanded some new institutional expression, and the reformed Papacy provided such an expression more effectively than any political institution could have done, since it transcended national and territorial rivalries and possessed in the hierarchy and the Canon Law the necessary instruments for its realization. It was, moreover, far more flexible than the Empire, since it could create special forms of relation, not only with local churches and monasteries, but also with the territorial powers, in addition to its universal authority. Thus Gregory VII encouraged the rulers of the more remote Christian territories, such as Spain, Denmark, Hungary and Croatia, to accept the protection of the Holy See and become vassals of St. Peter. And though this did not imply any direct political control, it emphasized the new position of the Papacy as the centre of international society.

The new formulation of the theocratic idea was assimilated without great difficulty by the feudal society of the West, where the limitations of kingship were a matter of common experience. But it was a very different matter in the Empire where the Carolingian tradition was so strong and where the Church and the bishops were the mainstay of the imperial system. Here there was a conflict of ideals as well as of social forces, and for generations Christendom was torn asunder by the conflict. For the first time in the history of the West an attempt was made to enlist public opinion on either side, and a war of treaties and pamphlets was carried on, in which the most fundamental questions concerning the relation of Church and state and the right of resistance to unjust authority were discussed exhaustively.

This marks a new departure in the history of Western culture, for it meant that men had begun to reason about the principles on which Christian society was based, and to use the appeal to these principles as a means of changing the existing order. When Gregory VII wrote, "The Lord says 'I am the Truth and the Life', he did not say 'I am custom' but 'I am Truth'" (*non dixit Ego sum consuetudo, sed Veritas*), he was invoking a new kind of Divine Right which was ultimately to prove stronger than the divine right of kings.

At first the controversy started from common presuppositions and common theological principles. Both sides accepted the Augustinian theology of grace and justice, the Gelasian doctrine of the concordance of the temporal and spiritual powers and the Carolingian conception of Christendom as a theocratic unity. Above all, St. Augustine's *City of God*, with its tremendous vision of the Two Loves and the Two Cities whose opposition and conflict explain the course of history, formed the background of the whole controversy and was appealed to explicitly and repeatedly by both parties in support of their interpretation of the struggle.

By the Reformers the claim of the Emperor to dominate the Church is seen as another assault on the liberty of the City of God by the children of Babylon and the generation of Cain. To the Imperialists, on the other hand, the Reformers are the enemies of peace who destroy the unity of the one Body by separating the priesthood from the kingship, putting the weapons of carnal warfare in the hands of the Church.

Thus the question of the right of resistance became one of the main issues of the controversy. The adherents of the Empire—like the monk of Hersfeld who wrote the anonymous work *De Unitate Ecclesiae Conservanda*—condemned the right of resistance on grounds of Christian pacifism.

Peace, says the Lord, I leave to you, My peace I give unto you. Wherefore, whenever the sons of the Church are compelled to make war, they do this not by the teaching of Christ and the tradition of the Church, but from necessity, and by a certain contagion of Babylon, the earthly city, through which the sons of Jerusalem journey during their earthly life.[10]

What a mystery of inquity is now being worked by those who call themselves monks and, confounding the Church

10 Op. cit., I, ad fin.

*and the state in their perverse doctrine, oppose and set
themselves up against the royal power and the Holy See*[11]

so that

*for seventeen years and more, everywhere in the Roman
Empire there are wars and seditions, the burning of
churches and monasteries; bishop is set against bishop,
clergy against clergy, people against people, and father
against son, and brother against brother.*[12]

But in the eyes of the reformer this passive conservatism
was irreconcilable with the liberty of the Church and the
restoration of the true order of Christian society. Since the
Church was one, the Christian prince and the Emperor
himself held his office within the Church, subject to the
law of the Church and under the authority of its spiritual
rulers. The temporal authority was therefore in a sense the
authority of the Church in temporal affairs, exercised
through its temporal ministers. And if these ministers went
wrong it was the duty of the Church and of the Christian
people to call them to order and, if necessary, to dismiss
them in favour of a more suitable candidate. Stated in its
extreme form, as in the *Letter to Gebhard* by Manegold
of Lautenbach, this involves the substitution of an almost
democratic theory of social contract for the traditional principle of the divine right of kings, as well as a drastic justification of the employment of force against schismatics and
heretics, according to the words of the prophet "Cursed be
he who doeth the work of the Lord negligently and cursed
be he that keepeth back his sword from blood." That this
was not a matter of abstract theory is shown by the history
of the Saxon revolt, as recorded by Lambert of Hersfeld
and Bruno of Magdeburg, both of whom stress the conditional character of the allegiance of the Saxons to the
Emperor and the right and duty of defending their national
liberties and those of the Church.

But in spite of this predominantly theological atmosphere, there were already some writers who were prepared

[11] Op. cit., II, c. 42.
[12] Op. cit., I, c. 7.

to defend the cause of the Empire on its own ground in virtue of its own temporal prerogative. The most remarkable of these writers is Benzo, Bishop of Alba, a scholar and a humanist, who anticipates Dante in his enthusiasm for the Roman tradition and for the restoration of the universal authority of the Empire. Henry IV is the rightful successor of the great emperors of the past and of the heroes of ancient Rome, who has been sent by heaven to bring back the glory of the Empire to Italy, and through Italy to the world. This restored Empire was to be independent alike of the Church and of feudalism. It was to be an absolute monarchy based on the ancient Roman order and universal law and a restored system of general taxation. Thus in spite of its Utopian character the thought of Benzo of Alba seems to foreshadow the approaching renaissance of the political conception of the state.

In the eleventh century, however, in so far as a political state existed it was to be found, not in the archaic traditions of the sacred Empire, but in the new monarchy of the Normans who were the especial object of Benzo's hatred and denunciation. And so, too, it was not the Empire but the reformed Papacy which was the real heir of the Roman tradition of universalism and international order. For the Church was not only a much more universal and comprehensive society than the medieval state; it exercised many of the functions which we regard as essentially political. As F. W. Maitland used to insist, it is impossible to frame any acceptable definition of the state which would not include the medieval Church. It was a sovereign power which imposed its own laws and enforced them in its own courts by its own judges and lawyers. It possessed an elaborate system of appellate jurisdiction, an organized bureaucracy and an efficient system of centralized control carried out by permanent officials and supervised by the visits and reports of the legates who played such a prominent part in the international life of Christendom.

All this was the direct outcome of the reforming movement, for the emancipation of the Papacy from its dependence on the Empire and the separation of the spiritual authority of the bishop from his secular obligations as a member of the feudal hierarchy made it necessary to reconstruct the whole order of ecclesiastical administration and jurisdiction as an organized unity.

But the creation of this great machine of ecclesiastical government was not the original aim of the movement of reform, which as we have seen was inspired by the unworldly, spiritual ideals of men like St. Peter Damian. The reformers themselves were well aware that the growth of ecclesiastical power and wealth involved a danger of secularization from within which was as deadly though more insiduous than the external evils against which they fought. It is true that there were some supporters of the reforming movement who had something of Benzo of Alba's sympathy for the ancient Roman tradition, and who regarded the victory of the Papacy as a triumph of Latin civilization and order over the forces of Germanic and feudal barbarism. Thus the fine ode which the Archbishop of Salerno, Alfano, addressed to Hildebrand when he was still archdeacon, calls on the Papacy to break with spiritual weapons the rude forces of barbarism which opposed the Roman power and compares Hildebrand himself to the heroes of the past— to Marius and Caesar and the Scipios:

> His et archiapostoli
> fervido gladio Petri
> frange robur et impetus
> illius, vetus ut iugum
> usque sentiat ultimum.
>
> Quanta vis anathematis!
> Quidquid et Marius prius,
> quodque Julius egerant
> maxima nece militum,
> voce tu modica facis.
>
> Roma quid Scipionibus
> Caeterisque Quiritibus
> Debuit magis quam tibi,
> Cujus est studiis suae
> Nacta jura potentiae?[13]

[13] Migne, P. L., Tom. CXLVII, 1262. Translation: "How great the power of thy anathema! All that Marius and Julius

But there is no sign of this in Hildebrand's own thought and utterances. He was inspired far more by the scriptural ideal of a prophet of justice and judgment set over the nations and over the kingdoms, "to root up and to pull down, to build and to plant". It was the same spirit which inspired St. Bernard in the following century, and so many other Christian leaders. And it was because this prophetic spirit inspired the work of the reforming movement in the eleventh and twelfth centuries that it acquired the spiritual energy and the moral prestige that enabled it to animate and transform medieval culture during that decisive period of its development.

---

accomplished with vast slaughter of soldiers, you can do with voice unraised.

"Break the strength of their onrush by the sword of Peter, the chief apostle, that they may feel the ancient yoke to the end.

"What more did Rome owe to the Scipios and her citizens besides than to thee, by whose efforts she has gained the rights of her power."

Chapter VIII

The Feudal World: Chivalry and the Courtly Culture

IN THE eleventh century the movement of reform of which I wrote in the last chapter was no longer limited to the monastic life, but had become the inspiration of a wider movement of spiritual change which transformed the order of the Western Church and the spirit of Western culture. In this way there arose the new unity of medieval Christendom which was no longer dependent on the existence of the Empire as in Carolingian or Byzantine society, but had a superpolitical or international character and possessed its own independent centre of authority in the reformed Papacy. It is true that the Carolingian tradition survived with little essential change in the Holy Roman Empire under the Saxon and Salian emperors, but it no longer embraced the whole of Western culture. The most active and vital centres of new life were to be found elsewhere in the disorderly feudal society of the West Frankish realm, where the Carolingian tradition was almost extinct and the royal power itself had sunk to the lowest possible level.

Here the real unit of political life was not the kingdom but the new feudal states which had been built out of the ruins of the Carolingian state by rebellious vassals or successful military adventurers or even, in the case of Normandy, by the settlement of barbarian invaders from the distant North. These feudal states had been created by war and for war. Their whole structure and ethos were military, and the only force which kept society together was the primary bond of fidelity which united the warrior and his chief, as it had done in the days of the barbarian invasions.

Thus the rise of feudalism seems to mark a return to barbarism, in which the fundamental institutions of civilized society have practically disappeared and the world was ruled by "the good old law, the simple plan, That he should take who has the power, and he should keep who can".

But though feudalism was a reversion to barbarism, it also contained its own remedy. The very ferocity and barbarism of the early feudal princes made them ill men to quarrel with. It was one thing to flout the authority of the weak and distant Carolingian monarch, but it was a very different matter to revolt against men like Fulk Nerra of Anjou, or Baldwin of Flanders, or William the Bastard of Normandy. Such men were hard and cruel masters, but good "justiciars", who were able to protect their own lands from war and plunder and were determined to enforce respect for their authority on their unruly vassals.

And in fact no sooner were the feudal principalities firmly established than population began to increase, the roads were once more open to traders, and towns and markets revived. Each of these feudal states—above all Normandy, Flanders, Anjou, Blois, Champagne and Burgundy —became the focus of an intense social activity; and their very multiplicity and limited character as compared with the unwieldy bulk and universal claims of the Carolingian and German Empires favoured the progress of Western civilization. A state of the size of Normandy or Flanders was large enough to form a self-sufficient social organism, while not too large to be controlled and defended by a single head. Thus the petty states of France and the Low Countries in the eleventh and twelfth centuries played a similar part in early medieval culture to that of the Greek city-states in antiquity, or to that of the Italian principalities in the Renaissance. The revival of religious, intellectual and artistic life was connected, not so much with the Empire or even the monarchies, as with these feudal states. Even the ferocious Fulk Nerra of Anjou, who seems at first sight no more than a bloodthirsty barbarian, was a great founder of monasteries and rebuilder of churches, while his contemporary, William the Great of Poitou (993–1030), was the friend of Fulbert of Chartres and a cultured and magnificent prince, who delighted in reading and copied manuscripts for his library with his own hand. Above all, it is significant that the movement of monastic reform found its earliest patrons, not in the great Saxon emperors, but among the feudal princes of the tenth century. Cluny was founded by William of Auvergne, the Duke of Aquitaine, the reform of Gerard of Brogne owed its extension in the Low Countries to Arnoul the Old, whose predecessor Baldwin II had grown rich on the plunder of Church lands and who had distinguished himself even in that lawless age by the murder of Fulk, the Archbishop of Rheims. Later in the early eleventh century it was Richard II of Normandy who brought St. William of Volpiano from Dijon and made Fécamp the great centre of monastic reform in the north-west.

Thus the anarchy of the feudal "system" was compensated by the vitality and the recuperative power of the new type of society. From the beginning of the eleventh century onwards Western feudal society showed an extraordinary power of expansion which carried French chivalry and its institutions from one end of Europe to the other—from the British Isles to Portugal and Sicily and further still to Syria and the borders of the Arabian desert.

It is an expansion comparable to that of the Northmen in the preceding period, who had established their settlements and kingdoms from Dublin to Kiev. Indeed, the two movements are in some measure continuous, since it was the Christian Northmen of Normandy who were everywhere the spearhead of the new movement. But while the Vikings were rapidly absorbed by the countries in which they settled, and adopted the religion and institutions of the conquered peoples, the new feudal society was strong enough to preserve its spiritual identity and even to exert a creative influence in the field of culture. This is due to the fact that the feudal society of Northern France had achieved a new fusion or synthesis between the Christian and the barbarian elements in medieval culture. Hitherto these elements had coexisted in Western culture side by side with one another, but they did not form an organic unity. They remained two separate worlds—on the one side, the peace society of the Church, which found its centre in the monastic life and culture; on the other, the warrior society of the Western barbarians, which remained pagan at heart in spite of the external and partial acceptance of Christianity.

The Carolingian Empire seemed for a moment to represent the triumph of the Christian element and the unification of Western culture on Christian principles. But it was soon evident that the imposing theocracy of the Christian Empire was a pretentious sham, and that although the emperors who were most deeply imbued with the Carolingian ideals—like Louis the Pious, Charles the Bald and Charles the Simple—might set forth in their capitularies the principles of Christian government and detailed plans of moral and liturgical reform, they were incapable of defending their lands against the pagans or making their subjects obey them. The rule of law and the political authority of the state had disappeared, and the only remaining principle of social cohesion was the direct personal bond of loyalty and mutual aid between the warrior and his chief, and that of service and protection between the serf and his lord. There is an obvious resemblance between the feudal society and the traditional relation of the barbarian war leader to his *comitatus* or "*hyrd*". And, similarly, both societies are inspired by the same primitive code of honour and loyalty, of contempt of death and the spirit of implacable revenge.

Nothing could be further from the Christian ethos, yet although the feudal noble was the lineal descendant of the barbarian warrior he was, at the same time, a Christian knight, who possessed a certain loyalty to the wider society of Christendom, and a certain fidelity to the Church.

This dualism in the spirit of feudal society finds a striking illustration in a famous incident in English history. On August 11th, 991, a Viking fleet landed near Maldon in the estuary of Blackwater and met the men of Essex, led by their ealdorman Byrhtnoth, who was defeated and slain after a brave resistance. The event is recorded in two almost contemporary sources: the Latin *Vita Oswaldi*, composed by a monk of Ramsey, and the Anglo-Saxon *Lay of Maldon*, which has sometimes been called the greatest battle poem in the English language. In any case it is a classical expression of the heroic aristocratic ethos which is seen in *Beowulf* and the *Fight at Finnesburg* and in the oldest Scandinavian poetry. The death of the hero and the speeches of his followers who are determined to die with their lord belong so completely to this tradition that they reproduce precisely the situation, the emotional reactions and the poetic formulas of the old Northern pagan heroic poetry. But, in the other source, the monastic chronicler represents Byrhtnoth as a Christian champion of his country against the pagans, whose hands are strengthened by his piety and good works. And both these versions are essentially correct, since Byrhtnoth was not only a great warrior, but a devout Christian, like his nephew Aethelwine, "the friend of God", and he was venerated for centuries by the monks of Ely as one of their great benefactors.

Here we see the two component elements of the new feudal culture coexisting in their pure state, without mingling or confusion. But in the territories of the former Carolingian Empire, above all in Northern France, which was the focus of the new society, a process of fusion was already far advanced and was giving birth to new institutions, new ideas and a new literary tradition. Here the rise of the feudal culture represents the translation into specifically Christian forms of the spirit of the old Northern warrior tradition, so that the dualism of culture which had been characteristic of Western Europe during the last four or five centuries was at last transcended.

This creative activity of the new feudal culture finds its appropriate literary expression in the new feudal epic—the *chanson de geste*—which makes its appearance in Northern France in this period. This is perhaps the only—certainly the most outstanding—example of a genuine heroic poetry arising in historic times and dealing with historic persons and events. It is true that the existing *chansons* date mainly from the twelfth century, while the subject-matter is derived from the tradition and legends of the Carolingian age. But it is essentially the poetry of the feudal society which arose out of the ruins of the Carolingian Empire, and it reflects the social conditions of that age in the same way as the Northern heroic poetry reflects the social traditions of the age of the barbarian invasions.

Thus their world is already an archaic one, and is in many respects more akin to the post-Carolingian world than to the world of the twelfth century to which the existing poems belong. In all of them, for example, the bond of kin is emphasized as it was in the old tribal society. When Ganelon is tried for his treason, for instance, thirty of his kinsmen are found as his sureties or oath helpers, and when their champion is defeated in ordeal of battle all thirty are hanged—an example of the principle of the solidarity of the family which exceeds anything to be found in the barbarian codes of law. In the same way we find the old barbarian law of the blood feud and the right of the kin to the payment of blood money in full vigour. Even so late a *chanson* as *Garin of Lorraine* gives a vivid picture of the consequences that might follow even an unintentional act of homicide: the messengers riding from one end of France to the other summoning uncles and cousins and vassals to avenge their kinsman or their lord, and the ineffectual efforts of the innocent slayer to make composition by the payment of an enormous wergeld. Again, in *Raoul of Cambrai*, the interest centres in the tragic conflict between the bond of kin and the bond of feudal allegiance which leads Bernier the vassal to slay Raoul, his lord. Where, in all this, it may be asked, is the new Christian spirit to be found? For the *chansons de geste* are barbarous in the same way as the feudal society was itself—more barbarous in some respects than the courtly spirit of the old Germanic epic. But while the old heroic poetry was confined within its own inherited tradition and knew no loyalty beyond the ties of blood and personal allegiance, the new literature implicitly recognized the existence of a higher law and a wider spiritual loyalty.

The dominant motive of the *chansons de geste*—at least the earliest and most famous cycle—is not personal revenge or family feud, but the war of the Christians against the infidel—*gesta Dei per Francos*. The Carolingian wars against the Saracens of Spain hold the same central place in the feudal epic tradition as the war of Troy in that of ancient Greece. And it was here rather than in any national opposition of French to Germans, or Normans to Englishmen that the new patriotism of feudal Europe arose. This patriotic sentiment has a religious rather than a political character, since it is not related to any existing state; but to the wider society of Christendom as a whole, and thereby it introduces a new spiritual element into the barbarian ethos of the warrior culture. The warlike deeds of the champions are not an end in themselves, they are performed in the service of Christendom, *et la loi Deu essaucier et monter*. The knight who dies in battle for the faith is not only a hero, but a martyr, as Archbishop Turpin explains to Roland and his companions at Roncesvalles. "Lord Barons," he says, "Charles has left us here. For our king we ought indeed to die. Give your aid to uphold Christendom. You will have battle, you may be sure, for with your eyes you see the Saracens. Confess your sins and ask God's mercy. I will absolve you for your souls' health. And, if you die, you will be holy martyrs. You will have a seat in high paradise."[1] So, too, when Vivien is defeated at the battle of Archamps, he repents that he has prayed to our Lady to preserve his own life, when God Himself did not do so, but suffered death on the cross for us to save us from our mortal enemies, and he prays instead that he may keep his faith till death without fear.[2]

[1] Seignurs baruns, Carles nus laissat ci.
 Pur nostre rei devum nos ben murir.
 Chrestientet aidez a sustenir.
 Bataille avrez, vos en estes tuz fiz,
 Kar a vos oilz veez les Sarrazins.
 Clamez vos culpes, si preiez Deu mercit.
 Asoldrai vos pur voz anmes guarir.
 Se vos murez, esterez seinz martirs.
 Seiges avrez el greignor pareis.
                    Chanson de Roland, 1127–35.
[2] Quant l'out dit, le bers se repentid.
 Mult pensai ore que fols e que brixs
 Que mun cors quidai de la mort garir,
 Quant Dampnedeu meïsmes nel fist,
 Que pur nus mort en sainte croiz soffri,

In the same way the feudal relation itself, the bond between the knight and his lord, was moralized by the introduction of religious motives. One of the greatest of the reforming bishops of the early eleventh century, Fulbert of Chartres, explains in his letter to William the Great of Poitou how the feudal relation constitutes a complex of reciprocal moral rights and duties centring in the *sacramentum fidelitatis*, and since the relation was in principle a free personal contract it inevitably depended more upon moral sanctions than would be the case in an ordinary political relation. And so the ancient barbarian motive of personal loyalty to the war leader was reinforced by higher religious motives, so that the knight finally becomes a consecrated person, pledged not only to be faithful to his lord, but to be the defender of the Church, the widow and the orphan, as the ceremony *ad benedicendum novum militem* in the medieval pontificals describes.

In this way the knight was detached from his barbarian and pagan background and integrated into the social structure of Christian culture, so that he was regarded as one of the three indispensable organs of society, like the priest and the peasant, each of whom, as Gerald of Cambrai says, needs the services of the other as members of one body. And though this may have had little immediate effect on the actual behaviour of the feudal warrior, it provided a spiritual archetype which ultimately had a transforming effect on the standards and ideas of medieval society.

At the same time, the period which saw the rise of the institution of knighthood also witnessed an organized attempt to limit or suppress the evils of private war and feudal lawlessness by the institution of the Peace of God and the Truce of God. This movement seems to have originated with the bishops of Central and Southern

Pur nus raindre de noz mortels enemis.
Respit de mort, Sire, ner dei jo rover
Car a Tei meïsme nel voilsis pardoner.
Tramettez mei, Sire, Williame al curb nes,
V Loowis qui France ad a garder.
Par lui veintrum la bataille champel.
Chançun de Williame, 816–26.

France, who first pronounced an anathema against the plunderers of the Church and those who robbed the peasants of their cattle at the Synod of Charroux in 987, but the Abbey of Cluny was associated with the movement from the beginning, and its great abbot, St. Odilo, together with the Lorraine reformer, Richard of St. Vannes, helped to extend the movement to Northern and Eastern France. Everywhere the bishops took the lead in the establishment of such leagues of the peace, the members of which swore to protect the lives and property of non-combatants, above all of the clergy and the peasants.

Radulf Glaber has described the enthusiasm with which the people thronged to these assemblies crying, "Peace, Peace," and the noble verses which Fulbert of Chartres composed on the subject show the spirit which animated the movement:

O band of the poor, he writes, give thanks to God Almighty who, strong to renew, no less than to create, has brought back to the right way an age that was abandoned to evil. He has succoured thy long travail, O heavy laden, by granting thee the renewal of peace and quiet. Now, the nobles that had long discarded the restraints of law, set themselves manfully to do the right. The thought of the gallows makes the robber hold his hand and the unarmed wayfarer sings aloud in the presence of the highwayman. The straggling vines are pruned once more and the waste land is tilled. The spear is made into a pruning hook and the sword into a plowshare: peace enriches the lowly and impoverishes the proud. Hail, Holy Father, and grant salvation to all who love the quiet of peace. But as for those who love war, break them with the power of thy right hand, delivering the sons of the evil one to hell![3]

This poem is no doubt connected with the efforts of King Robert the Pious (996–1031) to extend the peace movement. He not only supported it in his own realm, but made a serious attempt to extend it to Christendom as a whole,

[3] *Analecta hymnalogica*, L, p. 288. Raby, *Christian Latin Poetry*, 261–62.

in concert with the Emperor St. Henry II, who was also a great supporter of the movement for religious reform.

But this attempt to suppress the evil of private war by direct action on the part of the bishops and the faithful is more significant as a symptom of the birth of a new spirit than as an effective method of social reform. The warrior element in feudal society was too powerful to be suppressed by sworn leagues of the peace: unless the latter became transformed into a militant revolutionary movement, as was indeed the case with the great league of the Capuchonnés in Auvergne in the twelfth century.

Far more successful was the attempt of the Church to find a new outlet for the warlike energies of feudal society by turning them against the external enemies of Christendom. For the proclamation of the Crusade for the reconquest of Jerusalem by Urban II at the council of Clermont in 1093 produced a wave of religious enthusiasm which was none the less real because it also appealed to the natural instincts of the unregenerate feudal warrior. According to Foucher of Chartres, the Pope associated his appeal with the ideas of the peace movement and the Truce of God, and called on the peace-breakers and men who lived by the sword to win pardon for their sins by becoming soldiers of Christ and shedding their blood in the service of Christendom.

For the first time feudal society had found a purpose which transcended local particularism and united Western Christendom in a common enterprise under the leadership of the Church. In many ways it was a unique movement, owing to the combination of a spontaneous popular movement with a number of organized military expeditions inspired by political aims. To an outside observer like Anna Comnena, who has described the Crusade so vividly from the standpoint of a civilized Byzantine princess, it seemed like a new wave of barbarian invasion.

For the whole of the West, she writes, *and all the barbarian tribes which dwell between the further side of the Atlantic and the pillars of Heracles, had all migrated into*

*Asia through the intervening parts of Europe and were mak-
ing the journey with all their household. . . . For these
Frankish soldiers were accompanied by an unarmed host
more numerous than the stars or the sand, carrying palms
and crosses on their shoulders—women and children too.
And the sight of them was like many rivers streaming from
all sides and they were all advancing on us through Dacia
generally with all their hosts.*[4]

But no disorderly wave of popular excitement can explain the success of the First Crusade. In any age it would
have been an achievement of the first magnitude to march
an army overland from France through Asia Minor to
Antioch and Jerusalem, to defeat the Turkish and the Egyptian forces and to establish a chain of Christian states along
the Syrian coast, and inland as far as Edessa on the
Euphrates. It marks a turning point in the history of the
West: ending the long centuries of weakness and isolation
and cultural inferiority and bringing the new peoples of
Western Christendom back to the old centres of Eastern
Mediterranean culture.

This achievement was rendered possible only by the over-
mastering unifying power of religious passion. And if it was
the religion of the *chansons de geste* rather than that of the
monastic reform, the crusading movement helped to establish a bond of sympathy and common interest between
them. For it was the great Cluniac Pope, Urban II, who
launched the first Crusade at a critical moment in the
history of the struggle between the Papacy and the Empire,
when the Emperor and the kings of France and England
were all under sentence of excommunication and when,
therefore, Christendom could not look to them for leadership. And in the second generation of the Crusades it was
the greatest of all the monastic reformers, St. Bernard, who
took the leading part in preaching the Crusade and who
also gave his powerful counsel and support to the new
Military Order of the Temple in which the religious ideals
of Christian Knighthood found their fullest expression.

The great Military Orders, like the Crusades themselves,

[4] Anna Comnena, *Alexiad*, XV, trans. E. A. S. Dawes.

were a bridge between lay and ecclesiastical society. While feudalism had tended to secularize the Church by assimilating the benefice of the bishop or abbot to the fief of the baron, the Crusades and the Military Orders introduced the religious principles of vows and voluntary obedience into the institution of chivalry. The Crusader was detached by his vow from all his feudal and territorial obligations and became the soldier of the Church and of Christendom. And in order to obviate the danger of anarchy resulting from this emancipation from feudal obligations, the institution of the Military Orders provided a new principle of authority and organization based upon strictly religious conceptions similar to those of the monastic order. The new social status created by these institutions was a strictly international one which belonged to Christendom as a whole and not to the Empire or the kingdoms. Accordingly the rise and fall of the great Military Orders, particularly the Templars, is an index of the progress and the decline of the unitary tendencies in medieval Christendom.

So long as the Crusades continued, the unity of Christendom found expression in a dynamic militant activity which satisfied the aggressive instincts of Western man, while at the same time sublimating them in terms of religious idealism. Thus the Crusades expressed all that was highest and lowest in medieval society—the aggressive acquisitiveness of a Bohemond or a Charles of Anjou and the heroic self-abnegation of a Godfrey of Bouillon and a St. Louis.

This ambivalence was equally characteristic of the institution of chivalry itself, which long outlasted the crusading movement and left a permanent imprint on European society and culture. Each of the great world civilizations has been faced with the problem of reconciling the aggressive ethos of the warrior with the moral ideals of a universal religion. But in none of them has the tension been so vital and intense as in medieval Christendom and nowhere have the results been more important for the history of culture. It was no longer, as in the age of the barbarian invasions, a tension between two societies and two social elements, between the warlike ethos of the pagan conquerors and the Christian culture of a more highly civilized conquered population. On the contrary, in feudal society the tension was *within* the same society and even within the same class. We see, for example, in Ordericus Vitalis's *Ecclesiastical History* how the same stratum of population, and even the same families, produced ascetics and warriors, leaders of the monastic reform and robber barons, so that individual character rather than social tradition was the decisive factor.

Thus the tension between the two ideals and the two ways of life now becomes an internal psychological one, which sometimes manifested itself by the individual conversion of the knight into the monk, but which more often took the form of some compromise between the two ideals, such as the vow of Crusade, membership of the Military Orders, or the attempt to transform knighthood into the secular arm of the Church and the spiritual power. The gradual leavening of the heroic ethos by the influence of the Church finds its literary expression in the *chansons de geste*, which represent the authentic spirit of feudal society, in contrast to the romantic poetry of the troubadours and the courtly epic which seem to belong to an entirely different world.

For the age of the Crusades also saw the development of a new secular ideal of chivalry which seems the direct antithesis of St. Bernard's ideal of Christian Knighthood and the disciplined austerity of the Military Orders, while at the same time it was equally remote from the barbaric heroism of Northern feudalism. This new ideal is the creation of the South. It arose from the contact between the feudal society of Languedoc and the higher civilization of the Western Mediterranean, which was still the centre of Western Islamic culture. It found expression in a new way of life and a new literature—the lyrical poetry of the troubadours—which was to have an immense influence, not only on Western literature, but also on Western standards of behaviour.

The distinctive features of this new movement were the cult of courtesy and the cult of love. It was concerned, above all, with the refinement of life—with creating a new pattern of social behaviour which centred in the ideal of romantic love, and it was reinforced by an elaborate code of manners which appears sophisticated and subtle even by modern standards, and must have stood out in abrupt and startling contrast to the brutality and violence that still characterized feudal society.

Thus the new movement has all the marks of an exotic growth. It has no roots in the earlier medieval culture of the West. It is neither Christian, nor Latin, nor Germanic. It appears abruptly in South-Western France about the time of the First Crusade without any preparation or previous development. Yet it must have had a pre-history, as is shown by its literary expression which is as exotic and original as the social ideals that it embodies. For the earliest-known lyrics of the early troubadours possess all the marks of a style and a literary tradition that had already reached maturity.[5]

I have argued elsewhere[6] that the origins of the new style are to be found in the rich and brilliant society of Moslem Spain, with which the Dukes of Aquitaine had been brought into contact through their annexation of the half-Spanish Duchy of Gascony after 1030, and by their crusade against the Moors of Saragossa which led to the conquest of Barbastro in 1064.

It is impossible to discuss here the arguments for and against the influence of Western Islamic culture on Provençal literature and the new courtly ideal. I can only refer to the more general aspects of the process of culture-contact which took place during this period. It is unquestionable that in spite of the mutual intolerance of the two cultures the young peoples of the West were sometimes receptive towards the higher and more sophisticated culture of the older civilization, as we see in the case of the transmission of Arabic philosophy and science during the

[5] Cf. Guillaume IX of Aquitaine, Nos. VI, VII and X of Jeanroy's edition in the *Classiques Français du Moyen Age* (1927).
[6] "The Origins of the Romantic Tradition", *Mediaeval Religion*, pp. 121–54 (1935).

twelfth century through the activities of the school of translators at Toledo and elsewhere. And if this was the case in clerical society which was most on its guard against the infiltration of alien doctrines, it is likely that lay society was even more ready to accept the influence of the higher culture in matters not directly related to religion or politics.

The civilization of the Southern Mediterranean which had reached its highest development in the age of the Fatimid Khalifate and the Khalifate of Cordova in the tenth and eleventh centuries inevitably produced a deep impression on the men of the North, who knew only the harsh and comfortless life of the feudal stronghold. And in the age of Crusades, when the Mediterranean was once more open to Western shipping, and the Italian maritime republics were growing rich by trade with Islamic lands, there was no lack of intercourse between the two worlds.

There is a charming passage in the Chronicle of Fra Salimbene in which he describes his one and only glimpse of this kind of life in one of the rich orientalized houses of the great merchant city of Pisa.

Going begging for bread with our baskets we happened on a cortile which we entered. And there was a leafy vine spread out overhead. Its verdure was delightful to behold and it was a pleasure to rest beneath its shade. There were leopards and many strange beasts from across the seas on which we gazed, for it is a pleasure to see what is new and strange. And there were youths and maidens in the flower of their youth, richly dressed and of charming countenances.

And they held in their hands violins, viols, zithers and other instruments of music from which they made melody, accompanying the music with appropriate gestures. No one there moved, no one spoke, all listened in silence. And the song was so new and so delightful, both on account of the words and the variety of voices and the manner of singing that it filled the heart with joyousness. No one spoke to us. We said nothing to them. And the music of the voices and the instruments never ceased all the time we stayed there, and we remained there a long time and knew not how to go away. I know not (God knows) whence came such a vision of so much delight, for never before had I seen anything like it, nor has it been granted me since ever to see it again.[7]

It may be objected that this scene took place in Christian Italy, not in Moslem Spain. But this illustrates my point regarding the penetration of the southern Islamic forms of culture into medieval Christendom. We see the same process taking place in Salimbene's age on a much wider scale at the court of the Emperor Frederick in Sicily and Apulia, and in the previous century the last Norman kings of Sicily went even further towards the adoption of the outward forms of the court life of the Islamic world, and showed themselves generous patrons of Moslem scholars and men of letters. There is, moreover, some fragmentary evidence that in the eleventh century this southern culture was already asserting its charm on its conquerors, for Ibn Bassam, the Portuguese Moslem historian,[8] has preserved a vivid picture of one of the leaders of the Aquitaine crusade of 1064, seated on a divan in oriental dress while he listened enthralled to a Moorish lady singing to him in Arabic.

For it was through music and poetry and the vision of a new and delightful way of life that the influence of the higher culture of the Southern Mediterranean penetrated feudal society. The courtly culture and the Provençal poetry were the carriers of this exotic spirit. They were not merely foreign to the older traditions of feudal chivalry, they were hostile to its spiritual ideals. As against the other-worldliness and asceticism which dominated Christian thought and inspired St. Bernard's crusading ideal, their spirit was frankly worldly and hedonistic. Love and honour, wealth and liberality, beauty and joy—these were the true ends of life in comparison with which the joys of heaven and the pains of hell were pale and shadowy.

Thus the courtly culture was a kind of anti-crusade, a

[7] *Chronica Fratris Salimbene de Adam*, ed. Holder-Egger, M.G.H., SS., XXXII.

[8] He is quoting from the lost work of Ibn Hayyan, the great Spanish historian, who was a contemporary of the events described.

propagandist movement for the development of a new secular aristocratic culture, which travelled in the opposite direction from the Crusades but along the same roads— from the Mediterranean to Northern France and Italy, and ultimately to Germany and England and Wales. And it is possible to follow the path of this diffusion in detail, at least in one of its most important channels. For the heiress of Aquitaine, the granddaughter of the first troubadour, Eleanor of Poitou, became successively Queen of France and Queen of England, and her daughters were Marie of Champagne and Alix of Blois and Mathilda of Saxony, and under their patronage all these five courts became in turn centres of diffusion for the courtly culture and literature in Northern Europe.

This development is a remarkable example of a purely cultural movement in the narrower sense of the word, a movement that has neither grown out of the soil nor been inspired by religious aims, but which belongs entirely to the intermediate region of conscious art and conscious social behaviour. Anomalous as such movements are in relation to the development of the great world cultures, they are not without their importance, as we see in certain aspects of Hellenistic and Renaissance culture. But the case of the courtly culture of medieval Europe is peculiarly striking owing to the fact that it coincided with the creative movement of medieval religion and traversed it. And the result was a conflict and tension in the heart of Western culture between two divergent conceptions of chivalry and two conflicting standards of behaviour.

This conflict was complicated by the fact that it overlaid the older conflict between the ideal of the barbaric warrior and that of the Christian knight to which I have already referred. Thus when the courtly culture reached the North in the second half of the twelfth century, these conflicts found expression in the new romantic literature which arose at the Angevin court and in the courts of Northern France and Flanders and the western and southern German lands. The Arthurian legend which had been created as a kind of national myth of the Anglo-Norman-Angevin dynasty afforded free scope to the imagination of the new school of poetry and became the centre of a vast development of courtly epic and romance. But here even from the beginning, we see a poet like Chrétien de Troyes accepting the exotic ideals of the new courtly poetry, in deference to his patroness, Mary of Champagne. "Matter and style," he says, "are given and furnished by the countess. The poet is simply trying to carry out her concern and intention."

Finally in the great prose cycle of Lancelot and the Quest of the Grail, in the thirteenth century, the tension between the courtly ideal and the Christian tradition is quite conscious and explicit and becomes a central theme of the whole cycle, as is shown in the dramatic contrast between Lancelot and Galahad; Camelot and Corbenic; the worldly chivalry with its cult of courtesy and its antinomian ideals of romantic love, and the heavenly chivalry that is symbolized by the quest and the vision of the Holy Grail. But here already there is an attempt at synthesis and reconciliation. Galahad is the son of Lancelot, and the latter joins, though without success, in the spiritual quest. And their divergent ideals are held together by the same code of courtesy and the common institutions of the "high order of chivalry". It is easy to find other examples of this effort of reconciliation. Hugh de Berzé, the repentant trouvère who made his recantation in *La Bible au Seigneur de Berzé*, could at the same time defend the ideals of courtesy. "Laughter and song, jousting and adventuring and holding court, such was the custom. Yet these aforetime did not for that forfeit paradise, for he who is angry and gloomy and melancholy may well lose paradise, and he who is full of joy and gaiety can well gain it, so long as he keeps himself from sin."[9]

Nevertheless the conflict of the two ideals found a tragic expression when the brilliant society which had given birth to the courtly culture went down in blood and ruin before the Crusaders from the North, led by the Abbot of Citeaux and Simon de Montfort. And the conflict of culture is reflected in the contrast between the characters of the leaders, on the one side the weak and irresolute Count Raymond of Toulouse and the dissolute King Peter of

[9] *La Bible au Seigneur de Berzé*, 127.

Aragon, both of whom were poets and great patrons of culture; and on the other side that thirteenth-century Ironside, the devout and merciless Simon de Montfort. The courtly culture of the South showed its essential frailty when it was brought to the hard test of war and found no unity of purpose and no worthy leadership. There was perhaps one exception, the young Raymond Roger of Beziers, who was the first victim of the crusade, and whose fate is commemorated in the noble lament of an anonymous troubadour.

They have slain him. Never has there been such a crime and folly so displeasing to God, as the act of these renegade dogs of the race of Pilate who killed him. As for him, he was like Jesus who died to redeem us. Has he not crossed by the same bridge to save his people?

Rich in lineage, rich in pride, rich in valour, rich in counsel, rich in prowess; there was never a man to be compared to you. In you we have lost the fountain of joy.[10]

But it is characteristic of the dualism of the ideals of chivalry that when the poet is brought up against a really tragic situation, he abandons the sophisticated style and the hedonistic ethos of the Provençal tradition and returns to the imagery and the ideals of Christian chivalry, and writes more like a crusader than a troubadour.

In fact from the beginning of the thirteenth century the exotic and the Christian elements in the tradition of chivalry interpenetrate one another in an inextricable confusion. Some of the clearest expressions of the pagan hedonism of courtly culture are to be found in the literature of the North, as in that exquisite little masterpiece, *Aucassin and Nicolette*, which seems to belong to Picardy or Hainault, though it shows clear marks of oriental influence. And on the other hand we find in Italy a really profound and fruitful assimilation of the ideals of the courtly culture by the spiritual life of medieval Christendom. We see this above all in the case of St. Francis, who owed more to the vernacular culture of the troubadours than to the Latin

[10] Trans. Jeanroy, *Poésie Lyrique des Troubadours*, II, 213.

culture of the Schools and the old monastic orders. In fact the life of St. Francis shows a conscious, but entirely spontaneous and unliterary transposition of the ideal of courtesy to the higher plane of the Christian life, thus freeing it from its conventional aristocratic limitations and endowing it with a transcendent cosmic significance.

He went honourably upon the stones, writes the thirteenth-century Dominican Jacopo da Varazze,[11] *for the love of Him that so called stone. He gathered the small worms out of the ways, because they should not be trodden by the feet of them that passed by. He commanded in winter to give honey unto bees that they should not perish for hunger. He called all beasts his Brethren. He was replenished of marvellous joy for the love of his Creator. He beheld the sun, the moon and the stars and summoned them to the love of their Maker.*[12]

I shall be speaking further on the influence of St. Francis on medieval religion. Here I will only point out the decisive importance of his life in the desecularization and spiritualization of the courtly culture. For he is the real creator of that vital union of the two traditions which had so great an influence on the development of both medieval spirituality and medieval vernacular literature.

But we must not overestimate the importance of this spiritual transformation, for it never entirely overcame the secular hedonism of the courtly culture within its own social environment. This secular element survived both the decline of Provençal culture and the rise of Franciscan spirituality. It was still the dominant element in the later chivalry, so well and sympathetically described by Froissart, which, when we consider the horrors of the Black Death and the Hundred Years' War, seems like a brilliant veneer that conceals the corruption of a dying society.

The secularization of chivalry was increased both by the loss of the crusading ideal and by the increasing wealth

[11] *The Golden Legend,* by M. B. James de Voragine, translated by Chaucer.
[12] *The Golden Legend,* Caxton's translation, Kelmscott ed., p. 897.

and luxury of Western court life, as we see it for example
at the Burgundian court at the end of the Middle Ages: so
that the figure of the medieval knight changes almost in-
sensibly into that of the Renaissance courtier. Yet even so,
the higher spiritual ideals of chivalry were never completely
discredited or lost. They were passed on through the later
Middle Ages from Joinville's *Life of St. Louis* to the *Life of
the Good Knight Bayard* by the Loyal Servitor, and from
Chaucer to Sir Philip Sidney. It is possible that the element of dualism and tension which was inherent in the
tradition of chivalry and courtesy from the beginning gave
it a power of adaptation and survival which the more completely integrated institutions of medieval Christendom did
not possess. However that may be, it is certain that the ideal
of Christian chivalry has always retained its attraction for
the Western mind and its influence on Western ethical
standards in spite of the criticisms of moralists like Ascham
and the tragic irony of the greatest minds of the Renaissance: Cervantes and Shakespeare.

Chapter IX

The Medieval City: Commune and Gild

THE DEVELOPMENT of the feudal society and the institutions related to it, notably the institution of chivalry, represents only one aspect of the revival of Western culture in the Middle Ages. No less important was the rebirth of the city which transformed the economic and social life of Western Europe. During the Dark Ages, and especially in the Carolingian and post-Carolingian age, Western Europe had become an almost entirely agrarian society, in which the life of the city played a smaller part than perhaps in any society that has reached a similar stage of civilization. But from the twelfth century onwards the medieval world was once more a world of cities in which the life of the city and the civic spirit were hardly less intense than in the classical age of Greece and Rome. Nor was the medieval city a repetition of anything that had gone before. It was a new creation, unlike the cities of antiquity or those of modern times and differing also, though in a lesser degree, from the types of city which were to be found in the East at the same period.

This new type of European city had a considerable influence on the religious development of Western Europe during these formative centuries. The late Ernst Troeltsch, following Max Weber, went so far as to maintain that it was the medieval city which first provided the favourable conditions for a thorough-going Christianization of social life such as had existed neither in the city culture of the ancient world, which was based upon slavery, nor in the

feudal agrarian society which had been built up so largely
by the strong at the expense of the weak.

It was, he writes, *only when the city which arose out of
the disintegration and surplus of feudal landownership had
united its varied population, drawn from all sorts of different social origins, that a ground was prepared on which
the higher qualities of medieval society could be purified
from the crudity and violence of feudalism. The very condition of existence of the city as an essentially economic
association is peace, the freedom and the common interest
of all the citizens, together with freedom to work and the
basing of property on personal effort and industry.*

*In all these respects the city corresponded to a great ex-
tent with the demands of Christian ethics. As a non-
military peaceful community of work, using the military
element only for its defence and still devoid of capitalistic
urban features, the medieval city was a pattern of Christian
society as we find it in Thomist theory. From the political
and economic point of view the period of civic culture which
begins in the eleventh century may be regarded as a preparation and foundation of the modern world. But for the
historian of ethics and the religious life it also appears, with
its cathedrals and its intensive church life, its religious con-
fraternities and gilds, its care for the spiritual and material
welfare of its inhabitants and its educational and charitable
institutions, as the highest point of the development of the
medieval spirit.*[1]

It is easy to show the reverse side of this development—
the intensity of class conflict and the ferocity of the in-
ternecine strife which fill the chronicles of the Italian and
Flemish cities. Nevertheless, there are several factors in the
development of the medieval city which bear out Troeltsch's favourable verdict.

For in the first place the city, like the monastery, was an
oasis of security and peace in a world of insecurity and war.
It was a place of refuge where the unwarlike could gather

[1] E. Troeltsch, *Soziallehren der christlichen Kirchen und
Gruppen,* pp. 250–51.

under the protection of the Church. The early cities of Carolingian times owed their existence to the Church. They were the residence of the bishops and the centre of administration of the diocese, and also contained a number of monasteries in addition to the chapter and the episcopal school. Apart from the ecclesiastics and their dependants, and the garrison of knights and men-at-arms charged by the bishop or the count with the duty of defending the walls, there was practically no independent class of townspeople. The Carolingian city was not an economic centre, apart from its market which provided the necessities of life for its inhabitants. It was in fact a sort of temple city, such as we find existing in prehistoric times in Mesopotamia or later in Asia Minor.

The distinctive element in later medieval city life—the merchant class—did not make its appearance until the tenth or eleventh century, and even then its importance was mainly confined to certain favoured regions, above all, the shores of the Western Mediterranean, the plain of Lombardy, and the valleys of the Scheldt, the Meuse and the Rhine, and in Eastern Europe to the two great trade routes which linked the Baltic with the Caspian and the Black Sea by way of the Volga, the Dnieper and the Don.

In Western Europe this new development was generally based on the principle of voluntary association under religious protection—a principle peculiarly suited to the needs of new classes that had no place in the established territorial hierarchy of the feudal state. These associations had a double character. On the one hand, they originated in the fellowship of the highway where men must travel in company for mutual protection, as organized caravans of pilgrims or merchants; and, on the other, in the voluntary religious association—the confraternity, *charité* or gild which united for charitable or social purposes under the patronage of some popular saint.

It was to associations of these kinds that the development of medieval city life in North-Western Europe was primarily due. Such groups of merchants were to be found in Flanders, as early as the tenth century, settled under the walls of a feudal fortress or an ecclesiastical town, and as the commercial movement grew, they spread throughout North-Western and Central Europe. By degrees the free and voluntary merchant association began to deal in an unofficial way with all the needs of the new communities. In this way it produced spontaneously the organs of a new municipal government which was utterly unlike anything that the classical city-state or the territorial feudal state had known, since it was by origin the limited functional organ of a single unprivileged class. The self-constituted group of merchants under their elected head met together to take counsel for their common interests and raised voluntary funds for their common needs. As they increased in wealth and numbers, they tended to become a complete self-sufficient organization which could carry on an independent existence apart from the regular organs of the feudal state. And as the power of the merchants grew and they became more accustomed to common action, they finally aspired to take over the political, juridical and military functions that had formerly belonged exclusively to the bishop, the count or the representatives of the feudal state.

In this way there arose the *commune*, which was one of the greatest social creations of the Middle Ages. The commune was an association in which all the inhabitants of a town, and not the merchants alone, bound themselves by oath to keep the common peace, to defend the common liberties and to obey the common officers. In principle, it had much in common with the sworn "leagues of the peace" of which I spoke in the last chapter, although it had a wider scope and a more permanent character. Its members described themselves as "the men of the peace", the "sworn brethren", partners in a common "friendship", bound every man to help his brother in the common need.

But although the commune had a definitely revolutionary aspect as an assertion of popular independence against the episcopal authority, it was far from being anticlerical in the vulgar sense of the word. On the contrary, both in Italy and in Northern France and Germany it was closely related to the movement of ecclesiastical reform and it was often under the leadership of popular preachers of Hilde-

brandine ideals that the towns rose in armed revolt against
their bishops.

The most striking example of this is the insurrection of
the Pataria in Milan, which played such an important part
in the reform movement in 1065 under the leadership of
Erlennbald, the first of the new tribunes, who ruled the
city "like a Pope and like a king, by the sword and by gold,
by sworn leagues and covenants", as a hostile chronicler
writes. It was here in Lombardy that the communal movement attained its greatest development, so that finally in
1176 the forces of the Lombard League were strong enough
to meet the Emperor Frederick Barbarossa himself and
defeat him in pitched battle at Legnano. Here the communal movement was inspired by the same intense religious enthusiasm that characterized the Crusades. The men
of Milan went out to fight for the liberties of their city and
the rights of Holy Church around the Carroccio—the great
ox wain on which the Mass of battle was said and which
bore the standard of St. Ambrose, the palladium of the
city.

In fact the alliance of the league of Lombard cities with
the Papacy against the Empire marks the emergence of a
new power in medieval society, and henceforward the
cities take a leading part in the public life of the West.

It is true that conditions in Italy were different from
those in Northern Europe, which I have been describing
hitherto. For in the Mediterranean world the Roman and
Byzantine traditions of city life survived to a far greater
degree than in the North, and there was never the same
tendency to class segregation and the development of the
town as the organ of specialized economic classes that we
find in Northern Europe.

In Italy the leading citizens of the town were the lesser
nobles of the surrounding country, and the class conflict
preceded and was intermixed with the feuds and rivalries
of the nobles, which corresponded to the private wars of
northern feudalism. Moreover, the fact that the Church
in Italy was essentially a city institution, which carried on
the tradition, and usually preserved the frontiers, of the
Roman *civitas* made the bond between city and country

much closer than in Northern Europe and strengthened the sense of civic unity and patriotism.[2]

Hence in the course of the early Middle Ages Italy became a land of city-states which is comparable only to ancient Greece in the richness and diversity of its civic life. From the great maritime republics such as Venice and Pisa and Genoa, which were wealthier and more powerful than many a medieval kingdom, down to the little hill cities of Umbria and the Marches which controlled only a few square miles of fertile territory, we find every type of community, agreeing only in the intensity of their local patriotism. In all of them the coexistence of nobles and plebeians in a common polity produced a social life unlike anything to be found in Northern Europe. No doubt class feeling was strong, as it had been in ancient Greece, but the conflict was not one between the urban bourgeoisie and the rustic nobility as in the North, but between the different classes which shared the common life of the city.

At first the commune was governed by consuls who were chosen in the full assembly or *arrengo* of the citizens. But as the political power of the cities developed, the consuls became dependent on the council of the leading citizens, who were nobles. On the other hand the growth of trade and industry increased the importance of the merchants and craftsmen, and they also demanded a share in the city government. In the thirteenth century the people, organized in their gilds, and combined in wider associations like the Credenza of San Ambrogio at Milan, the Society of San Faustino at Brescia or the Society of San Bassiano at Lodi, attempted to wrest the control from the nobles. Finally, above all in Tuscany, the nobles became an ostracized class, who were either excluded from office, or driven from the city altogether, so that the political exiles and the disenfranchised became an important element in Italian city politics.

[2] The symbol of this intimate relation between Church and city is to be seen in the common baptistery which is such a striking feature of the Italian cities, especially in Tuscany, and we see in Dante how both the civic patriotism and the religious devotion of the poet were concentrated on this as the sacred heart of Florence (*Paradiso*, XXV, 1–11).

This jealousy of any class or individual which claimed an exceptional position was characteristic of Italian communal life and led to the elaboration of a series of constitutional devices for the supervision and control of the magistrates. This was the inevitable consequence of the direct participation of every citizen in the work of government, which, as in ancient Greece, involved the rotation of office and short periods of tenure as well as the supremely democratic system of election by lot instead of by vote.

The political development of the great maritime cities followed a different course, owing to the fact that the nobles themselves were engaged in commerce, so that even the Doge of Venice, who was the equal of kings and intermarried with Byzantine and German princesses, had a share like other Venetians in trading ventures. These cities had been the leaders in the economic revival of the Mediterranean, and possessed a cosmopolitan outlook unknown elsewhere in Western Europe. Venice, above all, had remained immune from barbarian conquest and control throughout the Dark Ages, and in the eleventh century was still largely Byzantine in culture and social life. The development of the Western cities, on the other hand, was hampered by the predominance of the Moslem powers in the Western Mediterranean, and the rise of the economic prosperity of Pisa and Genoa depended on trade with Spain and North Africa rather than on the Byzantine world. At the beginning of the twelfth century Donizo of Canossa writes of Pisa as a semi-oriental town.

Qui pergit Pisas videt illic monstra marina,
Haec urbs Paganis, Turchis, Libycis, quoque Parthis
Sordida, Chaldæi sua lustrant littora tetri.

Yet these cities were none the less in the van of the Christian advance against Islam, and their peoples were animated by a strong crusading spirit which finds expression in the Latin verses of the Pisan poets of the eleventh and twelfth centuries. From a literary point of view these poems are far inferior to the crusading epic of Northern feudalism—the *chanson de geste*—but on the other hand they are very close to the events that they relate and reflect the essentially civic character of the crusading movement in Italy. Already, a generation before the First Crusade, the Italian cities had burst open the doors which had so long shut off Western Europe from the civilized Mediterranean world, and the foundation of the great Duomo at Pisa in 1063, which was built with the spoils of the Saracens after the conquest of Palermo, is a witness to the combination of civic pride, commercial enterprise and crusading idealism which characterized the maritime republics.

The effects of the reopening of the Mediterranean on Western trade and shipping were by no means confined to the Italian maritime cities; the cities of Provence and Catalonia, above all Marseilles and Barcelona, shared in the expansion. When Benjamin of Tudela visited Montpellier in 1160 he found it thronged with Christian and Moslem merchants from all parts—from Algarve, Lombardy, the Empire, Egypt, Palestine, Greece, France, Spain and England, and he adds that people of all tongues meet here, chiefly in consequence of the traffic of the Genoese and the Pisans.

In this way Mediterranean influences penetrated inland, from Venice into Lombardy and across the passes into Germany, from Pisa into Tuscany, from Genoa across the Mont Cenis and from the Riviera up the valley of the Rhone to Burgundy and Champagne. Here the merchants from the Mediterranean met those from the other great centre of Western economic activity—the towns of Flanders; and the great fairs of Champagne developed during the twelfth century into an international commercial centre and a clearing house for financial transactions between men of different nationalities.

As this stream of commerce grew wider and deeper, it gradually transformed the economic way of life in Western Europe. New industries sprang up, new towns were founded and the old episcopal cities revived and acquired communal institutions. From the town the new life reached the countryside and in some cases even led to the formation of rural communes by groups of villages, as in the well-known example of the commune of Laonnais where seventeen villages acquired a charter of communal liberties from Louis VII in 1177. But even apart from these exceptional cases the revival of town life brought liberty to the peasant, either directly by migration to the growing cities, or indirectly by favouring the commutation of labour for money payments and increasing the possibilities of enfranchisement.

It was in this atmosphere of economic renaissance, the expansion of commercial life, and increasing opportunities of personal freedom, that the great flowering of the religious culture of medieval Christendom took place; a flowering which finds its artistic expression in the new Gothic style of architecture and sculpture which had its origin in Northern France in the twelfth century and spread from one end of Western Europe to the other during the next hundred and fifty years.

No doubt Viollet le Duc went too far when he defined Gothic architecture as the architecture of the communes— a lay art inspired by the new spirit of popular liberty— since the monks also, above all those of the Cistercian order, had an important share in its early development. Nevertheless, there is a close relation between the two movements, since the new art originated in the regions of Northern France in which the communal movement was strongest, and the great cathedrals which were the supreme achievements of the new style were the centres of the civic life of the new cities, like the city temple in antiquity.

Moreover the new style spread and became diversified with the expansion of town life, until by the later Middle Ages it had transformed the appearance of every city in Northern and Western Europe and inspired the new civic architecture of the Low Countries and the Hanseatic towns of the Baltic.

For the new city produced a new people and a new art, and although both were conditioned by economic forces and depended materially on the revival of commercial and industrial activity, they were also inspired by new spiritual forces which to a considerable extent preceded the economic revival. Thus the ways of pilgrimage are older than the trade routes. St. Gilles was a centre of pilgrims before its famous fair developed and before Marseilles and Montpellier became centres of merchants. It was the pilgrimage to St. Michael of Monte Gargano that brought the Normans to Southern Italy before the Italian merchants crossed the Alps, and it was the pilgrimage to Jerusalem, and not the Levant trade of Pisa and Genoa, that inspired the crusading movement.

Finally, and above all, it was the religious confraternity or "charity"—the free association of individuals under the patronage of a saint for mutual aid, spiritual and material—which was the seed of the great flowering of communal life in the merchant and craft gilds which were the most striking feature of medieval urban society. The life of the medieval gild was a microcosm of that of the commune, and its intense solidarity made its membership more important in the life of the individual than that of the city itself, since it was primarily through the gild that the ordinary man exercised and realized his citizenship. The constitution of the craft gilds was essentially the same throughout Western Europe; and in the course of the thirteenth and fourteenth centuries it came to play the leading part in the life of every medieval town, from great cities like Florence and Paris and Ghent down to little towns with only a few hundred inhabitants.

There was, however, a great difference between the part played by the gilds in the life of the free cities of Italy and Flanders and Germany and the more modest functions that they performed in countries like England and the France of the later Middle Ages which possessed a strong royal government. The position in Italy was unique, inasmuch as the nobles—at least the lesser nobles—from the first took a leading part in the common life of the city, and the gilds to which they belonged—such as the bankers, the merchants and the lawyers—inevitably possessed a much greater social prestige and political influence than the gilds of the craftsmen and shopkeepers. Hence it was in Italy that the gilds first succeeded in dominating and practically absorbing the government of the commune and concentrated its authority in the hands of their own representatives—the Priors of the Greater and Lesser Arts.

It is, however, in Northern Europe, in the cities of Flanders, that we find the most remarkable development of the craft gilds as a political force. Here in the fourteenth century the gilds of the less privileged workers, above all, the weavers who were the largest element in the population, rose against the merchant aristocracy and set up a kind of medieval dictatorship of the proletariat. Under the rule of the gilds of the clothiers the three great cities of Flanders —Ghent, Bruges and Ypres—reached their highest point of development and for a short time played an important part in European politics. But this was a unique achievement, due to the exceptional condition of the Flemish industrial cities which possessed a great international market. In more normal cases the craft gilds were subject to the control of the civic authorities and formed a hierarchy of corporations through which the economic and social life of the town was regulated in the most minute detail. In this way the medieval city succeeded in reconciling the interests of the consumer with the corporate freedom and responsibility of the producer. As the late Henri Pirenne wrote: "The medieval urban economy is worthy of the Gothic architecture with which it is contemporary. It created in every detail, and one might say *ex nihilo*, a system of social legislation more complete than that of any other period of history, including our own."[3]

It was this integration of corporate organization, economic function and civic freedom which makes the medieval city, as Troeltsch remarks, the most complete embodiment of the social ideals of the Middle Ages, as we see them in their most highly developed form in the writings of St. Thomas and his contemporaries. Medieval political philosophy was dominated by the ideal of unity. Mankind was one great society, and above all the regenerated human race, that portion of mankind which was incorporated in the Church was united by its membership of Christ, its Head, by its allegiance to the divine law and by its dedication to

[3] H. Pirenne, *Les Villes du Moyen Age*, p. 182.

one transcendent end. This unity formed a complex hierarchical organism, a body with many members, each having a vital function to fulfil, each with its own office and
ministry for the service of the whole.

This doctrine of society involves the principle of hierarchical subordination at every stage, but unlike the Aristotelian theory it does not involve total subordination or the
institution of slavery. For every individual member of the
whole is an end in himself, and his particular *officium* or
ministerium is not merely a compulsory social task but a
way of the service of God through which he shares in the
common life of the whole body. No doubt in practice a
man's place in the social hierarchy may be determined by
heredity or social competition, but in principle the theory
favours the conception of vocation and the internal autonomy of each particular organ.

Now, as we have seen, there was already a tendency in
the feudal order to recognize the organic nature of society
and the reciprocity of rights and duties in the social hierarchy. But the feudal system rested in the last resort on a
foundation of serfdom and on the power and privilege that
were won and maintained by the sword, so that the feudal
state could never entirely escape from the condition of
anarchy and disunity out of which it had arisen. The medieval city, on the other hand, was essentially a unity—a visible
and tangible unity, sharply defined by the circle of its walls
and towers and centred in the cathedral, the visible embodiment of the faith and spiritual purpose of the community.
And within the city, the autonomous corporate organization of the different economic activities in the economic
and social life of the community, by means of the gild
system, corresponds perfectly with the doctrine of the organic differentiation and mutual interdependence of the
members of the Christian society. Thus the medieval city
was a community of communities in which the same principles of corporate rights and chartered liberties applied
equally to the whole and to the parts. For the medieval
idea of liberty, which finds its highest expression in the life
of the free cities, was not the right of the individual to
follow his own will, but the privilege of sharing in a highly

organized form of corporate life which possessed its own constitution and rights of self-government. In many cases this constitution was hierarchical and authoritarian, but as every corporation had its own rights in the life of the city, so every individual had his place and his rights in the life of the gild.

These rights were not purely economic or even political, for one of the most remarkable features of medieval gild life was the way in which it combined secular and religious activities in the same social complex. The gild chantry, the provision of prayers and masses for deceased brethren, and the performance of pageants and mystery plays on the great feasts were no less functions of the gild than the common banquet, the regulation of work and wages, the giving of assistance to fellow gild-men in sickness or misfortune and the right to participate in the government of the city. For it was in the life of the Church and in the extension of the liturgy into common life by art and pageantry that the community-life of the medieval city found its fullest expression, so that the material poverty of the individual man was compensated by a wider development of communal activity and artistic and symbolic expression than anything that the more materially wealthy societies of modern Europe have known.

In this, the medieval city was more completely a *commonwealth*—a full communion and communication of social goods—than any society that has ever existed with the exception of the Greek polis, and it was superior even to the latter, inasmuch as it was not the society of a leisured class supported by a foundation of servile labour. Erasmus, who saw at Strasburg one of the last examples of the full gild constitution of the Middle Ages that still survived in the age of the Renaissance, was conscious of this when he wrote,

Videbam monarchiam absque tyrannide, aristocratiam sine factionibus, democratiam sine tumultu, opes absque luxu . . . Utinam in hujusmodi rempublicam, divine Plato, tibi contigisset incidere![4]

[4] "I saw monarchy without tyranny, aristocracy without fac-

It is true that the full development of the gild system in the polity of a free city was an exceptional achievement, which, like Greek democracy, was only realized in exceptionally favourable circumstances and for a brief period, as in Flemish towns in the fourteenth century, at Siena under the government of the Riformatori (1371–85), and at Florence under Michele di Lando and the Ciompi (1378–82). In France and England the rise of the national monarchy deprived the cities of their political independence and ultimately of their internal autonomy. Nevertheless, even here, they made an essential contribution to the life of the medieval state. By taking their place in the feudal hierarchy, side by side with the barons and the clergy, they brought a new representative principle into political life. First in Southern Italy and Spain, later in England and France, and finally throughout Western Europe from Sweden to Portugal, the "good towns" became one of the great estates, "universities" or "brazos" of the realm, and were summoned to send their proctors or representatives to give counsel and aid to the king and obtain "the common assent of the realm".

It is in this system of representative estates that the medieval conception of society as a community of communities finds its most complete expression. The kingdom as a whole is a *universitas*—the commune of the realm—and it is made up of a number of different *universitates* in which each order or organ of society is conceived as a corporate whole.

No doubt this idea was so deeply rooted in medieval thought that it had already found expression in feudal society before the rise of the new system. Indeed the primary estates of the realm were the clergy and the barons—the lords spiritual and temporal—and the towns only attained a place in the council at a later period as "the Third Estate". But it was not until the coming of the towns, which could only take part in political life through their elected representatives or proctors, that the representative principle

tions, democracy without tumult, wealth without luxury . . . Would that it had been your lot, divine Plato, to come upon such a republic."

became an essential part of the estates system, and it was this principle which gave the medieval assemblies of estates their new character and their constitutional importance. From this point the medieval state ceases to be a feudal hierarchy based on the principle of land tenure, and becomes a true political community in which nobles and commons co-operated for common social ends. The institution of constitutional representative government which has become the characteristic political form of modern Western culture has its roots in this medieval development, and even during the Middle Ages it had already acquired full, though premature, expression in exceptional cases, such as the Cortes of Aragon and Catalonia where the estates possessed complete control of legislation, as well as the right of supervising the administration of their grants by a permanent committee of the estates, known as the *Diputacion General*.

Thus the medieval ideas of the organic nature of society, of corporate rights and duties and the mutual co-operation of the different specialized social functions in the life of the whole underlie the development not only of the corporate institutions of the medieval city but also the representative constitutional organization of the later medieval kingdom. And at every stage of this development these ideas find a corresponding expression in the thought and institutions of the Church. Thus the feudal hierarchy of early medieval society corresponds with the integration of the monastic communities into great hierarchical orders like the Cluniac and the Cistercian. The development of the communes and free cities is associated with the rise of the universities and with a new type of religious Order—the Friars—which is no longer based on endowments and the ownership of land but is organized to fulfil a particular social function; and the later development of the system of estates finds its ecclesiastical counterpart in the Conciliar movement which developed the principle of representation on a still wider basis than that of the medieval state, and attempted to create constitutional representative organs for the entire body of Christendom.

Clearly these are not two independent developments.

The life of medieval society was one, and its religious and secular institutions only represent different functions of the same organism, as medieval thinkers from John of Salisbury to Nicholas of Cusa continually insist. There is, however, a striking contrast between this unitary and universalist tendency in medieval thought and culture, and the sharp dualism of Church and World characteristic of the older Christian attitude to secular culture, which, as we have seen, still dominated Christian thought during the Dark Ages. The change was due not merely to the changed relations of the Church to a society which was Christian by profession and regarded its religious faith as inseparable from its citizenship. It was also due to the revolutionary change of thought by which medieval philosophy had assimilated the Aristotelian ethical and sociological principles and integrated them into the structure of Christian thought, so that the Law of Nature—the moral law revealed by the light of reason—was confirmed and developed by the spiritual law revealed by faith. This does not of course abolish the fundamental Christian distinction between nature and grace, reason and faith, the World and the Church, but it puts the emphasis on the concordance and harmonization of the two orders rather than on their opposition and conflict. The divine law which is of grace does not abolish the human law which is based on natural reason. It is a law of liberty which sets man free from the limitations and servitudes of the temporal order and opens a wider spiritual horizon to Christian civilization. This conception of the progressive incorporation of all the different levels of existence and value in a divine order provides an appropriate theological ideology for the complex corporative development of medieval society in which every religious and social function finds its autonomous organic expression, from the trade gild which serves the material needs of the city up to the monastic community which exists only for prayer and contemplation—each with its own law and its own institutions, but all sharing alike in the common life and faith of one all-inclusive spiritual whole.

Nor was it only the philosophers who were conscious of

the continuity of nature and grace and the capacity of every social institution to be informed by a higher spiritual purpose. What could be more Thomist than the words in which the Yarmouth chronicler speaks of his gild merchant.

If, he says, *the bond of love and friendship is laudable among mere rational men, then how much more is that which is between Christians, who are tied by the strongest bond of faith and religion; but above all by those Christians who form one fraternity bound and linked together by a solemn oath.*[5]

In every aspect of the later medieval culture we find this conception of a hierarchy of goods and values and a corresponding hierarchy of estates and vocations which bind the whole range of human relations together in an ordered spiritual structure that reaches from earth to heaven. Nevertheless the completeness and symmetry of the Thomist synthesis should not blind us to the fact that it rests on a very delicate balance of opposing forces and different traditions which can only be maintained by a strict adherence to an order of ethical and metaphysical requirements that rests in the last resort upon an act of faith. There is all the difference in the world between the Pauline doctrine of the mystical organism of the Divine Body in which every part achieves it own spiritual perfection and subserves the ends of the whole and the Aristotelian idea of society as a natural organism, sufficient to itself, in which the different classes exist solely for the sake of the whole, and where the ruler and lawgiver imprint form on the inert matter of the social body, so that the lower classes, which are concerned with the mechanical arts or with unskilled labour, have a purely instrumental character.

Now, as St. Thomas has shown, it is quite possible to incorporate the organic materialism of Aristotelian politics into the organic mysticism of the Christian view of society, but only on condition that the state itself is recognized as an organ of the spiritual community and not as the sovereign end of human life. That is to say, that social theory

[5] Gross, *The Gild Merchant*, II, 278.

and social practice must deal with the part in terms of the whole and not as a final end.

And this means that the lesser corporate bodies—cities, gilds, universities and estates—are not merely instruments or organs of the state, but possess a further relation and responsibility to the wider spiritual society of which they also form part. As the gild has a loyalty to the king as well as to the city, so it has a loyalty to Christendom as a whole, as well as to the kingdom or principality to which its city belongs.

Now this principle was recognized generally in medieval society in its great period, and it was this that gives medieval civilization its peculiar character. But it was difficult to reconcile this conception of a graduated series of communities, each with its own principle of quasi-political authority, with the Aristotelian theory of a single community which was autarkic and autonomous, and possessed exclusive sovereignty over its members. It was possible to maintain the universalism of medieval thought only by transferring the attributes of the Aristotelian state to some wider whole. If this whole was the Church, as Aegidius Romanus and Alvarius Pelagius maintained, it resulted in a theory of Papal monarchy or theocracy which threatened the independence of the temporal power even in its own sphere. If it was the Empire, as Dante believed, then it is the Empire and not the Church which becomes the divinely appointed organ through which human civilization attains its ultimate end. This end Dante defines in Aristotelian or rather Averroistic terms as the continuous actualization of the potential intellect, i.e. the realization of all the potentialities of the human mind. And the Emperor is the formal principle of human unity and moves the wills and actions of men by a single law, in the same way as God, the First Mover, imparts a single law of uniform motion to the heavens.

All this is much nearer to Averroes or Avicenna than to the teaching of St. Thomas. But at the same time it is equally remote from the real spirit of Aristotle's politics, which was concerned with the study of the nature of the Greek city-state as it actually existed rather than with the vision of an ideal world-state. It is only when we come to Marsilius of Padua, less than a generation later, that we find a theory of the state in which the medieval Christian tradition is entirely dominated and transformed by the spirit of Aristotelian naturalism, so as to leave no place for the medieval conception of one universal Christian society. It is true that Marsilius still maintained the organic nature of society, but it was in the purely Aristotelian sense which no longer possesses any link with the Pauline and theological tradition. The priesthood is no longer the principle of spiritual unity, the soul of the social organism; it has become one among the many organs of the community, the *pars sacerdotalis*, subject to the ruling class, the *pars principans*, and devoid of any transcendent authority. The principle of unity is to be found in the will of the human legislator which alone possesses coercive legal power. Now the human legislator, in Marsilius's view, is nothing else but the community itself, the *communitas* or *universitas civium*, which is the ultimate source of law[6] and the constituent power behind the *principatus*, the ruling class that is its organ or instrument. The same principle holds good for the Church which is the *communitas fidelium*, but since Marsilius assumes that his state is a Christian one, the two communities are the same, and there can be no division in the ultimate source of authority in Church and state.

In all this Marsilius undoubtedly represents one aspect of the medieval civic development—the lay element in the Italian city-state as represented by the lawyers and officials as against the friars and the churchmen; and his adaptation of Aristotelian political theory shows how easy it was for a citizen of the medieval Italian city-republic to return to the tradition of the Greek polis with its socio-political monism and autarky.

The older medieval political philosophy, from the Carolingian age to the twelfth century, was not really concerned with the theory of the state at all but with the relations of spiritual and temporal authority—of the two hierarchies that

[6] *Nos autem dicamus, secundam veritatem et consilium Aristotelis, causam legis effectivam, primam et propriam esse civium universitatem (Defensor Pacis, I, Ch. XII).*

coexisted in the one body of Christendom. The state in the classical and modern sense of the word first re-emerged in the Italian city-state with its intensive political life, its strong civic consciousness and its complex and artificial constitutional systems. It is therefore no accident that the thinkers who revived the Aristotelian and classical doctrines of the state and applied them to contemporary society were almost without exception Italians, like St. Thomas Aquinas, Aegidius Colonna, Marsilius of Padua and Bartolus of Sassoferrato. And so when these writers speak of *civitas* and *respublica*, they are always thinking primarily of the city-state they knew; even though they enlarged their definitions so as to include larger political units like the medieval kingdom or the empire.

But in the case of Marsilius we are conscious of new currents of social and religious thought which no longer belong to the pattern of medieval culture, but point forward to a new world. No doubt his conception of the *universitas civium* as the ultimate principle of social authority is grounded on the political realities of the Italian city-state, in which it was always theoretically possible to appeal from the Podesta and the councils to the *parliament* or general assembly summoned by the great bell of the commune, as we see in the countless revolutions and changes of government in the Lombard and Tuscan cities. But when Marsilius goes on to apply the same principle to the Church and abandons the whole principle of hierarchical authority in favour of the *communitas fidelium*—the judgment of the general body of the faithful, of which the clergy are the ministers and employees—he seems nearer to sixteenth-century Zurich or seventeenth-century New England than to the age and country of Dante and St. Catherine of Siena.

Chapter X

The Medieval City: School and University

THE RISE of the medieval city was accompanied by far-reaching changes in the intellectual life of Western society and in the traditions of medieval education. And since those traditions were primarily religious these changes produced corresponding changes in Western religion and in the relation between religion and culture.

As we have seen, the early Middle Ages, in the Carolingian age and the centuries that preceded and followed it, were marked by the preponderance of the monasteries, not only in the spiritual discipline of the religious life but no less in the intellectual development of Christian culture. They have been called the Benedictine age of Western culture, since from the rise of the new Christian culture of Northumbria in the seventh century down to the revival of city life and the rise of the communes in the twelfth century, the continuity of the higher culture was maintained in Western Europe in the Benedictine abbeys which were the great sources of learning and literary production.

No doubt in theory the episcopal cities were also centres of learning, and it was the bishop rather than the monastery who was directly responsible for carrying out the programme of Christian education as laid down in the capitularies of the Carolingian emperors. Moreover, the personal influence of the ruler often caused the Court and the School of the Palace to be centres of intellectual activity and cultural leadership. But in both cases the actual achievement was due to the monks, who were equally prominent in the episcopal cities and in the courts of Anglo-Saxon, Carolingian and German rulers. It is difficult to separate the traditions of the school of York from that of Bede and Benedict Biscop, and the tradition of the school of the Carolingian palace from that of Tours, and Corbie, and Fulda. Even in the eleventh century, when the economic revival of Western Europe had already begun, Monte Cassino under the abbacy of Desiderius (1058–87) was the most advanced centre of culture in Italy; while north of the Alps the Abbey of Bec under Lanfranc and St. Anselm (c. 1045–93) not only possessed one of the most famous and influential public schools of the time, but in the early writings of Anselm himself attained a level of intellectual achievement such as Western Europe had not known for more than six centuries since the days of St. Augustine.

Nevertheless, by the eleventh century Bec and Monte Cassino were exceptional, and the leadership in education and learning was passing to the cathedral schools of Northern France and Lorraine, such as Reims, Chartres, Laon, Tournai and Liége. This development had started in the previous century at Liége under Bishop Notker, and at Reims under Gerbert of Aurillac, who was *scholasticus* or master of the school from 970 to 982. The tradition was carried on by St. Fulbert at Chartres and by Adalbero at Laon, and extended in the course of the eleventh century to Tournai and Paris and Tours and Angers and Le Mans. But perhaps the most remarkable example of the eleventh-century cathedral school is to be found at Liége, where the monastic schools of the diocese produced a sort of rudimentary university to which scholars were attracted from many parts of Europe, not only from France and Germany, but from Anglo-Saxon England and (in the case of Cosmas of Prague) from remote Bohemia. But the struggle between the Empire and the Papacy and the loyalty of Liége to Henry IV destroyed the pre-eminence of this "Second Athens" at the very moment when the intellectual revival was becoming pronounced.

Guibert of Nogent, who wrote in the beginning of the twelfth century, describes in his autobiography how before his day and even in his youth there was such a lack of schoolmasters that they could hardly be found save in the most important cities, and even their knowledge was scanty and "hardly equal to that of the wandering clerks"—*clericulis vagantibus*—of "modern times", when, as he writes elsewhere, letters were so flourishing and the number of schools so great that they were accessible even to the poorest.

For about this time, in the last decade of the eleventh century and the first two decades of the twelfth, there was already a remarkable revival of culture and literary activity which was not identified with any particular cathedral school but was common to the Western provinces of France—Maine, Anjou, Touraine and Normandy—and found its patrons in the Anglo-Norman court of Henry I and that of his sister, Adela of Blois. The leading figure in this movement was Hildebert of Lavardin, teacher and Bishop of Le Mans and afterwards Archbishop of Tours (1056–1133), perhaps the most accomplished Latinist of all the Latin poets of the Middle Ages. Closely associated with him were Marbod of Angers (1035–1123), Chancellor and head of the school of Angers and afterwards Bishop of Rennes, and Baudri of Meung sur Loire (1046–1130), who studied at Angers and became Abbot of Bourgeuil (1089) and Archbishop of Dol in 1107, and more remotely connected were Reginald of Faye, south-west of Tours (c. 1040–1109), who became teacher at St. Augustine at Canterbury from 1097, and Raoul of La Tourte (c. 1063–1110), the Master of the monastic school of Fleury.

These men were not philosophers or theologians, but poets and humanists who prided themselves on their knowledge of the classics and delighted in the society of scholars and learned ladies with whom they exchanged letters and copies of verses. Thus before the schools of Paris had become famous and before the new vernacular literature had been developed at the feudal courts, there was already an ecclesiastical courtly culture which foreshadowed the later development of Western humanism and set a new ideal of literary education and social intercourse.

It is hardly an exaggeration to say that this type of ec-

clesiastical humanism represents the central tradition of
higher culture in the West. It looks back to the revival of
learning in the Carolingian period, which also had been
represented in the same region by Alcuin at Tours, Theodulf at Orléans and Lupus Servatus at Ferrières; and forward to the early Italian humanism of Petrarch in the
fourteenth century. Throughout the twelfth century it was
exceptionally flourishing in the Anglo-Norman and Anglo-
Angevin kingdom and had an important centre in the
households of Archbishop Theobald (1139–64) and St.
Thomas Becket (1164–70) at Canterbury, as well as at the
royal court.

Here the spirit of medieval humanism found its most
complete embodiment in John of Salisbury, the great
English scholar, who after his studies at Paris and Chartres
became the secretary of Archbishop Theobald and was later
the companion of St. Thomas in his exile and at his death,
finally becoming Bishop of Chartres in 1176. His works give
a more complete picture of the intellectual life of his time
than anything in medieval literature. For he was not only a
humanist and a student of the classics like Hildebert or
Marbod, he was also fully initiated into the new dialectical
and philosophical studies of the schools as represented by
his teachers, who included Abelard and Gilbert de la Porree
as well as William de Conches and Richard l'Eveque. He
was, moreover, one of the pioneers of the Aristotelian
revival and perhaps the first to realize the philosophic
importance of the "New Logic", especially the Topics,
which transformed the old scholastic art of disputation into
a theory of science and a science of thought.[1]

Yet at the same time he was fully alive to the dangers
that threatened the new university culture—not only the
tendency towards a barren intellectualism—*dialectica exsan-
guis et sterilis*—but still more the Philistine view of education as a utilitarian preparation for a successful professional
career. In these respects John is faithful to the tradition of
Chartres which in the early part of the twelfth century
under the brothers Bernard and Thierry and their disciple
William of Conches had rivalled Paris as a centre of

[1] Cf. *Metalogicon*, III, v: *De utilitate Topicorum*.

philosophy and surpassed it as a school of classical and humane learning. Chartres was the last and greatest of the pre-university cathedral schools, and thanks to John of Salisbury and the two educational treatises of Thierry and William of Conches, the *Heptateuchon* and the *Dragmaticon*, we have fuller information about the educational methods and ideals of the school of Chartres than we possess for the great medieval universities in the following century.

But when John of Salisbury wrote, the university movement was already far advanced. Paris and Bologna were thronged with crowds of students from every part of Christendom, and the Bohemian life of the needy and turbulent scholars had already become a favourite subject for poets and satirists. This new class was no longer contented with the patient scholarship and strict discipline of the old cathedral schools as represented by Chartres. It was an intellectual proletariat of needy and ambitious students, contemptuous of the past, impatient of restraint, following the fashionable teacher and doctrine of the moment.

Already at the beginning of the twelfth century the fame of Abelard had made Paris one of the most popular centres of teaching in France, and by the middle of the century the multiplication of schools and the competition of rival teachers had made it the intellectual capital of Christendom. During the twelfth century the schools of Paris gradually achieved their corporate organization, which culminated in the formation of the great *universitas* or corporation of "masters" or licensed teachers under the control of the Chancellor, and it became the archetype and standard of most of the universities which were subsequently constituted in Northern Europe.

But though Paris surpassed all other medieval universities in its intellectual activity and in its corporate authority as the intellectual organ of Christendom, it was equalled and perhaps surpassed both in seniority and in social prestige by the great Italian university which represents a different tradition and a different type of organization. The University of Bologna held a similar position in Italy to that which the University of Paris held in France. As the latter university became the great international school of theology and philosophy for the whole of Western Christendom, so Bologna from the beginning was the great international centre of legal studies. But while the University of Paris throughout the Middle Ages was essentially a clerical institution, Bologna was largely a lay university where the lawyers and officials, who played such a large part in the government of the Italian cities, received their education.

No doubt the development of the study of the Canon Law which was associated with the work of Gratian about 1140 made Bologna an equally important centre of training for the administrators and lawyers of the medieval Church. But it was as a school of Roman law that Bologna first became famous in the days of Irnerius (c. 1090–1130), and it was the civilians, not the canonists who set the standard and determined the course of studies.

Already in the first half of the twelfth century the doctor of Civil Law enjoyed extraordinary prestige, as we see from the part taken by the Four Doctors of Bologna at the Diet of Roncaglia in 1158.[2] Moreover, the students at Bologna also possessed a much higher position, due in part to their more mature age and higher social position, than the clerical students of Paris and Oxford. From a very early date they began to manage their own affairs and control their conditions of study, so that Bologna and the Italian universities which followed its tradition were essentially student corporations that ultimately asserted their control over their teachers whom they treated as their employees rather than their masters.

This strange system which is so different from the hierarchical ecclesiastical order of the Northern universities is closely related to the development of Italian communal institutions. The universities were in fact student communes based, like the city commune itself, on the moral and legal bond of the common oath. This relation has been

---

[2] Rashdall writes that "no teachers perhaps in the whole history of education had hitherto occupied quite so high a position in public estimation as the early doctors of Bologna".

admirably described by Dr. Rashdall in the following passage from his classical book on the Medieval Universities.

The conception of citizenship prevalent in the Italian republics, he writes, *was much nearer to the old Greek conception than that which prevails in modern states. Citizenship which is with us a mere accident of domicile was in ancient Athens and medieval Bologna an hereditary possession of priceless value. . . . Prolonged exile was therefore a serious penalty to which a body of young men of good position, many of them old enough to be entering on political life in their own cities, would naturally submit with reluctance. The student universities represent an attempt on the part of such men to create for themselves an artificial citizenship in place of the natural citizenship which they had temporarily renounced in the pursuit of knowledge or advancement; and the great importance of a* studium *to the commercial welfare of the city in which it was situated may explain the ultimate willingness of the municipalities—though the concession was not made without a struggle—to recognize the student universities.*[3]

It is difficult to overestimate the influence of Bologna on the revival of jurisprudence and the study of Roman law in Western Europe. It was the great centre to which students of law resorted from all over Europe and from which teachers like Vacarius in England and Azo and Placentinus in France went out to carry the seeds of the new learning. But it was in the life of the Italian city-states that this influence was strongest. Almost every important city tried to attract teachers from Bologna and to possess a law school of its own, and the numerous universities which were founded in Italy in the Middle Ages, with the exception of Frederick II's state creation at Naples, were all based on the Bolognese model of a free student corporation and devoted themselves, above all, to the study of law.

All this may seem remote from the history of the relation of religion to Western culture. But the medieval revival

[3] Rashdall, *Medieval Universities*, edited by Powicke and Emden, I, 164.

of Roman law was intimately related to the growth of the new Canon Law which played such a great part in the integration and organization of medieval Christendom.

The growth of the new Canon Law coincided with the reform of the Papacy and was an essential condition of the centralization of authority and jurisdiction in the Pope and the Roman Curia. But it was not until Gratian, a monk of Bologna, produced, about the year 1140, his great treatise, the *Decretum*, in which all the existing material was classified and arranged in the spirit of the new jurisprudence, that the study of the subject was put on a scientific basis. Henceforward Bologna became the great centre for the teaching of Canon as well as of Civil Law. Alexander III, one of the greatest of the medieval pontiffs, was the pupil and commentator of Gratian. Innocent III was the pupil of Uguccio of Pisa, who taught at Bologna in the latter part of the twelfth century.

In fact throughout the central period of the Middle Ages from 1150 to 1350 it was the canonists and the University of Bologna rather than the theologians and the University of Paris who stood nearest to the Papacy and had the strongest influence on the government and organization of the Church. This was deplored by the conservatives like St. Bernard and Gerhoh of Reichersberg, and by idealists like Roger Bacon and Dante. It was, however, to the Canonists that the actual organization of the medieval Church was due. The fact that this work was done by men trained in the same school and the same traditions as the Civilians who during the same period were organizing and rationalizing the medieval state was of the first importance for the history of Western institutions. And it was in the life of the Italian cities that this process of interaction was most complete. The rulers and officials of the city-state and the administrators of the Church were drawn from the same classes, educated in the same universities and shared the same intellectual background; so that there was a continual process of mutual criticism which stimulated the growth of an educated public opinion, such as did not yet exist in Northern Europe.

In Northern Europe the influence of Bologna and the

revival of legal studies made themselves felt from a very early period on the higher level of ecclesiastical and royal government. It is true that Bologna was by no means the only centre of legal studies. Apart from the Italian universities, like Padua, which were immediately derived from it, it was the model for many other later foundations like Lerida, while in France Orléans and Toulouse possessed important schools of law. Nevertheless as Paris possessed a unique prestige as the centre of Christian philosophy and theological studies, so Bologna—*Bononia docta*—was the legal teacher of Europe from which, as Honorius III writes in his Bull of 1220, "went forth the leaders who rule the Christian people"; so that for centuries Paris and Bologna were the opposite poles round which the world of medieval studies revolved. While the great Italian philosophers, like St. Bonaventure, St. Thomas, Matthew of Acquasparta and Aegidius of Rome gravitated to Paris, clerics from Northern Europe who looked forward to a public career in the Church studied at Bologna, where they constituted an independent corporation—the *Universitas Ultramontanorum*. And the Bologna degree—especially the double doctorate of Civil and Canon Laws—was generally regarded as the highest academic honour in the world.

But in spite of the contrast in spirit and institutions between Paris and Bologna, they both contributed equally to the transformation of Western education and to the formation of the professional intellectual classes which were henceforth to dominate Western culture. In the past the spiritual unity of Christendom had been realized in a common faith and a common moral or ascetic discipline which was the tradition of Western monasticism. It was only with the rise of the universities that Western culture acquired that new intellectual and scientific discipline on which its later achievements were dependent.

It is true that this aspect of medieval culture was for centuries ignored or derided. The Humanists despised the Schoolmen for their bad Latin, and the scientists and philosophers attacked them for their degenerate and "vermiculate" Aristotelianism.[4] It is only in recent times that men like A. N. Whitehead have recognized that modern science itself could hardly have come into existence had not the Western mind been prepared by centuries of intellectual discipline to accept the rationality of the universe and the power of the human intelligence to investigate the order of nature.

Clearly the fact that the educated classes of Europe for centuries underwent a rigorous and elaborate training in the art of logical thinking must have left a mark on European culture, as was recognized a century ago by Sir William Hamilton and J. S. Mill. But I believe we can go further than this, and see in the medieval scholastic discipline one of the main factors which have differentiated European civilization from the great religion-cultures of the East, to which the earlier medieval culture and that of the Byzantine Empire were so closely akin. No doubt the Roman tradition which survived in Western culture may have been responsible for the social activity and the constructive political sense that were distinctive of the Western Church since the days of St. Gregory or even St. Leo the Great, but this Roman tradition with its sense of the value of discipline and law and authority was essentially a conservative force. It was not thence that Europe derived the critical intelligence and the restless spirit of scientific enquiry which have made Western civilization the heir and successor of the Greeks. It is usual to date the coming of this new element from the Renaissance and the revival of Greek studies in the fifteenth century, but the real turning point must be placed three centuries earlier in the age of the universities and the communes. Already at Paris in the days of Abelard and John of Salisbury the passion for dialectic and the spirit of philosophic speculation had begun to transform the intellectual atmosphere of Christendom. And from that time forward the higher studies were dominated by the technique of logical discussion—the *quaestio* and the public disputation which so largely determined the *form* of medieval philosophy even in its

[4] Cf. Francis Bacon's famous passage in *The Advancement of Learning*, I, iii, 3.

greatest representatives. "Nothing," says Robert of Sorbonne, "is known perfectly which has not been masticated by the teeth of disputation," and the tendency to submit every question, from the most obvious to the most abstruse, to this process of mastication not only encouraged readiness of wit and exactness of thought but above all developed that spirit of criticism and methodic doubt to which Western culture and modern science have owed so much.

No doubt this passion for disputation and logical analysis also led to an immense waste of intellectual energy on barren controversies. At the beginning of the scholastic age John of Salisbury remarked that more energy had been spent during the last fifty years on the controversy concerning universals than the Romans had spent in the conquest of their empire. And at the end of the Middle Ages, the perverse subtilty of the Occamists and Terminists went far to justify the violence of the Humanist reaction. Nevertheless between these two points there was a period of great and fruitful intellectual achievement which was not confined to logical and metaphysical studies, but extended to every field of knowledge, including the natural sciences.

Hitherto I have been mainly concerned with the two great universities of Paris and Bologna which were the main centres of theological and legal studies and the archetypes of the whole university movement. But there was also a third tradition, represented by the schools of Salerno and Montpellier and Toledo and the court of Palermo, which was of the greatest intellectual importance, though it had little influence on the institutional development of the medieval university. For this was the channel by which Greek and Arabic science reached the Western world, and from which the medieval culture of the thirteenth and fourteenth centuries derived its knowledge of Aristotle not merely as a logician, but as a metaphysician, a physicist and a biologist.

We have seen how, during the Dark Ages, the Western Mediterranean had been separated from Christian Europe and had been the centre of a brilliant cultural development derived from the Islamic East. And it was here, rather than in the crusading states of Syria and the Latin Empire of Constantinople, that the East and West came into contact with one another, and the vital process of cultural transmission and adaptation took place.

The process began in Southern Italy, where in the second half of the eleventh century an African monk of Monte Cassino, Constantine, initiated the work of translation, and the school of Salerno became a meeting-place of Greek, Arabic and Jewish influences, at least in medical studies. But it was in Spain that the main work of translation took place, above all at Toledo, where the Archbishop, Raymond of Sauvetat (1126–51) established a school of translators which continued its activity through the twelfth and thirteenth centuries, so that Toledo for a time became equal to Paris and Bologna as a factor in medieval culture. The scholars of Toledo not only translated into Latin the whole Aristotelian corpus in its Arabic form, they also produced versions of the principal works of the great Moslem and Jewish philosophers and men of science: Al Kindi, Al Farabi, Al Battani, Avicenna, Ibn Gebirol and Al Ghazali. Finally there were original thinkers, like Domingo Gonzalez, the Archdeacon of Segovia, who first attempted to make a new synthesis between the philosophy of Avicenna (itself a synthesis of the Aristotelian and Neo-platonic traditions), with the Augustinian tradition of Latin Christianity.

The most striking thing about this movement was its cosmopolitan character. Jews and Arabs and Greeks cooperated with Spaniards and Italians and Englishmen. Already at the beginning of the twelfth century an English scholar, Adelard of Bath, who had been educated in the cathedral schools of Northern France, was travelling in Spain, Southern Italy and the Near East and translating the works of Euclid and the ninth-century mathematicians and astronomers of Central Asia such as Al Khwarizmi and Abu Ma'shar of Balkh. To Adelard and his successors—the Italians Plato of Tivoli and Gerard of Cremona, and the Englishmen Robert of Chester, Daniel of Morley and Alfred of Sereshel—this was like the discovery of a new world, and they called on their compatriots to leave their elementary studies and their barren arguments, and set themselves to school with the Arabs and the ancient Greeks who alone possessed the genuine tradition of scientific and philosophic knowledge.

One might well have supposed that the Mohammedan and pagan origins of the new learning would have prevented its acceptance by Western Christendom, but in spite of the opposition of conservatives and the suspicions of the guardians of orthodoxy the new teaching made its way with remarkable rapidity into the rising universities, so that by the middle of the thirteenth century the works of Aristotle were being studied and commented and discussed at Paris and Oxford and Toulouse and Cologne.

At Paris the main effort of the numerous *summas* and commentaries on the Sentences of Peter Lombard was directed to the interpretation of theology in terms of Aristotelian metaphysics and their mutual integration. At Oxford, on the other hand, under the influence of Robert Grosseteste and the Franciscan school, it was the scientific and mathematical aspects of the new learning that were most studied and gave the school of Oxford its original character.

Finally, the Aristotelian tradition was represented in its purest and most uncompromising form by the teaching of the Spanish Moslem Averroes (Ibn Rushd, 1126–98), whose works were translated after 1217 by Michael Scot (d. 1232), the court astrologer of Frederick II, and found enthusiastic disciples in Siger of Brabant and his followers in the University of Paris from 1270 to 1280, and at Bologna and Padua in the fourteenth century.

The result of this great influx of new knowledge and new ideas was to provide the universities and the international society of scholars and teachers who frequented them with the materials from which to construct a new intellectual synthesis. The dialecticians were no longer compelled to masticate and remasticate the old scholastic commonplaces. They had at last something solid to get their teeth into. And for a hundred years there was, in consequence, such a development of philosophical studies as the world had not seen since the great age of ancient Greece. The effect on general culture may be seen in a unique form in the *Divina Commedia* of Dante, the greatest literary achievement of the Middle Ages, in which every aspect of life and every facet of personal and historic experience is illuminated by a metaphysical vision of the universe as an intelligible unity. And behind the *Divina Commedia* there is the work of St. Thomas and St. Albert and a hundred lesser men, all of them devoted to the building up of a great structure of thought in which every aspect of knowledge is co-ordinated and subordinated to the divine science —*Theologia*—the final transcendent end of every created intelligence.

The great interest of this synthesis is not its logical completeness, for that was to be found already in a rudimentary form in the traditional curriculum of the earlier medieval schools, but rather the way in which the mind of Western Christendom reconquered the lost world of Hellenic science and annexed the alien world of Moslem thought without losing its spiritual continuity or its specifically religious values. No doubt all this was questioned by the later critics of scholasticism, like Luther and his contemporaries who maintained that medieval philosophy had abandoned evangelical truth to follow Aristotle and the vain deceits of human wisdom. But in order to maintain this view they were compelled to push their condemnation further, and to condemn the whole tradition of Western Catholicism right back to the age of the Fathers.

But if we look at the development of Western Christendom as a whole, it is clear that the intellectual synthesis of the thirteenth century was not a contradiction but the crown and completion of centuries of continuous effort to achieve an integration of the religious doctrine of the Christian Church with the intellectual tradition of ancient culture. This aim was already set out in a rudimentary form by the encyclopaedists of the sixth and seventh centuries like Cassiodorus and Boethius and Isidore of Seville, but it was not completely achieved until the thirteenth century with the recovery of the full inheritance of Greek philosophy and science, and with the creation of the new intellectual organs of Christendom—the university corporations and the Orders of Friars.

The co-ordination of these two organs by the deliberate policy of the Papacy in the thirteenth century marked the final and decisive step in the intellectual organization of Christendom. But it was not achieved without a severe struggle, for in spite of the revival of learning and the progress of the schools during the twelfth century, the attempts of the Popes and the councils to provide for the education of the clergy by a canonical system of endowed teachers in every episcopal and archiepiscopal see had been generally ignored or neglected. It is even possible that the increasing popularity of the new universities, especially Bologna, had a detrimental effect on clerical education as compared with the older type of cathedral school owing to their concentration on legal studies at the expense of theology. Consequently when St. Dominic founded his Order of preachers to combat the spread of heresy in Southern France, Honorius III and his adviser, Cardinal Ugolino, saw the opportunity to create a new institution which would carry out the programme of the Conciliar legislation and provide the theological teachers which the secular clergy had been unable to produce.

It was in the new universities, above all the University of Paris, that the new Order found its most fruitful field of work. For it was not only among the Albigensians of Languedoc that Christian orthodoxy was threatened by new forms of heresy. At Paris itself the introduction of Arabic philosophy and Aristotelian science was accompanied by the spread of pantheistic theories, and their condemnation in 1210 and 1215 had been accompanied by the prohibition of Aristotelian physics and metaphysics. Yet this prohibition could not be maintained indefinitely. Even William of Auvergne, the greatest representative of the older tradition of philosophy in the first half of the thirteenth century, who was bishop of Paris from 1228 to 1247, recognized the value of Aristotelian science and of the Arabic and Jewish philosophies that were based upon it. The problem was to construct a philosophic synthesis which would unite the scientific truth contained in the teachings of the philosophers with the religious truth represented by the tradition of the Church and the teaching of the theologians.

The solution of this problem was the intellectual mission of the new Order. As early as 1217 the first Dominicans were sent to Paris and Bologna. In 1221 they were at Oxford and in 1229 they were put in charge of the theological faculty of the new university that was established by the joint action of the Papacy and the King of France at Toulouse. Their example was soon followed by the Franciscans, in spite of their original diversity of aims; and from the middle of the thirteenth century all the leading theologians and philosophers with two or three exceptions belonged to one or other of the great mendicant Orders— Alexander of Hales and Bonaventure, Albert the Great and Thomas Aquinas, Roger Bacon and Thomas of York, Robert Kilwardby and John Peckham, Matthew of Acquasparta and Duns Scotus. But the dominant position of the Friars in the intellectual life of the medieval university was not attained without a struggle, and it required all the authority and persistence of the Papacy to overcome the resistance of the University of Paris. It was a conflict between the proudest and most independent corporation in Christendom and the concentrated powers of the new religious Orders supported by the Papacy. Both St. Thomas and St. Bonaventure were involved in the controversy and it threatened the very existence of the University, since the latter at the height of the struggle resorted to the desperate measure of putting an end to its corporate existence by a solemn act of dissolution.

The passion aroused by the controversy may be seen not only in the writings of the protagonists—e.g. in William of St. Amour's diatribe against the Friars, *On the Perils of the Last Times*, and St. Thomas's pamphlet *Contra Impugnatores Cultus Dei*—but also in the vernacular poetry of Rutebeuf and Jean de Meung, both of whom were violent partisans of the University. And we see in the *Romance of the Rose* how a quarrel which originated in the conflicting interests of two branches of the clergy—the regulars and the seculars—acquired a secularist and "anticlerical" character which foreshadows the future secularization of Western culture.

On the other side, however, there is no trace of any intention to lessen the prestige and authority of the University as such. On the contrary the Bull of Alexander IV in 1255 in support of the Friars—*Quasi lignum vitae*—shows very clearly that it was the policy of the Papacy to recognize the unique and sovereign position of the University of Paris in the intellectual life of Christendom. "The science of the schools of Paris," it declares, "is in the Church like the Tree of Life in the terrestrial paradise, a shining lamp in the temple of the soul. . . . It is at Paris that the human race, deformed by original sin and blinded by ignorance, recovers its power of vision and its beauty, by the knowledge of the true light shed forth by divine science."

There can, in fact, be little doubt that the creation of the universities and the formation of the new religious Orders alike formed part of the far-reaching design of the medieval Papacy for the intellectual organization of Christian civilization, which is one of the most remarkable examples of the planning of culture on a large scale that history has ever seen.

This ideal of the universal organization of human knowledge and human life by a spiritual principle was not confined to the international government of the Church; it is the dominant spirit of thirteenth-century culture. It is to be seen in rather a crude and naïve form in the work of encyclopaedists like Vincent of Beauvais and Bartholomeus Anglicus. It inspired Roger Bacon's immense survey of all existing and possible science, of which the *Opus Majus*, the *Opus Minus* and the *Opus Tertium* are the fragments. It finds an almost perfect literary expression in Dante's epic, and it was embodied in visible form in the great French cathedrals. But, above all, it found supreme expression in the philosophic systems of the thirteenth century— those great "cathedrals of ideas", as Professor Gilson has called them, in which all the acquisitions of Aristotelian and Arabic science have been organically incorporated with the Christian tradition in an intelligible unity.

But though this intellectual achievement marks the

culmination of the medieval development, it did not become the foundation of a unitary religion-culture as we might have expected. On the contrary, it inaugurated a period of intellectual criticism and cultural change which is of the utmost importance for the history of Western culture, but proved fatal to the synthesis of religion and culture that seemed to have been achieved in the previous centuries.

At first sight this is a surprising development, for Western civilization did not undergo any external catastrophe such as the Mongol conquest which overwhelmed the most flourishing centres of thirteenth-century Moslem culture in Central Asia. Nor was there any slackening of intellectual activity, and the university movement continued to grow. It was rather that the movement towards integration and unity which had dominated Western Christendom since the eleventh century had lost its impetus and no longer found leaders capable of carrying it forward to new achievements.

The fourteenth century was an age of division and strife, the age of the Great Schism, which saw instead of the Crusades the invasion of Europe by the Turks and the devastation of France by England.[5] And at the same time the intellectual resources of Western society which had been so much strengthened by the extension of the university movement no longer assisted the integration of Christian thought but were used negatively and critically to undo the work of the previous century and undermine the intellectual foundations on which the synthesis of the great thinkers of the previous age had been built. It is as though the spiritual tide which had been steadily making for unity for three centuries had suddenly turned, so that everywhere in every aspect of life the forces that made for division and dissolution were predominant.

[5] Cf. Denifle's remarkable work, *La désolation des églises, monastères et hôpitaux en France pendant la guerre de Cents Ans,* 2 vols., 1899.

Chapter XI

The Religious Crisis of Medieval Culture: The Thirteenth Century

THROUGHOUT the period of which I have been speaking during the last three chapters, the spiritual life of Western culture was dominated by the movement of religious reform which came to maturity in the second half of the eleventh century. The emancipation of the Church from imperial and feudal control and the assertion of the primacy of the spiritual power set free new spiritual forces and created the new international society of medieval Christendom. Few, if any, of the historians of the Middle Ages have done justice to the importance of the reforming movement as a continuous dynamic influence on medieval culture. Those who are most sympathetic to the medieval culture have been impressed by its religious unity and the harmony of medieval Christendom, while its critics have always stressed its traditionalism and its blind obedience to ecclesiastical authority. Neither party has paid sufficient attention to the element of conflict which characterized the creative centuries of the Middle Ages. For the great debate which began with the reforming movement of the eleventh century was not a temporary politic-ecclesiastical conflict that was ended in 1122 by the Concordat of Worms; it was inherited from generation to generation and passed from one country to another through the whole course of medieval history. And the creative centuries of medieval culture owed their unity, not to the absence of strife, but to the fact that the party of reform, which was the dynamic element in medieval culture, for a time attained a position of cultural leadership through its alliance with the governing element in the Church. When this alliance was broken at the close of the thirteenth century, the spiritual unity and the creative power of medieval culture gradually disappeared.

During the eleventh and twelfth centuries, however, the reforming movement was a principle of unity rather than division. It united the most active elements in Christian society in a common programme round a common centre of unity. It broke down the barriers of feudal class privilege and territorial particularism and gave new opportunities for spiritual leadership and the free choice of individual vocations. It brought the monk out of his cloister, the bishop out of his diocese and the knight out of his fief and made them all conscious of their place in the common life of Christendom and their participation in a common cause.

This widening of the horizon is to be seen first in the new monastic movements which preceded the general movement of reform and contributed so much to it. The age of reform was characterized by a new type of monasticism which was to become characteristic of Western Christendom. In order to carry out the work of monastic reform it had proved necessary to sacrifice the traditional autonomy of the individual monastery and organize a number of reformed communities under the direction and jurisdiction of a mother house. The most famous example of this tendency was the Cluniac movement, which organized a whole hierarchy of monastic communities under the absolute control of the Abbot of Cluny. By the time of St. Hugh (1049–1109) there were more than eight hundred monasteries affiliated to Cluny in France, Italy, Germany and Spain, so that the congregation had become a great international power in the life of Christendom. This process of organization was carried still further in the new monastic movements that arose at the beginning of the twelfth century, above all by the Cistercians, as organized by St. Stephen Harding early in the century, which was the first genuine religious *Order* in the later sense of the word. This first established the principle of corporate control by

an annual general chapter of the whole Order and a system
of mutual visitation and inspection. Thus the abbey was no
longer an end in itself; it was part of a larger whole, which
in turn was an organ of the universal society of Christendom.

This tendency towards the socialization of the monastic
ideal was at once a cause and an effect of the reforming
movement. The reformed Papacy was, as we have seen,
largely a monastic creation, and it found its ablest and most
disinterested helpers in the reformed monastic order. St.
Peter Damian, Humbert of Moyenmoutier, St. Hugh of
Cluny, Lanfranc and St. Anselm, Richard the abbot of
St. Victor at Marseilles, and many more, were monks who
left their cloisters to work for the reform of the Church.
Urban II, the Pope who carried the reforming programme
to triumph, and who was also responsible for the launching
of the First Crusade, was a former prior of Cluny. And in
the twelfth century this tradition of monastic reform finds
its supreme representative in St. Bernard, who was at once
the embodiment of the ascetic ideals of Cistercian monasticism and the greatest public figure in the life of his time.
In spite of his profound devotion to the monastic ideals of
contemplation and penance, he was also a great man of
action of the type of Gregory VII. His influence was felt
at every point where the interests of Christendom were at
stake, ending the Papal schism of 1130–38, restoring peace
between Christian princes and launching the Second Crusade. Above all, he was the champion of the Gregorian ideal
of uncompromising spiritual reform, and applied the principles of the eleventh-century reformers to the changed circumstances of a new age.

For, as we have seen, the victory of the Church created
new problems and new temptations. In so far as the spiritual authority of the Papacy was embodied in a concrete
system of international government, it was forced to make
use of temporal means, above all a system of revenue and
finance. And since there was as yet no system of ecclesiastical taxation, the medieval Papacy, like the medieval
state, was driven to use its rights of jurisdiction as a source

of revenue—a system which inevitably led to abuse and to the exploitation of litigants and local churches by the Curia and the Papal legates.

It was against these abuses that St. Bernard addressed the severe criticism of the Papal administration of his great treatise *de Consideratione*, which was addressed to his disciple the Cistercian Pope Eugenius III. He complains that the increase of litigation has turned the Curia into a secular law court.

The Palace resounds with the sound of laws, but they are the laws of Justinian, not those of the Lord. Is not the enriching of ambition the object of the whole laborious practice of the laws and canons? Is not all Italy a yawning gulf of insatiable avarice and rapacity for the spoil it offers? So that the Church has become like a robber's cave, full of the plunder of travellers.[1]

Against these evils of the Curia and this tendency towards an ecclesiastical imperialism which made the Pope the successor of Constantine rather than Peter, St. Bernard sets up the reformer's ideal of the prophetic and apostolic mission of a true Pope set over the nations to destroy, and root up, to build and to plant, "a mission that suggests the heavy labour of the peasant rather than the pomp of a ruler. For if you are to do the work of a prophet you need the hoe rather than the sceptre".[2]

In all this St. Bernard was far from wishing to diminish the claims of the reformed Papacy to universal authority. In fact these claims have never been more passionately asserted than in the tremendous passages which conclude this treatise. His condemnation was directed entirely against the secularizing tendencies which accompanied the growth of ecclesiastical power and centralization and had produced the same confusion between spiritual authority and temporal power as had existed in the old Carolingian imperial state Church against which the reformers had revolted. For the victory of the Papacy and the weakening of the power of the Emperor or the prince over the clergy had not

[1] S. Bern., *de Consideratione*, II, vi.
[2] Ibid.

fundamentally changed the nature of the medieval Church in its feudal and territorial aspects. As the great ecclesiastical magnates had formerly used the imperial or regal control of the Church to increase their political power and wealth, so now they used the Church's freedom and its claim to independent jurisdiction in order to strengthen their position still further. As an American historian has written:

> Certainly not the state nor yet the church was the ultimate winner in the great controversy. The prince-bishops and warlike abbots of Germany, with their worldly ways, their hard faces, their political interests, lords of church lands that were actually huge ecclesiastical fiefs, and the German feudality were the real victors of the war.[3]

The perplexity and despair of the reformers in face of this tragic confusion is clearly expressed by Gerhoh of Reichersberg (1093–1169), one of the greatest representatives of the spiritual party in the German Church during the twelfth century. He remained faithful to the cause of the Papacy on the question of the Investitures, and, during the great struggle between the Emperor Frederick I and Pope Alexander III, endured persecution and exile on behalf of his principles. But at the same time he censured the views of the extreme papalist party which asserted the direct power of the Papacy over the Empire. In his last work, which he entitled *The Fourth Watch of the Night*, written in exile two years before his death, he is concerned, like St. Bernard, with the perils that threatened the Church from the avarice and ambition of her rulers. He saw the coming of the end, not in the external distress and persecution of the Church, but in its corruption from within by the "Jewish and pagan avarice that reigns in the very Kingdom of Christ" and makes Rome a second Babylon. In despair he looks to the speedy coming of Christ as the only hope of the Church. *Come then, Lord Jesus,* he prays, *come to Thy ship, the Holy Church, which is labouring heavily in this Fourth Watch of the Night; come O Lord, rule in the midst of Thine enemies, the false priests who sell and rob in Thine house and the princes who tyrannize in the name of Christ. Come, Saviour Jesus, working salvation in the midst of the earth and the midst of the Church, making peace between the Kingdom and the Priesthood.*[4]

This sense of imminent crisis, of the pressing need for moral reform and spiritual renovation, runs through all the religious thought of the twelfth century. That century which seems to us the Golden Age of medieval Catholicism —the age of St. Anselm and St. Bernard, the age of the Crusades and the Cathedrals, of the new religious Orders and the new schools—appeared to contemporaries dark with the threat of the coming doom. Their attitude is summed up in the opening lines of Bernard of Morlais' great rhythm, *de contemptu mundi.*

Hora novissima, tempora pessima sunt, vigilemus,
Ecce minaciter imminet arbiter ille supremus. . . .[5]

This preoccupation with apocalyptic ideas is characteristic of the mind of the twelfth century. It shows itself in a crude popular form in the vernacular German drama of Antichrist (*c.* 1150) as well as in the learned World History of Otto of Freising and in the theological symbolism of Rupert of Deutz (–1135), Gerhoh of Reichersberg, Honorius Augustodunensis (*c.* 1120) and Anselm of Havelberg (–1158). Above all, it finds expression in the visions and prophecies of Hildegard of Bingen (1098–1179), one of the most original minds of the twelfth century and the first of the great prophetesses of the Middle Ages—the two St. Mechtilds, St. Angela, St. Bridget and St. Catherine of Siena. And it reaches its final culmination in the Calabrian Abbot, Joachim of Flora (–1202), who announced the coming of a new age, the age of the Spirit and the Eternal Gospel in which the Church will be renewed in the liberty of the spirit under the leadership of the new order of Spiritual Contemplatives.

[4] *De Quarta Vigilia Noctis,* 21. *Lib. de Lite,* Tom. III, M.G.H.
[5] The world is very evil; the times are waxing late;
Be sober and keep vigil; the Judge is at the gate.

These tendencies were by no means a proof of religious or cultural decline. On the contrary, they show how deeply men's minds had been stirred by the religious awakening and their awareness of the imminence of a new age. Nor were they confined to the educated minority—to the leaders of the reforming movement in the clergy and the monastic Orders: they had already begun to affect the new society that was coming into existence in the medieval city. As early as 1058 the reforming movement had become identified in Milan and the cities of Lombardy with the revolt of the popular faction against the bishops and the ruling nobles; and half a century later, in the Low Countries, the anti-Gregorian writer Sigebert of Gembloux complains of the revolutionary propaganda against the established order in Church and State that was heard in the workshops and factories, making the common people the judges of the clergy and denying the validity of the sacraments administered by married or simoniac priests.[6]

This uncompromising denunciation of the worldliness and corruption of the existing state of the Church by the reformers and still more the denial of the validity of the orders and the sacraments of the unreformed clergy by the more extreme representatives of the reforming movement, like Humbert of Moyenmoutier, recall the uncompromising rigorism which characterized the old Western heresies, like Novatianism and Donatism. Thus it is not surprising that the reforming movement coincided with the reappearance of heresy and sectarian activity in the West, and that there was even a certain confusion between the two movements, as we see in the case of the priest of Schere who was burnt at Cambrai, in 1077, as an heresiarch who stirred up the common people, although he was regarded by Gregory VII as an orthodox defender of the cause of reform. In the same way the Patarine movement in Northern Italy which began in close alliance with the reformed Papacy eventually became so contaminated with unorthodox elements that the name of Patarines eventually became the colloquial Italian term for heretics.

[6] Cf. esp. his letter to Archdeacon Henry in Martène and Durand, Thesaurus novus, I, 230.

We see how this transition from orthodoxy to heresy took place in the case of Arnold of Brescia, the disciple of Abelard and the opponent of St. Bernard, who was one of the leading figures in Italian society in the first half of the twelfth century. He first became involved in the conflict between the commune and the Bishop of Brescia—a struggle which began, as at Milan in the previous century, with an alliance of the commune and reformers against the imperialist bishop, but which was still carried on after the election of a reforming bishop supported by Rome. In Arnold's view the real cause of the conflict was the temporal power of the bishop and the wealth of the Church, and the true solution was to be found in a return to the poverty of the primitive Church. In this he did not go much further than many orthodox reformers, like Pope Paschal II himself who had attempted to solve the conflict with the Empire in 1111 by a wholesale abandonment of the temporal authority and privileges of the Church. But Arnold went much further when he asserted that priests who held property or exercised temporal authority could not be saved; that everything temporal must be resigned to the prince and the laity, and the Church must return to a state of evangelical poverty.

John of Salisbury, who gives a remarkably impartial account of Arnold's career, says that what he taught was in agreement with Christian ideals but quite irreconcilable with life,[7] and so long as he remained in exile in France and at Zurich, he seems to have been regarded as an unworldly and impracticable idealist. But when he returned to Italy and to Rome about 1147 he found himself once more in a revolutionary atmosphere highly favourable to the propagation of his ideas. In 1143 the Roman commune had risen against the Pope and proclaimed the restoration of the Republic. It was an expression of the same communal movement which had led the Lombard cities to revolt against episcopal control. But in Rome the bishop was the spiritual head of Christendom and the city was the heir and embodiment of the immemorial tradition

[7] Hist. Pont., 64.

of classical antiquity, so that the rise of the commune inevitably involved a conflict with international forces: its claim to civic independence touched the interests of the Papacy at its vital centre, while its assumption of the venerable title of "the Senate and People of Rome" was a challenge to the Germanic Empire.

The theories of Arnold of Brescia, which had a purely religious origin, provided the revolutionary commune with an effective ideological justification for its struggle with the Papacy, and for about seven years the reformer threw himself heart and soul into the struggle and became the apologist for the republican cause. But his attempt to arrange an alliance between the commune and the Emperor at the expense of the Papacy proved a failure. The Roman resistance collapsed before the armed power of Frederick Barbarossa. The German Emperor handed him over to the English Pope Hadrian IV and he was executed as a heretic at the same time that Frederick was crowned Emperor.

Thus Arnold's career is typical not only of the alliance between the new social forces and the religious idealism of the extreme reformer, but also of the attempt of the Italian intelligentsia to revive an association between the civic patriotism of the Italian cities and the old traditions of classical Rome.

The same tendency was to find expression in the later Italian Ghibelline movement—in Dante and Cola di Rienzi, as well as in Petrarch—and in all of them we see the same disproportion of spiritual aims and political means. This contradiction between the romantic idealization of "the sacred city of Rome, the mistress of the world, the maker and mother of all the emperors" and the complete failure of the republican party to face political realities finds a dramatic though comic expression in the interview between the deputation of the Senate and the Emperor Frederick in 1155 described by Otto of Freising in which each party considered itself as the only true heir of the tradition of ancient Rome.[8] Nevertheless the civic patriotism of the Italian communes was a real force, as Frederick I experi-

[8] *Gesta Frederici*, lib. II, cap. 29 and 30.

enced when the northern chivalry was broken at Legnano round the "carroccio" of St. Ambrose by the forces of the Lombard League.

And in the same way, in spite of the impracticable nature of Arnold of Brescia's programme, the revolutionary idealism of the religious reformers was also a real force which represented a serious challenge to the traditional order in the Church. During the second half of the twelfth century the Church in Northern Italy and Southern France was threatened by the rapid increase of heretical and sectarian movements, ranging from the oriental dualism of the Catharists, the Western representatives of the Bogomils,[9] through the Arnoldists and Speronists and Lombards to the Poor Men of Lyons and the *Humiliati* which were in origin orthodox lay movements for radical religious reform that came into conflict with the local authorities and gradually or partially lapsed into schism and heresy. These movements were particularly active among the new urban classes, as we see from the way in which the name *Textores*—Weavers—acquired a sectarian significance. But they also appealed to the anticlerical elements among the nobility and the ruling class in the communes. For example, the heresy of Ugo Speroni, which has only recently become known by the discovery of the treatise of Vacarius,[10] the pioneer of legal studies in England, was the result of the private theories of a distinguished lawyer and consul of Piacenza, while in Languedoc some of the greatest nobles in the land, families like Esclamonde of Foix, the widow of Jourdain de l'Isle Jourdain, were practising Catharists.

On the whole the Popes showed a far greater understanding of the importance of this challenge than the Hohenstaufen Emperors showed towards the revolutionary spirit of the communes. They recognized, almost from the beginning, that the sectarian movement involved two essentially dissimilar elements, which demanded two different methods of treatment. On the one hand, the Catharist or

[9] Cf. Ch. VI.
[10] Published by P. Ilarino da Milano in 1945 under the title *L'Eresia di Ugo Speroni*.

Albigensian heresy was not a reformist movement or even an unorthodox form of Christianity. It marked the reappearance of an ancient oriental religion as far or farther removed from Christianity than the religion of Islam. Consequently the Papacy used the same methods as it had employed against the Moslems—the method of the Crusade, and of an appeal to Christian princes to use their power in defence of the faith; a method which was supplemented by a missionary campaign for the reconversion of the affected regions and finally by a code of repressive legislation which gave birth to the Inquisition.

This marks a radical departure from the traditional theory, expressed in the sentence of St. Bernard, *Fides suadenda est non imponenda*. It was largely due to the influence of the revived study of Roman law, since the assimilation of heresy to treason by Innocent III in 1199, although it was in accord with the practice of the medieval state both in the East and the West, follows the precedent of the old civil legislation as represented by the Codex Theodosianus.[11] On this matter Papacy and Empire were at one, and the only question at issue was which power should control the process of repression; and the final organization of the Inquisition by Gregory IX in 1231 was determined by the unwillingness of the Papacy to allow Frederick II a completely free hand in applying his drastic legislation against heresy.

It is, in fact, difficult to separate the new attitude of the Church towards the suppression of heresy from the tendency of the Popes of the thirteenth century to assume a direct responsibility for the control of Christian society as a whole: a tendency which was no doubt conditioned by the circumstances of the great struggle with the Hohenstaufen Emperors and the influence of Roman law, but which was ultimately the logical conclusion of the same unitary theocratic conception of Christian society that had

---

11 The Manichaeans, in particular, had always been persecuted with exceptional severity. Under the code of Justinian they were liable to the death penalty, and this goes back before the conversion of the Empire to the time of Diocletian, who ordered their leaders to be burnt and their followers to be beheaded.

given birth to the Sacred Empire itself. But in contrast to this development of external and legal measures of repression, we find another method directly inspired by the spiritual ideals of the reforming movement and which sought to meet the demands of the dissident lay movements on their own ground. The Papacy recognized that the essential aims of these movements—above all the attempt to lead a life of poverty and evangelical perfection outside the monastic order—were orthodox in principle, and it attempted from the first to discriminate between the groups which rejected the priesthood and the sacraments of the Church and those which desired to fulfil their vocation within the hierarchical order.

Thus it was not until 1184 that a final breach occurred between the Waldensians and the Church, and as late as 1179 they had received conditional approval from the great canonist Pope Alexander III. At the same time the *Humiliati*—a lay movement similar to the Waldensians which flourished among the artisans and populace of Milan and the Lombard communes—never entirely broke away from the Church, but became divided into two branches, one of which received Papal approval and continued to flourish throughout the thirteenth century and later.

It is in relation to these movements that we must view the rise of the Friars Minor. In its origins the Franciscan movement has a considerable resemblance to the Waldensians. It differed from them, above all, by the fact that its founder was one of the greatest religious geniuses in the history of Christendom, a man of the most intense originality who had a profound influence on the spirit of Western Christianity and Western culture. But it also differed in that St. Francis was from the first entirely and wholeheartedly committed to the cause of Catholic unity so that in consequence the Papacy found in his Order an ideal organ for the evangelization of the new classes and the new society which had grown up in the new cities outside the traditional *cadres* of the territorial feudal Church. It is significant that the man who did more than any other to secure the recognition of the new order and its intimate relation with the Papacy was Cardinal Ugolino of Ostia, the future Pope Gregory IX, the organizer of the Inquisition and the leader of the great conflict with Frederick II. Yet this indomitable representative of militant theocracy was the devoted admirer and personal friend of the saint who went further than any Waldensian or Patarine in his pursuit of a purely evangelical way of life based on the literal observance of the words of the Gospel. It is however misleading to speak, as I have done, of the primitive Franciscan community as a religious *Order*. Nothing was further from the mind of St. Francis than the foundation of a monastic order of the traditional type, as we see in the passage of his last Testament in which, after his profession of faith and his loyalty to the Hierarchical Church, he returns once more to the origin and purpose of his way of life.

And after the Lord had given me some brothers, no-one showed me what to do, but the Most High Himself revealed to me that I must live according to the form of the Holy Gospel: this I had written down in few and simple words and the Lord Pope confirmed it for me.

Those of us who were clerics said the office like other clerics, and the laymen said the Paternosters. And very happily we stayed in poor and abandoned churches, and we were ignorant and subject to all men. And I worked with my hands and still wish to work; and it is my firm will that all the other brethren should do some manual labour which belongs to an honest way of life. And those who do not know how to work should learn; not out of cupidity to receive the price of their labour, but in order to give a good example and to banish idleness. And if we should not be given reward for our labour, let us have recourse to the bounty of the Lord and beg our bread from door to door.

The Lord has revealed to me that we should employ this form of salutation: "The Lord give you Peace."[12]

---

[12] Opuscula S. P. Francisci, 76–82. English translation in Karrer, St. Francis of Assisi, 274–76 (1947), and in Cuthbert's Life, 450–55.

For what St. Francis desired was not a new religious Order nor any form of ecclesiastical organization but the following of Christ—a new life which would shake off the encumbrances of tradition and organization and property and learning and recover an immediate personal contact with the divine source of eternal life, as revealed in the Gospel. How was it possible to reconcile such an ideal with the vast and complicated organization of ecclesiastical power represented by such a man as Gregory IX, and with the ancient heritage of intellectual culture and social tradition of which medieval Christendom was the bearer? In one sense it was not possible. The primitive rule was not realized. The Friars Minor became a religious Order, different in form and spirit from the older Orders but no less an integral part of the ecclesiastical organization, and the unlettered laymen of the primitive tradition became one of the great student Orders which dominated the universities and were renowned as philosophers and men of learning.

Yet in spite of all this the spirit of St. Francis remained a creative force in the life of the time, and even literature and art owed more to his inspiration than to any of his learned and cultured contemporaries. In spite of the changes in the character of the "Order" there always remained a remnant faithful to the spirit of their founder and the primitive observance, men like Brother Leo and Brother Giles who had been with the saint from the beginning and bore witness to what they had seen with their own eyes. And it is to this group and their successors in Tuscany and the March of Ancona that we owe the greater part of that remarkable body of tradition—both historical and legendary—in which the image of St. Francis and the spirit of the primitive fraternity have been preserved. But on the other side, the Franciscan movement influenced medieval religion and culture no less through its official ecclesiastical organization as a new religious Order.

Here its development owes much to the example of the other great Order of Friars, the Dominicans, which arose at the same period and was adopted by the Papacy as a new and powerful organ of the Church Militant. Nothing could be more dissimilar than the character and aims of the two founders. St. Dominic had devoted his life to combating the heretical movement in Aragon and Languedoc, and he felt the need of a new organization more flexible and more highly trained than the older religious Orders—one which could devote its whole energy to the struggle with heresy by preaching and the intellectual training of qualified teachers. In these respects his aims were similar to those of the founder of the Jesuits three hundred years later, and like the latter he was, above all, an organizer and a leader of men, whose aim it was to create a corporate instrument for the service of the Church. This was also the aim which Cardinal Ugolino had in mind for the Franciscans, and it is possible that he entertained the idea of a fusion between the two movements when he brought the two founders together at Rome in 1218.[13]

Any scheme of this kind was of course impossible to reconcile with St. Francis's profoundest convictions, nevertheless the influence of authority and the pressure of external circumstances did produce a certain assimilation between the two Orders. The Dominicans accepted the Franciscan principle of corporate poverty and became known as Friars instead of Canons.[14] And on the other side the Franciscans adopted the Dominican ideal of a teaching Order and shared their intellectual activity and their participation in the life of the medieval universities.

Nevertheless, in spite of this, each Order retained its own spiritual character. The Dominicans remained consistently devoted to their original ideal of a teaching Order—the Order of Preachers—while the Franciscans of both Observances and traditions preserved their original mission as preachers of the elementary and essential Christian truths to the common people. Yet both Orders rivalled one another in their activities in the universities and in the life of

[13] Cf. *Thomas of Celano*, II, 150; *Speculum Perfectionis*, 43. J. R. H. Moorman, *Sources for the Life of St. Francis*, 20–21 (1940).

[14] St. Dominic was himself a Canon Regular, and the Dominican Rule was based on that of St. Augustine and of the Premonstratensians, the "White Canons".

the medieval city, as we see for example in the movement to bring peace to the warring factions in the Italian cities in 1230 which was known as the Great Alleluia.

It was the Franciscans who first had the greatest influence on vernacular literature, through their use of verse and minstrelsy in their popular apostolate—a practice which had been initiated by St. Francis himself in his great Canticle of Brother Sun, and which later in the thirteenth century found its most remarkable expression in the *Laudi* of Fra Jacopone of Todi, the poet of the Spiritual movement. But in the fourteenth century it was the Dominicans who inspired the great movement of German mysticism which centred in the priories and nunneries of the Rhineland and Switzerland and produced a galaxy of mystics and spiritual writers—Eckhart, Tauler, Suso, Margaret and Christina Ebner and the sisters of Unterlinden and Töss and Engeltal.

Again, both Orders shared in the new missionary movement which begins with St. Francis's mission to the Egyptian Sultan El Kamil in 1219, and reached its culmination with the establishment of a Catholic Archbishopric at Pekin or Cambaluc in 1305. Here, however, the Franciscan contribution was the most remarkable, both in respect of personal originality, as with St. Francis himself or Ramon Lull, and the scale of their achievements. For the journeys of the Friars, no less than the voyages of Columbus and Vasco da Gama, mark the awakening of a European world consciousness and the end of the geographical Dark Ages.

There are, it seems to me, few more impressive documents in the history of medieval culture than the record of the journey of John of Plan Carpino in 1246–47 and William of Rubrouck in 1253–54 across the whole breadth of Central Asia to the court of the Great Khan in Inner Mongolia. Here we see two unknown worlds confronting one another; unable to comprehend each other's language and representing the opposite poles of human experience.

And Western Christendom could not have found a better representative than this companion of St. Francis, John of Plan Carpino, who travelled in apostolic fashion—in hunger and cold and nakedness—across the empty places of the world where, he said, the only signs of man were the bones of the dead and the ruins of dead towns, in order to bring to the successor of Ghenghis Khan the letters of the Pope bidding him cease from the slaughter of the inoffensive peoples of Eastern Europe. The reply which John of Plan Carpino brought back, in Persian and Turkish with a Mongol seal, was discovered not long ago in the Vatican archives by M. Pelliot, and a very remarkable document it is.[15]

This is a good example of the way in which the Papacy made use of the Friars as its personal agents and emissaries in the affairs of Christendom. Indeed from the time of Gregory IX onwards the relation between the Papacy and the Friars became ever closer, until the two great Orders came to form a disciplined *corps d'élite* under the direct command of the Papacy. An international body of this kind, detached from local territorial obligations and private interests, had always been a great need of the reformed Papacy, and therefore the creation of the Mendicant Orders together with the foundation of the universities marks the culmination of the movement towards international and superpolitical unity which was the ideal of medieval Christendom.

But unfortunately it came too late: the great age of the reforming movement was over, and the Popes who did most to favour and make use of the Friars were not men of the type of Gregory VII or St. Bernard but able lawyers and statesmen like Gregory IX himself and Innocent IV and Martin IV who were preoccupied with the intense political conflict with the Hohenstaufen and the fatal entanglements of the Angevin alliance.

Hence it came about that the prophetic and evangelical vocation of the early Friars became subordinated to the demands of ecclesiastical power politics, and this produced a rift in the reforming movement from which medieval Christendom never recovered. The Papacy issued from the conflict with the Hohenstaufen victoriously, but with a

[15] Pelliot, "Les Mongols et la Papauté" in *Revue de l'orient Chrétien*, 1922–23.

serious loss of moral prestige. In the following century it never regained the universal European position that Innocent III had held. Above all, it lost the leadership of the movement of reform. Henceforward during the later Middle Ages the reformers were predominantly anti-Papal in spirit, as were the Spiritual Franciscans and Wycliffe, or supporters of the secular power like William of Ockham and Marsiglio of Padua.

This tragic crisis of the medieval spirit is reflected in the greatest literary achievement of that age, the *Divina Commedia* of Dante. Nowhere can we find a more perfect expression of the power and the glory of the medieval cultural achievement which reached from Heaven to Hell and found room for all the knowledge and wisdom and all the suffering and aggressiveness of medieval humanity in its all-embracing vision of judgment. Yet at the same time it is a most drastic indictment of the medieval Church, and the great apocalyptic pageant of the concluding cantos of the *Purgatorio* expresses the revolutionary criticism of the spiritual Franciscans and the Joachimites rather than the orthodox conception of the Papal theocracy which was the ideal of Aegidius Romanus and St. Thomas himself.[16]

This crisis of the reforming movement and the decline of the unifying energy of medieval culture found outward expression in the two great external catastrophes of Dante's generation—the end of the crusading states and the destruction of the great crusading Order. The former was the inevitable result of the way in which the crusading ideal had been discredited and secularized by its use as a political weapon against Christian states like the Empire and the kingdom of Aragon. The destruction of the Templars by Philip IV, linked as it was with the attack on the prestige and independence of the Papacy by the simultaneous process against the memory of Pope Boniface VIII and the rehabilitation of Philip IV by the Papacy, was far more

---

16 We find the same revolutionary criticism two generations later in the very different vision of our English poet William Langland. In spite of his bitter hostility towards the Friars his poem is penetrated through and through by the ideas and ideals of the Franciscan Spirituals.

serious, since it marked the complete victory of the temporal power of the new monarchy over the international elements in medieval society. The imposing structure of medieval Christendom which had been built up by the idealism of the reforming movement, the organizing power of the Papacy, and the devotion of the religious Orders proved powerless to withstand the determined attack of a handful of unscrupulous officials like Guillaume de Nogaret and Pierre Flotte, who were the servants of the new monarchy and understood how to exploit the new techniques of power in a ruthlessly totalitarian fashion.

That such a collapse could have occurred shows that medieval culture was undergoing a process of revolutionary change. In fact the second half of the thirteenth century, which from many points of view seems to represent the culmination of medieval culture, also represents a turning point and a moment of crisis. For three centuries the development of Western Europe had been centripetal towards the unity of Christendom and the creation of an intellectual and spiritual synthesis. From the second half of the thirteenth century this movement is reversed and a centrifugal process begins which continues throughout the later Middle Ages until it culminates in the religious division and social changes of the sixteenth century.

This change was not, however, entirely determined by the internal forces of Western culture, for at the same period a series of changes was taking place in Western Asia that resulted in a general shifting in the axis of world culture. It was in this age that the region between the Mediterranean and the Iranian plateau which had been the focus of world civilization for four thousand years lost its position of cultural leadership and became stationary or decadent. Hitherto Europe had looked inward to Jerusalem and Byzantium and "Babylon" (i.e. Cairo) as to the centres of the world, and Western man had been the pupil and the imitator of older, richer and more advanced civilizations. Now for the first time Europe is forced to follow untrodden ways and to find new goals, and at the same time becomes conscious of its own powers, critical of accepted traditions and ready for new ventures.

Chapter XII

Conclusion: Medieval Religion and Popular Culture

THE AGE of Dante and Philip le Bel, which saw the translation of the Papacy of Avignon and the failure of the forlorn hope of the Emperor Henry VII to reassert the claims of the Holy Roman Empire, marks the end of the medieval development. The later Middle Ages open a new chapter in Western history. They are the time when Western man sets out with uncertain and hesitating steps on his great adventure for the discovery of a new world: not merely the discovery of new oceans and continents but the discovery of nature and of man himself as the crown and perfection of nature.

Yet in doing so Western man was not consciously turning his back on the spiritual ideals and the religious faith which had been the driving forces in medieval culture. When he started on his new journey his mind was still dominated by medieval ideals and he was seeking new channels for their realization.

We see this in many different departments of life. For example, the external expansion of Western culture by exploration and discovery is directly related to the earlier crusading movement through the work of Prince Henry the Navigator, who planned his programme of discovery in the service of his religious ideals.

In the same way, as I said at the beginning, the origins of modern science in the later Middle Ages are found, not among the Averroists of Padua, but with the disciples of Roger Bacon and William of Ockham, who regarded religious faith as the ultimate source of true knowledge.

But in the study of medieval culture it is necessary to remember that the higher levels of intellectual culture and political thought, on which the historian's attention always tends to be concentrated, form a very small part of the total picture, and that the creative activity of religion is most powerful where it is least recorded and most difficult to observe—in the minds of the masses and in the traditions of the common people. And thus in the fourteenth and fifteenth centuries, when the scholars were intent on the revival of learning and the statesmen were transforming the order of Christendom into a new state system, the mind of the common people was still immersed in the religious atmosphere of the medieval past.

We possess a precious and almost unique record of this popular religious culture in the first great vernacular English poem—William Langland's "Piers Plowman". For though Langland was an educated and even a learned man he represents the tradition and culture neither of the court nor of the schools. He is a voice from the underworld of the common people, speaking their language, using their imagery and sharing their ideals. And his poem seems to prove that the fundamental principles of the creative period of medieval religion had been more completely assimilated and incorporated by the new vernacular culture of the common people than it had been by the higher and more literary culture of the ruling elements in Church and state.

In the first place Langland represents the movement of spiritual reform which had been the inspiration of medieval religion for so long and which has now passed from the monastic orders and the Friars to the laity. In the second place, the reforming ideal is not conceived in terms of ecclesiastical organization and government, but as a new way of life as St. Francis had seen it, and there is the same insistence on the Franciscan ideal of poverty and compassion for the poor, although the Friars no longer in his eyes appear the true representatives of these ideals.

And in the apparel of a poor man and a pilgrim's likeness
Many times has God been met among poor people. . . .

And in a friar's frock once was he found
But it is far ago in St. Francis time.[1]

And Langland is no less Franciscan in the way in which he attempts to bring the life of Christ and the high mysteries of the faith into direct relation with the homely realities of common life. Indeed he goes even further on the same road, since his realism is no longer sublimated by the romantic idealism of the courtly tradition but expresses the harsh realities of common life with a crude and scathing directness. Langland represents an older tradition than that of the Troubadours. He does not belong to the new world of courtly culture and oriental romance and Provençal song, but to an older order which still maintained the native traditions of culture and still clung to the antique alliterative measures of Anglo-Saxon heroic verse. He seems at once more archaic and more modern than his great contemporaries like Chaucer. His stern ascetic moralism has nothing in common with the spirit of the *Romance of the Rose* and the *Decameron* but looks forward to Bunyan and backwards to the *Poema Morale* and the Anglo-Saxon homilies.

Yet in spite of all this Langland's work has incorporated all the vital elements in the medieval religious tradition, which had been transmitted to the popular culture by the vernacular preaching of the Friars, and created from it a vital unity of religion and culture which the more learned and highly cultivated classes had failed to achieve.

We have seen how the fundamental dualism of Christian thought had expressed itself during the earlier Middle Ages in the other-worldliness of the monastic ideal and in an unresolved conflict between the pagan traditions of the barbarian warrior society and the Christian ideals of peace and brotherly love. We have seen the great effort of the reforming movement to subdue the World to the Church by the vindication of the primacy of the spiritual power, by canonical reform and by the weapon of the Crusade. And we have seen how this heroic effort was weakened and

[1] B, xv, 202–23, 225–26.

broken at the close of the thirteenth century, so that in the later Middle Ages the old social dualism reappeared in a new form in the conflict between the Church and the new sovereign state which was ultimately to destroy the unity of Western Christendom. Nor was this conflict in any way solved by the Reformation, since it continued to operate more intensely than ever within the divided Christendom in the new confessional Churches and in the new national sovereign states.

But in Langland's vision we can see—if only for a moment by a flash of poetic and prophetic inspiration—how this dualism might have been surmounted and overcome. His view of life and his scale of values are no less other-worldly than those of the most ascetic representatives of the earlier medieval tradition. But they no longer find expression in the flight to the desert or withdrawal to the cloister. For Langland the other-world is always immediately present in every human relationship, and every man's daily life is organically bound up with the life of the Church.

Thus every state of life in Christendom is a Christian life in the full sense—an extension of the life of Christ on earth. And the supernatural order of grace is founded and rooted in the natural order and the common life of humanity.

Right as the Rose · that is red and sweet
Out of a ragged root · and rough briars
Springeth and spreadeth · and spicers desire it,
So Do Best out of Do well · and Do better doth spring.[2]

True wedded folk · in this world are Do well
For they must work and win · and the world sustain.
For of this kind they come · that confessors be called,
Kings and Knights, Kaysers and churls,
Maidens and Martyrs · out of one man come.[3]

There is moreover no room for any social dualism or political conflict between Church and state. For Langland remains faithful to the basic medieval conception of the One

[2] A, x, 119–123.
[3] B, ix, 107–111.

Society whose members are differentiated by rank and authority, but are all alike children of one father and servants of one master.

For we are all Christ's creatures · and of his coffers rich,
And brethren as of one blood · as well beggars as earls,
For on Calvary of Christ's blood · Christendom gan spring,
And blood brethren we became there · of one body won,
As quasimodo geniti · *and gentlemen each one.*
No beggar or serving boy among us · save sin made him so.[4]

Langland's poem is the last and in some respects the most uncompromising expression of the medieval ideal of the unity of religion and culture. He realized more clearly than the poets and more intensely than the philosophers that religion was not a particular way of life but the way of all life, and that the divine love which is "the leader of the Lord's folk of heaven" is also the law of life upon earth.

For Heaven might not hold it: it was so heavy of himself,
Till it had upon earth eaten his fill.
And when it had of this fold · flesh and blood taken,
Was never leaf on a linden · lighter thereafter,
As light and as piercing · as the point of a needle,
That no armour may hold it · nor no high walls.[5]

.   .   .   .   .

Therefore these words · be written in the Gospel,
Ask and it shall be given you · for I give all things,
And that is the lock of love · that letteth out my grace,
To comfort the careworn · cumbered with sin.[6]

This vision of Christendom as a labour of love is embodied in the great central figure of Piers Plowman who represents the threefold state of humanity. First he appears as man, the child of nature, the peasant who sustains the world by his labour. Secondly he is the Son of Man and the Son of God who saves the world by his blood,

[4] B, xi, 192–97.
[5] B, i, 151–56.
[6] E, i, 198–201.

Who comes in with a cross · before the common people,
Like in all limbs · to our Lord Jesus.

And thirdly he is the figure of the Church, the new spiritual humanity, anointed and enlightened by the Holy Ghost to carry on the work of unity and salvation.

Hence the symbolism of the poem leads Langland necessarily to view human life according to the pattern of the earth as a work of spiritual tillage and harvest. In this he is returning to the imagery of the Gospel and to the words of St. Paul, "We are fellow workers with God. You are God's tillage. You are God's building"; or, to use the words of the Vulgate which were so familiar to him, *Dei agricultura estis.*

In this image Langland finds an answer to the questions that were dividing the mind of medieval culture and destroying the unity of Christendom.

From the root of nature there springs the unexpected and unpredictable flower of grace and the fruit of the spirit, which is eternal life. Christianity is the labour of love to which every man is called according to his personal gifts and his social vocation, and the Church is the community of love—the house of unity into which the harvest of humanity is brought.

And he called that House Unity · which is Holychurch in
    English.[7]

Langland wrote at a time of deep distress and doubt, in the midst of the Hundred Years' War, on the eve of the Great Schism, when the great hopes of the reforming movement seemed to be lost. When, as he writes,

It seemeth now soothly · to the world's sight,
That God's Word worketh not · on learned or on lewd,
But in such manner as Mark · meaneth in his Gospel,
If the blind lead the blind · both shall fall into the ditch.[8]

Yet Langland's poem is itself a proof that all was not lost; that the labour of seven hundred years had not been

[7] B, xix, 325.
[8] B, x, 274–76.

in vain. For if the barbarians of the West had learnt to think such thoughts and speak such a language, it shows that a new Christian culture had been born which was not an alien ideal imposed externally, but was the common inheritance of Western man.

What have we done with this inheritance? At least we have *had* it. It has been part of our own flesh and blood and the speech of our own tongue.

And the importance of these centuries of which I have been writing is not to be found in the external order they created or attempted to create, but in the internal change they brought about in the soul of Western man—a change which can never be entirely undone except by the total negation or destruction of Western man himself.

If there is any truth in what I have been saying in these two courses of lectures, such moments of vital fusion between a living religion and a living culture are the creative events in history, in comparison with which all the external achievements in the political and economic orders are transitory and insignificant.

Appendix

Notes on Famous Medieval Art

FIGURE OF CHRIST
From the Bewcastle Rood (*c.* 700) *Warburg Institute.*

The Anglian High Crosses are among the earliest and most remarkable monuments of Western Christendom. Although they date from the first age of Northumbrian Christianity, they show an astonishing mastery of design and execution, unlike anything to be found elsewhere in Western Europe during this period. This new art owes its origin to the deliberate importation of Christian art and Christian craftsmen from the Mediterranean world by the leaders of the Anglian church, above all St. Wilfred and St. Benedict Biscop in the second half of the seventh century. But while the ornament, especially the vine scroll, shows clear signs of Mediterranean (Syrian) influence, the style is not purely imitative, but represents an original Anglian renaissance of classical Roman traditions. It is in fact a true "Romanesque" art which anticipates the Continental development by centuries. The Bewcastle cross has a particularly close association with the great age of the Northumbrian church, because it was erected in commemoration of King Alchfrith, the friend of St. Wilfred and the supporter of the Roman party at the Synod of Whitby (664). It stands on the site of an old Roman fort high up on the Cumbrian moors beyond the Roman Wall. The figure of Christ in Majesty resembles that on the earlier and even finer Rood at Ruthwell in Dumfriesshire. In both cases the face is unbearded, but carries a moustache. The

Bewcastle inscription is entirely runic, whereas at Ruthwell the corresponding figure has a Latin inscription—*IHS XPS IUDEX AEQUITATIS. Bestiae et Dracones cognoverunt in Deserto Salvatorem Mundi.* It seems that both of these great crosses were set up as triumphant assertions of the power of the Cross over the forces of outer barbarism.

LITURGY AND HIERARCHY

Ivory, Stadtbibliothek, Frankfort a. M. From Propylaen-Weltgeschichte, Vol. III.

This is one of a pair of ivory diptychs which originally formed the covers of a sacramentary. They are a fine example of the liturgical art of the Carolingian age, and show the figure of an archbishop wearing the Pallium and surrounded by his attendant clergy. In the first panel, now in the Fitzwilliam Museum at Cambridge, the archbishop is holding a book open at the Introit for the First Sunday of Advent, while he raises his right hand in benediction. The second panel, from the Stadtbibliothek at Frankfurt, which is shown here, depicts the liturgical action itself. The archbishop is standing before the altar, and the open book shows the beginning of the Canon of the Mass.

THE MEDIEVAL ABBEY

Durham Cathedral.

The Cathedral monastery at Durham is one of the most wonderful monuments of medieval culture in Northern Europe. For it is not only the finest and most complete example of Anglo-Norman architecture, it is also typical of the social development of the feudal monastery as a political and civic institution, a sacred city which ruled the land between Tweed and Tyne and protected the Northern Marches against the Scots.

But behind this feudal development there lies the ancient tradition of Northumbrian Christianity which made Durham the holiest place in the north, for it was the sanctuary of St. Cuthbert and the legitimate heir of the sacred traditions of the Holy Isle of Lindisfarne from which the monastic life first came to Northumbria. After the destruction of Lindisfarne by the Danes, the body of St. Cuthbert began a long pilgrimage through the north, and wherever the body rested, the see of St. Cuthbert had its centre. Finally, after a century at Chester le Street, it was brought at the end of the tenth century to Durham, still carried, according to tradition, by the descendants of the original bearers of the body, "the men of St. Cuthbert", who preserved a privileged position as tenants of the bishops. Finally, after the Norman conquest the monastic life was revived by three monks from Evesham—a Norman and two Anglo-Saxons—who had been inspired by their reading of Bede to restore the tradition of Northumbrian monasticism first at Jarrow, and finally, in 1083, at Durham itself. The monastery stands high on a rocky peninsula above the River Wear, defended on the north by the castle of the bishops which covered the neck of the peninsula. The cloister and the monastic buildings lie south of the cathedral.

MEDIEVAL KINGSHIP

Canute as Christian King. *British Museum* (Stowe MS. 944).

This drawing, from the *Liber Vitae* of Hyde Abbey (British Museum, Stowe 944), shows King Canute and his queen, Aelgivu (Emma), offering a gold cross to the altar of the abbey, while angels place a crown and a veil on their heads and point upwards to the figure of Christ in Majesty. The drawing is a fine example of the Winchester school, *c.* 1020, the classical style of Christian Wessex, and it shows not only how the Viking conqueror had acquired by his coronation the character of a Christian king, but also how the revival of Christian culture, which had been begun by King Alfred, proved strong enough to survive the political catastrophe of the second Danish conquest and to transform the culture of its conquerors.

The court art of Danish England owed nothing to the still vigorous tradition of Nordic paganism, it was the art of King Alfred's descendants; and King Alfred's foundation of Newminster (Hyde Abbey), in the same way, was the special object of the Danish conqueror's protection and benefactions.

The Medieval Knight

Tomb of William Longespee, Earl of Salisbury (d. 1226) in Salisbury Cathedral.

The medieval idea of knighthood finds its classical expression in the art of the thirteenth century, alike in architectural sculpture, as in the famous equestrian figure of Bamber (probably representing St. Stephen of Hungary), and still more typically in the tomb effigies which are so numerous in this country. An example is the tomb traditionally ascribed to William Longsword, the son of Henry II, and the father of William Longsword, the crusader who accompanied St. Louis to Egypt and died in the Battle of Mansourah, and whose cenotaph and effigy is also in Salisbury Cathedral.

In contrast to these figures which express the classical idea of Christian knighthood, the romantic or courtly conception of knighthood also finds expression in art, especially in painting. Thus the famous Manasse codex of the German poets, which was produced at Zurich at the beginning of the fourteenth century, shows the knight either as a youthful, rather effeminate figure with long hair and flowing robes, or in full armour with the great tilting helmet, mounted on a barded destrier. In the latter case, though the figure is supposed to represent a particular poet like Hartman von Aue or Ulrich von Lichenstein, the face and even the human figure have entirely disappeared. Man and horse have become transformed into a sort of heraldic monster, a fantastic bird-headed hippogriff. And the fact that the same age has produced such completely different representations of the same institution is a striking example of the dualism that underlies the most brilliant development of medieval culture.

The Oriental Influence in Medieval Culture

The Death-bed of William II of Sicily. From the Berne Manuscript of Peter of Eboli, *de rebus Siculis carmen.* Propylaen-Weltgeschichte, Vol. III.

The brilliant culture of the Norman kingdom of Sicily was steeped in Oriental and Byzantine influences, and the life of the court resembled that of a Saracen ruler. This illustration shows the dying king attended by his Arab physician and astrologer, with the mourners bewailing his death in Oriental fashion.

Similar conditions existed at the Spanish courts, and the Escorial Manuscript of the Book of Games, by Alfonso the Wise, depicts the king among his Moorish secretaries and men of learning.

No aspect of medieval culture has been more neglected than this intensive process of cultural intercourse between East and West which took place in the Western Mediterranean during the central period of the Middle Ages.

THE GERMAN PRINCE BISHOP FREDERICK I, ARCHBISHOP OF MAGDEBURG, 1142–52.
> From his tomb in Magdeburg Cathedral. Propylaen-Weltgeschichte, Vol. III.

The metropolitan see of Magdeburg was founded by Otto I in 968 as the centre of ecclesiastical jurisdiction for all the lands beyond the Elbe, and throughout the Middle Ages it was one of the chief bridgeheads of German expansion towards the east. During the twelfth century the archbishops collaborated with the Margraves of Brandenburg in the systematic colonization of the Eastern Marches by settlers from the west. Archbishop Frederick was one of the leaders of the crusade against the Wends in 1147, which on the whole had a disastrous effect on the conversion of the Slavs by increasing the antagonism between Christians and pagans, and it was his successor Wichman who did most to organize the colonization of the lands between the Elbe and the Havel by Flemish and Dutch settlers.

PRINCE HENRY THE NAVIGATOR. 1394–1460.
> Third son of King John of Portugal and Philippa of Lancaster, Master of the Order of Christ. From the Paris Manuscript of Azurara's Conquest of Guinea, c. 1453. Propylaen-Weltgeschichte, Vol. IV.

Henry the Navigator is one of the typical figures of the period of transition between the Middle Ages and modern times. He was the last of the crusaders and the first of the conquistadores. He devoted his whole life to the struggle against Islam in Africa, taking a prominent part in the conquest of Ceuta in 1415, in the disastrous siege of Tangier in 1437, and the capture of Alcacer in 1458. This was entirely in the medieval tradition, as it were a continuation of St. Louis' last crusade against Tunis. Where Henry differs from his predecessors is in his development of geographical discovery and colonization in the service of the crusading ideal. It was his aim to establish a new Christian dominion in West Africa so as to turn the flank of Islam, and possibly establish relations with some Christian kingdom which was supposed to exist beyond the frontiers of Islam. Year after year he sent his ships west and south along the African coast, until at last in 1445–46 they passed Cape Verde and discovered the world of tropical Africa. It was this discovery that first broke down the limits of Western Christendom, so that even before the discovery of America the vast possibilities of a new world were opened to medieval Europe, as we see in the letter of the humanist Politian to King John II of Portugal in 1491. But at the same time the crusading ideal became contaminated with the negro slave trade and the quest for gold, both of which were inaugurated by Prince Henry. In spite of this, he remains a thoroughly medieval personality: a crusading prince after the pattern of St. Louis, devout, chaste and ascetic; and it was as the head of a military order—the Order of Christ—and under the banner of the crusade that all his expeditions and settlements were made.

INDEX